LET MY PEOPLE LEARN

THE BIOGRAPHY OF DR. WIL LOU GRAY

DaMaris Ayres

THE ATTIC PRESS
1988

Attic Press, Inc.
Stony Point
Grenwood, SC 29646

ACKNOWLEDGMENTS

The author gratefully acknowledges the technical assistance and encouragement rendered by Caroliniana Library; the South Carolina State Library; Robert A. Pierce, *The State* ; Earl Jackson, University Press; Dr. Yvonne Jones and Nancy Montgomery, my co-workers at Willow Lane School, Department of Youth services; George Smith, Wil Lou Gray Opportunity School; Dr. Marvin Efron and the Board of Trustees of the Opportunity School. Special thanks go to Gray family members, the alumni of various "Opportunity Schools," Miss Gray's friends and former co-workers, and to Evelyn Branch's fantastic memory.

Photographs and illustrations were provided by the Gray family, the Opportunity School staff, Dr. Manuel Gaetan, P.E., Brad Huckeriede, South Carolina Educational Television, and the University of South Carolina. Michael Del Priore generously contributed a copy of Miss Gray's portrait for the front cover. The front jacket was designed by my husband.

The quality of this book would not have been possible without the cooperation, patience, and technical skill of the Eastside Printing staff, who allowed me to hover over my "brainchild" while the manuscript was prepared for publication.

AUTHOR'S NOTE

This book was written during the lifetime of Wil Lou Gray, with the exception of the final chapter which concerns the last two years of her life. Therefore, the story has been told in the present tense. Also, any material which has been quoted is verbatim, with the writers' original spelling and grammatical construction.

This book is dedicated to the memory of my parents who taught me to love learning and to persist until seemingly impossible dreams are attained.

TABLE OF CONTENTS

page

FOREWORD

Wil Lou Gray moved mountains, but she always stood in their shadows. Thus, it may take a few decades of perspective to establish the lofty niche this gritty grand dame etched in South Carolina's history.

Certainly, Miss Gray was the state's most effective crusader for universal literacy. She was more than a crusader. She was, most of all, a doer, and that is one secret of her greatness.

She was a persuasive and perpetual motion machine who struck fear in the hearts of legislators and journalists as she ever lobbied them on behalf of great, even controversial, causes. But she was never viewed as a fanatic or a harpy.

In an ara of segregation and bigotry, Miss Gray campaigned for equal education for all races, for her people and causes were everywhere. As a Southerner, she violently disagreed with proponents of white supremacy, segregation, and Jim Crow laws. But she was never dismissed as an idle dreamer or revolutionary.

Though ever pleasant, she was perhaps the most persistent woman I have ever known. She expended her energies, not on ideological reveries, but on real life accomplishments. One editor marveled that this diminutive woman possessed a "whim of steel" when it came to transforming a dream into a reality. A legislator, pondering her war for adult education, branded this gentle woman a nuisance "worse than chewing gum in your hair." At my offices at *The State* newspaper, editors sometimes hid or fled when word seeped out that she had entered the building. They knew they would soon be at her persuasive mercy.

Unlike some of today's activists, Wil Lou Gray never flapped her wings at the moon. She simply persisted until she got things done.

But her perseverance was born of compassion. Former Governor Dick Riley put her determination in perspective. "Anybody who accomplishes as much as she did has to push people," he said, "but she never pushed them for herself. She never quit working to help other people."

As a child, Miss Gray, from a well-to-do Laurens family, was saddened when she saw her neighbors pencil their "mark" rather than their signature. Her alarm over illiteracy was heightened when she began teaching in a one-room school in Greenwood County and at a rural school in Laurens County. Thus a spark flared into a fire of passion for the plight of the downtrodden, leading to thirty years of championing their right to read. She traveled dusty, uphill roads, toiled into the night, and scrimped to invest her money in a cause at a time when women were expected to grace the home, not crusade for change.

Miss Gray's people were the ragged, doll-carrying kids; the eleven-year-old who kept house and cooked for a family of eight; tiny Mary, fifteen, starved by a squalid environment, who at first only sat, "almost autistic-like" and watched others; the boy who had never seen an automobile and ran wild in the mountains after his mother died; Mrs. Jones, sixty-three, worked in a mill at age eight. All were her "children," and they all loved her as she loved them. Each produced his own real-life novel of sorts that Wil Lou Gray held close to her heart. They were the uneducated people whom Miss Gray, holder of a graduate degree from Columbia University, wanted to transform from "present liabilities to society's assets."

As a woman, she, along with her family, including her father, early pushed for woman's suffrage when it was a most unpopular cause. As a human being, she espoused rehabilitation in the prisons and, though often frustrated, tried to provide educational programs to help prisoners. It's understandable that, even by yesteryear's narrow standards, she was never considered a wild-eyed liberal but simply a humane, compassionate woman.

Miss Gray never wrote an autobiography, even though her story inspired people almost as much as her presence and deeds. But she savored written thanks from her "children." Those tributes from her former students alone produce touching stories which, perhaps, she hoped to relive in her quieter days. Of course, those quieter days never came. Miss Gray stayed busy until she died after her one-hundredth birthday. In fact, she was always too busy doing for others to write about herself. Fortunately, she opened her records to the woman she named her official biographer, DaMaris E. Ayres, who had researched the early history of adult education in South Carolina while pursuing graduate studies at the University of South Carolina.

It was left to Ms. Ayres, unabashedly sympathetic to and admiring of her subject, to produce this volume that records Miss Gray's triumphs and disappointments. The author conducted hours of taped interviews and pored over mountains of papers for more than a decade.

This story is one of unbridled "wholesome optimism," which, Miss Gray believed, "combined with a broad, deep human sympathy, are necessary elements in any true culture."

When Miss Gray died on Saturday, March 10, 1984, *The State*, along with other South Carolina dailies, extolled her contributions. In the lead editorial three days later, I wrote that this warrior would "not only be remembered for educational contributions she made to an underdog state during her fruitful one hundred years of life, but also for her persistent determination to achieve her purpose."

The most appropriate physical tribute to Miss Gray is the "Opportunity School" that she founded at the former Army air base in Lexington County. It won state support and is now known as the Wil Lou Gray Opportunity School, a fitting memorial to its founder.

But the biggest monument, a human one, remains those underdogs whom Miss Gray inspired to find a happier, more useful place in society.

Robert A. Pierce,
The State

CHAPTER I

Life in Laurens

Here is the place where Loveliness keeps house,
Between the river and the wooded hills.
                                    Madison Julius Cowlin

The town of Laurens, South Carolina, the birthplace of Wil Lou Gray, lies in the northwestern Piedmont section of the state. Its rolling, wooded hills and meandering Little River, then as now, paint a picture of rustic beauty.

At the time of Wil Lou's birth in 1883 Laurens was a typical small Southern county seat, with fifty-three places of business arranged around a square presided over by a beautiful, stately courthouse in a central location. Houses rented for approximately one hundred dollars annually, while the best business locations could be leased for little more than this amount. Lumber, brick, stone, and cement were building materials all locally produced. Land sold for five to twenty dollars per acre, but in some townships in Laurens County there was no land for sale. After the destruction caused by the Civil War and the hardships imposed during Reconstruction, many farms were owned by absentee landlords who paid a small share of the farms' profits to those freedmen and poor whites who lived on the land and tilled the soil. Since landowners had no money to pay workers, and recently freed slaves and poorer whites had no money with which to buy land of their own, this system of "sharecropping" evolved. The principal crop produced was cotton, which found a ready market in the county's four textile mills.[1]

1

Gradually, the effects of the Industrial Revolution, which had begun in England and then traveled across the Atlantic to New England, were becoming evident in the South. The entire nation was discovering untapped resources which accelerated the growth of a new Machine Age. An inexpensive process for making steel was discovered and the invention of the dynamo enabled machines to convert the energy of steam or water power into electricity. Petroleum was found to have many uses, such as kerosene for heat and lighting, and gasoline or diesel to power the newly invented internal combustion engines. These innovations led to the mass producing of automobiles in the late 1890's.[2] However, the first "horseless carriage" did not appear in Laurens until 1905.[3]

Wil Lou Gray's father and other close relatives owned several farms and small businesses. However, it was becoming evident that the small business was to be swallowed by giant corporations. Moreover, most small farms were to be engulfed by larger operations using the farm machinery being mass produced and the scientific knowledge being disseminated by such agricultural colleges as Clemson, established in 1889 by "Pitchfork Ben" Tillman.[4]

The educational picture at this time was bleak. In all of Laurens County in 1883 there were one hundred schools in nine districts. There were two private schools, Laurens Female College and Clinton Male High School, with combined enrollments of fewer than one hundred fifty students. The average salary for male teachers was twenty-five dollars per month, while women received an average of twenty-three dollars. Conditions in the isolated rural schools were deplorable. Buildings were usually one-room affairs, unpainted, heated by a pot-bellied stove, with crude furnishings and little equipment or materials with which to teach. Since there were no telephones, electricity, or indoor plumbing even in Laurens itself until the late 1890's, of course all rural schools in the area were without any modern conveniences until long after they were taken for granted in the city schools. Today we are appalled that one teacher was required to teach all students who enrolled, no matter what their ages or grade levels. Moreover, the lack of a compulsory attendance law, apathetic, uneducated parents, poorly qualified teachers, and a largely unconcerned public, all combined to produce an abysmal level of illiteracy.[5]

In the state as a whole, conditions were fully as deplorable.

> . . . in 1877, the state government came under considerable pressure to reduce educational expenses, especially for Negro schools. Many whites disliked the whole educational program because it was begun by the Radicals, it implied racial equality, it might 'spoil' good Negro field hands, and it might improve the Negro's political potential . . . By the time the Constitution of 1895 was written, the state had raised its expenses per white pupil to $3.11 annually, while reducing expenses per Negro pupil to $1.05.[6]

According to the Superintendent of Education's Annual Report in 1885, the average annual salary for a male teacher in South Carolina was $27.50, while females earned $24.48. There were 1,137 white male, 1,205 white female, 982 Negro male, and 449 Negro female teachers. There was an average attendance of 70 days. There were 3,562 schools serving 178,023 students. For that entire year, only $214.39 was spent on library books by the state of South Carolina! Moreover, since the Census of 1880 reported that there were 101,189 white and 180,475 Negro children between the ages of 6 and 16 living in the state, this meant that more than 100,000 of this age group did not attend school.

How auspicious it was for the state of South Carolina that during such times as these, on August 29, 1883, a child was born who was destined to become an educational pioneer of international acclaim, devoting her entire lifetime to the betterment of her people through education.

3

NOTES

[1]South Carolina Handbook (Charleston, S.C.: Walker, Evans, and Cogswell, 1883), pp. 710-11.

[2]Leonard C. Wood et al., *America: Its People and Values* (New York: Harcourt Brace Jovanovich, 1975), pp. 362-65.

[3]Harriet Gray Blackwell,*A Candle for All Time* (Richmond: The Dietz Press, Inc., 1959), p. 174.

[4]Ernest M. Lander, Jr., *A History of South Carolina 1865-1960* (Chapel Hill: University of North Carolina Press, 1960), p. 139.

[5]Ibid., pp. 125-26.

[6]Ibid., p. 127.

REFERENCES

Blackwell, Harriet Gray. *A Candle for All Time*. Richmond: The Dietz Press, Inc., 1959.

Bolick, Julian Stevenson. *A Laurens County Sketchbook*. Laurens: Mrs. Julian Stevenson Bolick, 1973.

Lander, Ernest M., Jr. *A History of South Carolina 1865-1960*. Chapel Hill: University of North Carolina Press, 1960.

South Carolina Handbook. Charleston, S.C.: Walker, Evans and Cogswell, 1883.

South Carolina State Department of Education Annual Report. Columbia: State Department of Education, 1885.

Wood, Leonard C., et al. *America: Its People and Values*. New York: Harcourt Brace Jovanovich, 1975.

CHAPTER II

Halcyon Days

Go ye into all the world . . .
St. Mark

Wil Lou Gray was named for her father, William Lafayette Gray, and her mother, Sarah Louise Dial Gray. Those who knew her parents well felt that Wil Lou had inherited personality traits from both, such as business acumen from her father, and a saintly degree of patience and compassion from her mother.

William was from a large family of twelve children whose father, Robert Adams Gray, was a teacher, and a confirmed believer in providing the best education possible for all his children, preferably at a Methodist institution. William's father had always been especially concerned about his children's religious training and had regularly recruited teachers from Wofford College to live in his home and tutor his large family. Therefore, it was not by accident that William, after graduating from Laurens City School, rode a horse thirty-five miles to enroll at Wofford College, a Methodist school in Spartanburg. His father was justifiably proud of his son's accomplishments while at Wofford, for though William had to wear blue jeans and shirts made entirely at home from cotton grown on the farm, he became a member of Kappa Alpha fraternity and an outstanding student and leader.[1]

After graduating from Wofford, twenty-year-old William taught in a school located at Chestnut Ridge for a term and then became principal of the Laurensville Male Academy for two years. It was while teaching at

5

Chestnut Ridge that he met his future wife, Sarah Lou Dial, while boarding in the home of her parents, a common practice for schoolteachers in isolated areas.

At the same time he was teaching at the Academy, William was studying law under Colonel B.W. Ball, a prominent Laurens attorney. After passing his bar examination successfully, he joined the legal practice of John L.M. Irby. However, very early in his legal career (in fact, his first week of practice) he became bitterly disillusioned with so-called "justice." One of his first clients, a Negro accused of murdering his wife and setting fire to their home to hide his guilt, retained the services of the fledgling lawyer and swore his innocence. As soon as the trial was over and the client was set free because there was no *corpus delicti,* he immediately confessed to the young attorney that he really was guilty and in a drunken rage had killed his wife with an ax, poured kerosene over her body, and set the house on fire.[2] William Gray promptly decided it was time to return to farming and other business interests in Laurens. However, he put his legal training to good use in conducting his many businesses, and later in the General Assembly where he was instrumental in the enactment of several laws leading to educational reform.

There were many similarities between the families of Wil Lou's mother and father. Albert Dial, Senior, Wil Lou's maternal grandfather, also produced a large family, even surpassing Robert Gray, for Sarah Lou had fourteen brothers and sisters. Grandfather Dial also wanted the very best education for all his children and gave them a strong religious background although he seldom attended church. He was the president of the First Bank of Laurens and a prominent man in the community, having inherited a large estate which had been deeded to his ancestors by the King of England.[3]

Sarah Louise Dial, or Lou as William always called her, also was a college graduate. Her freshman year she had attended Furman College in Greenville, which at that time was for women only, but transferred to Spartanburg Woman's College where she received her degree.[4]

After her marriage to William Gray, Lou was busily engaged in taking care of their home and spending a large share of her time working for the First Methodist Church of Laurens. She felt that families should worship together and she became just as dedicated to the Methodist church as she had formerly been to the Baptist faith.

Wil Lou was the middle child born to William and Lou Gray. With her parents and two brothers, Dial, who was older, and the younger Coke (named for a Methodist bishop), Wil Lou lived a simple life in a house not sumptuous, but more than adequate for that day and time. This house had been a wedding present to William and Lou from her father. Downstairs there were a kitchen, two dining rooms, a parlor, one bedroom, and a bathroom. Upstairs there were three bedrooms and another bathroom. Encircling almost the entire house was a two-storied veranda which provided a favorite occupation for Wil Lou, rocking or swinging to her heart's content and from this vantage point calling to any chance passerby. Even as a young child Wil Lou loved to talk and she never met a stranger.

The Gray home was heated by several fireplaces. A cookstove fueled by wood or coal kept the kitchen cozy in the wintertime, but unbearably hot in the summer. Kerosene lamps provided lighting, but it was not until 1896 that homes in Laurens could be wired for electricity. The next year indoor plumbing was a novel convenience, and Wil Lou was glad that her father was always among the first to take advantage of any new scientific discovery. She was grateful that she no longer had to visit the little house out back, especially when the thermometer might plunge below the freezing mark during a typical Laurens winter season.

Before the advent of modern plumbing, Wil Lou nostalgically remembers the covered well outside the kitchen door. As she lowered the metal bucket on its creaking chain and pulley, she anticipated the sweetness of the cool water, which her father so much preferred to any other that he walked home several times a day from his office in town whenever the hot Southern sun produced a thrist. Many, many years later, when a sample from the well was sent to Clemson College laboratories for analysis, it was found to be teeming with bacteria and scientists warned against drinking it. This was the only time that Wil Lou ever heard her father regret the impact that scientific progress was exerting on their lives.

William Gray's tenant farms produced abundant food, and hams, pork shoulders, and slabs of hickory-smoked bacon were preserved in barrels of salt or hung in the Gray's storeroom. The cook rendered lard, a by-product of the autumn butchering season, which was so necessary

7

for preparing Southern fried chicken and peach or blackberry cobblers, favorite foods in the Gray household. Watermelons, berries, peaches, and pears were brought in from the farm to be enjoyed in season and made into preserves for later use. The middle of summer, Mrs. Gray and the children stayed at Aunt Lou Dial's home for an entire week to can and preserve the bountiful harvest of the farm gardens and orchards. Wil Lou, her brothers, and many cousins generally were underfoot, vying for the privilege of licking sugary spoons and kettles or competing in shelling peas and stringing beans. Wil Lou felt her presence was indispensable, for her small hands were often the only ones which fit into the Mason jars that had to be washed in soapy water and then sterilized.

Sugar and flour was bought by the barrel, and food that was available in cans at the general store was bought by the case. Chickens and turkeys were always kept at home to provide fresh eggs and poultry. Bread, usually biscuits, was baked at home, but an occasional treat such as cinnamon buns could be bought from a bakery wagon which made its rounds several times a week. Milk was bought in from the farms for the cook to make butter in a crockery churn with a wooden paddle. The butter was shaped in a wooden mold which left a decorative imprint on top. Twice a week the ice wagon stopped at the Gray home and left fifty- or one hundred-pound blocks of ice for the wood and galvanized tin-lined icebox. Wil Lou always looked forward to this in the summertime, for she knew it meant homemade ice cream on Sunday afternoon when the family returned from church. She and her brothers had been known to dispute possession of the dasher as soon as it came from the wooden bucket, so now they begrudgingly took turns licking this delightful confection as it dripped from the cream-covered frozen blades.

The family always ate well, but their normal everyday meals did not compare to the repasts prepared for guests, which were classic examples of Southern hospitality. The dinner prepared for Bishop W.W. Duncan and the Methodist Board of Stewards was a typical example of such a festive company meal.

> ... The first course was oyster stew, where plump oysters showed dark in Jersey milk thickened with rolled snowflake crackers, where golden globules of butter glistened on top, and an occasional tiny scarlet crab accented the surface.

8

The main dinner featured broiled chicken with rice, and giblet gravy to which sliced boiled eggs were added. Macaroni, rich with butter, cheese and eggs, was hot in a casserole, and sweet potatoes in a white agate pan, candied until they were practically crystallized, were even more appetizing than usual because the top was dotted with lemon slices that looked like translucent Teneriffe wheels. An ample cake of homemade butter, embossed with roses made by skillfully using a teaspoon to shape a design while the butter was still soft, was on the table. It was to go with the hot biscuits and pear preserves. Waldorf salad in scooped out red apples and garnished with whipped cream was colorful at each place.

A damask cloth five yards long covered the table, extended to its full length. Two Rudelstaadt porcelain leaves, filled with salted almonds, flanked the centerpiece of snowdrops and jonquils from the garden. And coffee, served with whipped cream and lump sugar, accompanied the dessert of ambrosia and pound cake.[5]

Gregarious little Wil Lou was happy that her hospitable father knew so many dignitaries and invited them to his home. He must have been proud of his children because he always included them in these social affairs so he could show them off.

The Gray family was fortunate, for Wil Lou's father could afford to pay others to perform most household chores. Wil Lou well remembers the talented seamstress who came to the house to make almost all of the family's clothing, including the many-layered petticoats and pantaloons of flannel or cotton which she had to wear. Also any heavy laundry was sent out to a washerwoman, while the cook took care of the weekly washing and ironing. This cook and her family lived in a cottage provided for them on the Gray property, and Wil Lou fondly recalls how she and her brothers often played with the children because they were all about the same ages.

The Gray children had to be content with simple childhood pleasures. Their father had given them a goat which pulled them in a wagon all over town. Wil Lou loved books, and when she was not reading one herself, she was pleading for her mother to read to her. Attending Sunday School, church socials, and family get-togethers were also favorite pastimes for Wil Lou, who always loved being with people, the more the merrier.

The Gray children were reared in a devout religious atmosphere and church attendance was a regular family affair. Perhaps this contributed to Wil Lou's childhood ambition of becoming a foreign missionary when she grew up. Her family remembers that Wil Lou's countenance would brighten radiantly whenever a reference was made to the mission field. However, she does remember slightly "backsliding" once when she set an alarm clock to ring in the middle of her father's early morning devotions, which she felt were at times entirely too lengthy for sleepy-eyed youngsters. Even at the tender age of three, Wil Lou remembers being impressed by her mother's show of faith during the historic earthquake of 1886. While the phenomenon which killed forty people in Charleston and injured one hundred others was vibrating the very ground on which the Gray home stood, Wil Lou's mother calmly herded her children to the front porch and sat on the steps with one arm around Dial and the other around her daughter. Just as the children were being soothed by the singing of a lullaby, the panicstricken cook and her brood burst in the back door, weeping and wailing and loudly repenting of their many transgressions, since the end of the world was seemingly at hand.

Unfortunately, Wil Lou's mother became ill with tuberculosis when Coke was still a baby, and Miss Mollie Bonham was employed as a housekeeper when Mrs. Gray could no longer cope with the children and housekeeping. Wil Lou remembers Miss Mollie with affection, but feels she was more than a little partial to the baby, Coke, and could never seem to get along with their cook.

Wil Lou recalls several incidents from her childhood which illustrate that she was a normal, healthy child full of curiosity, and not above getting into mischief now and then. She remembers how her brother Dial, and his friend from next-door, Jim Dunklin, promised to reward her with a dime if she chewed some Mule tobacco they had found, which had been purchased to use as a moth preventive in stored winter woolens. Curious to try anything new, after only a few moments of valiant chewing, she was caught, not red-handed but green-faced, clutching the front porch railing for support. Since she could not open her mouth to tell her mother what was wrong for fear of getting the boys into trouble, she literally swallowed her pride, along with the cud of tobacco, and went inside to add insult to injury, a dose of foul-tasting medicine to cure her apparent stomachache. Even today she cannot abide tobacco in any shape or form!

10

Another time, Wil Lou's father had just returned from a business trip to New York where an acquaintance had convinced him that whiskey had medicinal properties which had helped his invalid wife rest better at night. Her father would try anything to give comfort to his beloved Lou, so he purchased a bottle of whiskey. Wil Lou was very curious about the novel substance, for the family had always been strict prohibitionists and teetotalers; therefore, the first time her mother's nurse was absent and her mother asleep, she climbed upon a chair to reach the bureau where the exotic bottle with its amber liquid was so tantalizing. She opened the cap and took a huge mouthful, rather than an experimental ladylike sip. Choking and feeling as if she were on fire, she stumbled across the room to the fireplace where she spit out the foul-tasting liquid, not knowing what happens to alcohol when ignited. To small Wil Lou, the ensuing blaze which leaped out at her and seemed to pursue her across the room was like the fires of hell she had heard about so often in church. The memory of that scene and the sensation in her burning throat convinced her so thoroughly of the evils of the demon rum that she has remained a confirmed teetotaler to this day! She felt so guilty about this incident that she never did confess to her family what she had done, and she was very thankful that her mother had not awakened and again caught her in the act of wrongdoing.

Then on several occasions Wil Lou was not above deliberately disobeying her mother in order to visit her beloved friend from next-door, Mary Dunklin, whom she had nicknamed "Mamie." Wil Lou considered Mamie as her very best friend, although Mary was ten years older, while Mary remembers Wil Lou during this time as "an echanting child, plump as Cupid, with very fair skin and red-gold curls."[6] Mr. and Mrs. Gray were both very fond of the Dunklin family and did not want Wil Lou to make a nuisance of herself with too many visits.

The evening before Mary was to leave for Columbia College, Wil Lou's parents walked over with going-away gifts, and since Wil Lou had selected and purchased a frivolous lace-trimmed handkerchief for her special friend and idol, she thought she was certainly entitled to accompany her parents and present her gift personally. However, it was an unseasonably chilly night and the children were left at home with Miss Mollie. When they were told to wash their feet in a basin in front of the fireplace before going to bed upstairs, Wil Lou, indignant at being left behind by her parents, deliberately spilled water all over the carpet. Outraged, Miss Mollie exploded, "I never seed sich a girl as you!" Undaunted, Wil Lou retorted, "And I never seed sich a woman as you!" However, it was not Wil Lou's nature to be impudent for more than a moment and she soon had talked herself back into Miss Mollie's good graces.

Inexorably, the condition of Wil Lou's mother worsened and a full-time nurse was employed to take care of her. Unfortunatley, the doctor's prognosis was pessimistic and despite all of the loving care given her, Lou Gray died in January of 1892, when Wil Lou was nine. William had realized for some time the inevitable loss which was to come, but he could not make himself tell the children. He persuaded their Uncle Nat, Nathaniel Dial, to prepare the children for their mother's untimely death. Wil Lou's first reaction was, "My mother won't die because God answers prayer, and I have been praying and praying that my mother will get well."

Unknowingly, her mother herself had prepared Wil Lou to accept death without fear or grief many years before. When Wil Lou was about six, she was playing with a neighbor's child who convinced her to go across the creek to another neighbor's home where a baby had recently died and the family was holding a wake before the funeral. When Wil Lou returned home, of course she had to tell her mother of her first experience with death, viewing "a dead baby wearing a white lace dress and bonnet." When her mother explained that the baby had gone to be with God's angels, Wil Lou was comforted.

As the family gathered around the gentle Lou in her last moments, Wil Lou has always remembered hearing her last words, "I see the angels coming," as she died with a smile on her lips. Wil Lou refused to cry until she was alone, for she felt she must be strong for her brothers and father and learn to care for them as her mother had always done.

After the sadness of the funeral, Wil Lou's father thought it best for the children's welfare to leave the home which was so empty without their mother's presence and to live for a time with comforting relatives. Therefore, he took them to stay with Dr. Jerome Christopher and his wife Laura, who was Lou's sister. Although they had no children of their own, their large rambling house in the country was always full of love and children for whom they were caring temporarily, and Wil Lou remembers many happy times there. She even felt it a privilege to be allowed to earn her own spending money by picking cotton. She also learned a valuable lesson from her Uncle Jerome that she remembered on many occasions when she was about to undertake some daring new project. With a tin pail in hand she was about to venture into the nearby woods to pick blackberries. When she told Aunt Laura where she was going, she was admonished, "If you must go, be sure and look out for snakes." Overhearing this warning, Dr. Christopher called out, "Wil Lou, be sure and look out for blackberries."[7]

Meanwhile, William Gray bought another tenant farm and immersed himself in his farming and church activities which he had been neglecting during his wife's illness. Miss Mollie had retired and built for herself a small home with the money she had earned while working for the Gray family, but the cook remained to take over the housekeeping chores for Mr. Gray.

Each Sunday afternoon found Wil Lou and her brothers eagerly awaiting the arrival of their father. He never failed to make the weekly drive to Gray Court, ten miles north of Laurens, a village which had been named for his father. Not only did he enjoy these trips because of his children, but he had been born at Gray Court and he welcomed the chance to visit with his brother Bob Gray and his sister, Dora Tolbert, who lived nearby.

This was the status of the Gray family for almost three years, but finally romance once again entered the picture. William Gray was an extremely fortunate man, for in his lifetime he had won the hearts of two beautiful, intelligent ladies who were devoted wives and mothers. Wil Lou was absolutely delighted when her father disclosed that he had proposed marriage to her beloved Mamie, and had been accepted. Mary had graduated from Columbia College by this time and was teaching in Laurens. As a matter of fact, she was Wil Lou's first-grade teacher, and despite the great affection they felt for each other, she sent her young charge to stand in the corner whenever Wil Lou was naughty.

Despite the difference in ages, for William was thirty-nine and Mary was twenty-two, their marriage seemed to be ideal. The family could now be reunited and Wil Lou and her brothers were thankful once again to have a loving mother. They again rejoiced a few years later when the family circle was enlarged by the advent of Harriet, always called Hattie, and later, William Lafayette Gray, Jr. The children were always very

13

devoted to each other and Mary loved her stepchildren just as much as she did those to whom she had given birth. None of the children ever thought it strange that Mary always referred to their father, whether in speaking to him personally or after his death, as "Mister Gray."

After the children had rejoined their father and new mother, Mary Gray was not pleased with Wil Lou's placement in Laurens City School. Supposedly she was behind other children her age in learning, proof that the rural schools at that time were far inferior to those in town. By the time Mary had tutored Wil Lou for a year she was able to skip a grade completely and rejoin her former classmates who were the same age.

Then later Coke developed a serious visual problem which had to be corrected by surgical specialists in Baltimore when he was only nine years old. He was able to perform well in grammar and high school with Mary's help, but it would have been impossible for him to go away to college and do well. Therefore, Mary tutored him at home in the usual college subjects and he learned so much that he was never hampered by the lack of a college degree and both he and Dial became successful businessmen.

The excellence of the new stepmother's teaching ability and the devotion she felt for her new charges must have helped to contribute to Wil Lou's decision to become a teacher herself. As she matured, she came to realize that although the number of missionaries was never sufficient to meet the demand, there was also a desperate need to give aid to those in the local area and help enrich their lives through education.

With this goal in mind, Wil Lou decided to further her education at Columbia College, a South Carolina Methodist school for girls, after her graduation from Laurens High School in 1899. (In those days it was typical to graduate after completion of the tenth grade.)

Mary Gray was quite fashion conscious and always saw to it that Wil Lou was well dressed. As a result, she and a seamstress designed a wardrobe which was the envy of all the young ladies at Columbia College. However, Wil Lou cared little about such feminine concerns as the latest styles. While she was yet in high school, her father had cropped short her auburn locks, a favor she had demanded because her unruly curls and tender scalp made hairdressing a painful chore. Even then, Wil Lou was years ahead of her time.

In her four years at Columbia College Wil Lou followed the standard

14

curriculum of the day. She remembers courses in United States and world history, English, geography, elocution, science, Latin, French, and German, but her very favorite subject was civics. She was not talented linguistically and foreign languages were very difficult for her; however, she excelled in her English classes. She did not learn much about science, for that class was taught by a lady who was a music major and knew little or nothing about the subject she had been assigned to teach. Classmates encouraged Wil Lou to distract the professor with discussions of music theory whenever she attempted to teach the science lesson for that day, but Wil Lou later regretted that she had wasted this time without learning anything.

Wil Lou earned above average grades at Columbia College although she was fonder of socializing than studying and quite often waited until the last moment before preparing for examinations. She seemed to have acquired the same gift for leadership that her father had displayed. She was a member of the Wightman Literary Society and served as its president her senior year. During that same year she was editor-in-chief and business manager of the *Criterion,* the school magazine. When she assumed this office, the publication was about to be discontinued because it was so heavily in debt, but Wil Lou personally assumed the obligation and managed the magazine so successfully that it soon revived, returned her investment, and began paying its own way.

Wil Lou wanted with all her heart to be a member of the Choral Club because all of her best friends had joined. Even though she realized she could not carry a tune, she was determined to participate in this activity with her friends. She stood next to her roommate who had a beautiful soprano voice, but her friend pointedly moved across the room from Wil Lou. When no one wanted to stand next to her because of her off-key singing, she finally took the hint and gave up her musical aspirations.

Wil Lou had learned to love politics at her father's knee and while in college had often visited the General Assembly meetings to observe South Carolina legislators in action. She was surprised and delighted one day when her father unexpectedly appeared at her dormitory and invited her to accompany him as he attended the inauguration of William McKinley. Wil Lou most remembers this historic occasion because of the bitter Washington cold they had to endure during the outdoor ceremony on the White House grounds.

Wil Lou's favorite teacher at Columbia College was Miss Cofield, her history professor. At the end of her senior year the prospective graduate was rejoicing over the successful completion of her studies and the imminent commencement exercises while talking to Miss Cofield. She was rudely brought down to earth when her mentor remonstrated, "It seems I remember a curly-headed young lady who failed to fulfill a pledge. I could not in good conscience allow you to graduate until you have passed a test in South Carolina history." Then Wil Lou remembered! In order to be accepted at Columbia College, prospective students had to pass examinations in several subject areas, and Wil Lou had failed to pass a test in South Carolina history. However, she was allowed to enter college since her other scores were very high, with the understanding that she would take the test again the next year. This she had promised to do, but had become so busy she had procrastinated and completely forgotten this vow. After Miss Cofield's reminder, there was nothing to do but seclude herself in her room for two days with nothing but history books for company, and not come out except for meals until she was thoroughly steeped in the historical background of her state. When she passed the test with flying colors, she once again could rejoice that she was about to graduate.

Wil Lou had hoped that her entire family could come to her commencement, but William was only a few months old and Mary felt she could not travel with him. Hattie was then not quite five years old and Wil Lou persuaded her father to bring her with him so she could visit the college which was becoming traditional for young ladies in the Gray family to attend. Little Hattie was ecstatic that she could go see her beloved "Boo" graduate from college, and every day she went upstairs and gazed with rapture at the graduation dress that had been fashioned for Wil Lou.

> This dress was made of the finest Swiss organdy, with pleated frills edged with lace over the shoulders, a basquelike waist, three-quarter-length sleeves, a gored skirt accented with quilled ribbon, trimmed the bottom of the skirt which was three inches above the floor. Three-quarter-length kid gloves, a lace fan, white satin slippers and her grandmother's pearls completed her graduation costume.[8]

For many years after, the sight of this dress hanging in her closet would bring back memories of those idyllic days at Columbia College.

Immediately after commencement Wil Lou enrolled for the summer term at Winthrop College in Rock Hill. She wanted to teach school in the autumn and since Columbia College at that time did not offer courses in education, psychology, and others we consider prerequisites for teachers today, she realized she was ill-equipped to teach school immediately.

Wil Lou's father wanted her to stay at home for a while rather than go to summer school, for he felt that a graduate of a fine Methodist institution like Columbia College was fully equipped to handle any job. However, Wil Lou reminded her father that he was not prepared to be a lawyer merely as a result of graduating from Wofford, but had to seek further training before engaging in that profession. When Wil Lou reasoned thusly, her father conceded that she must do as she felt compelled and follow her star. Attending the summer session at Winthrop College was only the first step along an educational path she was to travel for more than half a century.

Wil Lou as a young child in 1885

The Gray home in Laurens, S.C.

As president of the Wightman Literary Society in 1902-03

Wil Lou as a graduate of Columbia College in 1903

Wil Lou as a high school graduate after completion
of the tenth grade

NOTES

[1]Harriet Gray Blackwell, *A Candle for All Time* (Richmond: The Dietz Press, Inc., 1959), pp. 84-85.

[2]Ibid., pp. 87-88.

[3]Gray Family Archives, n.d.

[4]Ibid.

[5]Blackwell, *A Candle for All Time,* p. 151.

[6]Ibid., p. 62.

[7]Kohn, Erin, "Wil Lou Gray," *South Carolina's Distinguished Women of Laurens County* (Laurens County Historical Society, Columbia: R.L. Bryan Co.), 1972.

[8]Blackwell, *A Candle for All Time,* pp. 165-66.

REFERENCES

Blackwell, Harriet Gray. *A Candle for All Time.* Richmond: The Dietz Press, Inc., 1959.

Gray, Wil Lou. Columbia, South Carolina. Interview, 18 July 1975.

Kohn, Erin. *South Carolina's Distinguished Women of Laurens County.* Columbia: R.L. Bryan Co., 1972.

Tolbert, Marguerite. *Gray Family Archives.* n.d.

CHAPTER III

Debut at Jones School

Go ye therefore, and teach all nations . . .
St. Matthew

In September 1903, Wil Lou approached her first teaching assignment with the unflagging enthusiasm with which she was to meet each new challenge in life. With her typical independence, she refused the proffered help of influential relatives, and on her own she applied for the sole teaching position at Jones School in nearby Greenwood County. This appointment was approved by the local board and Wil Lou was launched upon an educational career that was to span fifty-four years of active teaching and supervising.

Jones School was a typical South Carolina rural school of the time. There was only one teacher for all ten grades. The physical plant was uninspiring with a potbellied stove for heat in winter, painted planks for blackboards, wooden benches for seats, and a building under which hogs had wallowed all summer. There was not even an outhouse (Dr. Jones thought them unsanitary), and the teachers and the students alike had to venture into the surrounding woods for privacy when the need arose.

Wil Lou had assumed she would board in the large country home of Dr. Walter Jones, the chairman of the board and the most prominent man in the community. Delivered by Coke to Dr. Jones's home, Wil Lou was tired, hot, and dusty after the five-hour ride from Laurens by horse-and-buggy. Then as they neared the house, Wil Lou felt instantly revived

19

because it looked so much like the spacious country homes of her many aunts and uncles where she had so often visited, and she knew she would at once feel right at home. She could not help but feel disappointed when after a brief visit, they were directed to the home of Dr. Jones's daughter, where he had arranged for Wil Lou to board.

Lydie Graham, her husband, and young son lived in a tiny, three-room cottage. When Coke was preparing to leave, he called his sister outside and doubtfully asked her if she really wanted to stay. But Wil Lou had promised to teach here and she felt bound by her commitment. She directed Coke to tell her parents that everything was fine and not to worry about her. She knew that Coke had not seen what she could perceive. He noticed only the external appearance of the cramped living space, while she saw the immaculate, white, handmade counterpanes, the inviting plumpness of the two featherbeds, the cleanliness of the kerosene lamp chimneys, and the spotless kitchen floor. Moreover, the friendliness of "Miss Lydie" and her family and the cordial welcome they had given her, made her realize that she could be happy here even if it was not at all like her own home in Laurens.

During her summer of study at Winthrop, Wil Lou had been very impressed by the teaching of Miss Annie Bonham, who later founded the innovative open-air school called Bon Air in Columbia. One of the first precepts she taught a future teacher was to arrive in the community a few days early in order to get acquainted with her new environment. Therefore, Wil Lou arrived on Saturday so she could have a chance to meet the community at Sunday services. The school served a dual purpose since an itinerant minister held services there Sunday afternoons. At this first meeting, the people of the community must have been impressed by the friendliness and enthusiasm of their new teacher.

Before Wil Lou met her students at Jones School, she had expected them to have received excellent instruction the previous year, for their teacher had been a good friend of hers, a graduate of Converse College at Spartanburg, and her expectations were soon confirmed. The new teacher found that she had some students at almost every level, from first grade to high school; therefore, she had to teach everything from the ABC's to the beginners, to Latin and algebra for the upper-level students. Wil Lou worked as hard and probably learned more than her students, for each night and weekend found her engrossed in preparing her lessons.

20

She particularly had to spend much time in reviewing Latin declensions and conjugations and solving the problems in higher mathematics, since these subjects had never been easy for her.

One night she had fretted over an algebraic equation which she just could not solve. She worried all during a sleepless night about what to do, for surely the teacher should be able to solve any problems in the textbooks. Still unenlightened, the next morning she started down the steps on her way to school with a prayer in her heart, "Lord, please give me the answer to that problem before I get to school," and instantly the correct solution popped into her head. She was chagrined that a mere misplaced decimal point had been the cause of her dilemma!

After her first week of teaching, Wil Lou decided it was time to follow another of Miss Bonham's practical guidelines, "Get out and know your parents!" For embarking on this mission, Wil Lou decided she should wear one of her best dresses, a bright blue polka-dotted foulard, to properly impress her students' parents, for she felt they must live very drab lives. It was the vogue at this time to have a train on "best" dresses, and Wil Lou's was no exception. She was making her rounds quite well although the high-buttoned shoes on her tiny feet were quite dusty from the red clay roads, and the train of her dress was trailing limply behind her in the dust before she had walked far. She probably would have returned home smugly satisfied with her dutiful visits accomplished, but for one untoward incident when the Meekin's dog took exception to her unusual appearance and tried to bite her. Not succeeding in that, he ripped a sizable chunk from her train. Undaunted, Wil Lou completed her rounds carrying the remains of a very bedraggled train over her arm. Later Wil Lou discovered that her stepmother had always detested the material she had selected for this particular dress, but she had remained silent because she felt it was time for the young lady to begin selecting her own clothes. However, she could not resist laughing when Wil Lou reported this incident, and commented, "I don't blame that dog, Wil Lou. Any self-respecting dog would have resented that dress."

Fortunately, other endeavors fared better. Miss Bonham also suggested involving the community in group activities, so Wil Lou, always ready to encourage the reading of good literature, decided to form a book club for adults. Each member was to buy one book each year, trading it to another member as soon as it had been read, and then the books were to be discussed at a monthly meeting.

Wil Lou wanted everyone, especially her pupils, to read good books, but unfortunately there was no library at Jones School. Then she happened to see an article in the *State* newspaper which might help her remedy that situation. The General Assembly had passed the first State Library Law, which provided that state aid would be offered for the purchase of library books if the school, district, and county would pay an equal share of ten dollars. Dr. Jones quickly agreed that this could be done and Wil Lou set to work to help raise the funds. She decided that a taffy pull to involve both the children and their parents would be a fun way of raising money for the new library. The result was a most successful Saturday night social affair, but the schoolroom floor was left in a sad state. The syrupy ingredients had spilled everywhere and one could hardly walk out the door without leaving shoes glued to the sticky floor. Since the school was to be used the next afternoon for church services, Wil Lou was at the school bright and early the next morning. With the help of only one little pupil, she built a fire to heat water on the wood stove, and for the first time in her life, Wil Lou Gray got down on her knees and scrubbed a floor. She has always heard in church that when your ox is in the ditch, it is all right to pull him out on the Sabbath, and although her conscience told her that she had helped to push the ox in on Saturday night, her qualms were eased when the congregation arrived to a neat, clean, although slightly damp schoolroom.

There was a humorous postscript added to this story many years later. When Wil Lou had chosen the books for the library, she knew absolutely nothing about what kind of books appealed to young rural readers. Therefore, she had ordered mostly the great classics which her stepmother had taught her to love and which she had enjoyed so much in her college courses. When she heard years later that a terrible storm had blown down the schoolhouse and completely destroyed the volumes of Shakespeare, Dickens, Thackeray, Scott, and many other great writers she had ordered, she heaved a sigh of relief that she need no longer be embarrassed about that first library.

While Wil Lou was studying at Winthrop, she had another favorite teacher, Mr. Hughes, who taught English and geography. Not only did she leave his classes with a finer appreciation of poetry, but she learned ways to make these studies exciting for her pupils. Since she had learned in his classes to make globes and maps of papier-maché, she decided that was an appealing way of teaching geography which involved children of all ages. The students brought to school all the old newspapers they could find. These were soaked in water and then molded into the mountains and valleys of a contour map drawn on heavy brown wrapping paper and glued to the surface of the globe. The finished products were colored with various dyes and hung in the room for both decoration and instruction. This was an after-school activity, and had been going on for some days when parents began complaining about their children getting home so late, especially the ones who had to walk several miles to school. Jones School had no clock, and Wil Lou had no watch. Consequently, both the teacher and her young charges were enjoying this activity so much, they never realized how late they were staying. Dr. Jones, who lived nearby, saved the day when he volunteered to go out on his porch at the proper closing time each day and ring a dinner bell so Miss Gray knew when to dismiss school. Later she wondered if the children's enthusiasm really stemmed from this educational project or whether they were glad to prolong it because it was better than milking cows and performing other evening farm chores.

The busy autumn of Wil Lou's first year of teaching quickly passed and the time for the Christmas holidays was fast approaching. Wil Lou was so busy planning and rehearsing the traditional school program that the community expected on Christmas Day, she forgot to be disappointed about missing Christmas Eve and morning with her family in Laurens for the first time. Wil Lou had worked hard to achieve the effect she wanted. The children had decorated the large tree which had been brought in from the adjacent woods with popcorn, cranberries, and apples. She had searched long and hard for the tiny little candles which were to be attached to the tree's branches adding the perfect touch and just the right amount of light for the festivities. She had gathered quilts from all over the community and tacked them over each window for the candlelight to be most effective. Unfortunately, on Christmas morning she discovered the candles had been misplaced. It was not until much later in the day that a naughty little boy confessed that he had hidden them. At the last minute all of the quilts had to be removed from the windows so the program could begin. However, all ended well with the proper Christmas spirit as the children recited their "pieces" perfectly,

23

the audience joined in the singing of the carols, and everyone exchanged gifts. As Coke was driving her home to Laurens after they had eaten Christmas dinner with Dr. Jones and his family, she reviewed the events of the past few months and decided that she had never been so happy in her entire life.

During the long drive home, Wil Lou, as usual, talked constantly and Coke must have been a patient listener. She told him about one of her favorite students, eighteen-year-old Coleman Cork, who walked six miles a day to school because he wanted to prepare himself for college. It was primarily for him that Wil Lou had struggled to be a good Latin and algebra teacher. Her instruction must have been effective, for she was later gratified to learn Coleman had graduated from Due West College and then attended the University of South Carolina, earning an advanced degree in the College of Law.

Another older adolescent who came to her for help had dropped out of school in the fifth grade because he had a severe hearing impairment. Wil Lou encouraged him to remain in school and assured him that her voice would be completely audible at all times. Indeed, she attributes her ability to project her voice to reach any audience to her early experience in teaching this almost deaf student. He must have remembered and appreciated this young teacher's effort, for after he married, he named his first daughter Wil Lou.

After Coke and Wil Lou arrived in Laurens for the Yuletide festivities, there was an entire week during which the young teacher could regale her family with all of her first-year experiences thus far. Her bubbly enthusiasm was contagious and caused her family to concede that she had made a wise choice when she decided to become a teacher.

Returning to Jones School and Miss Lydie's after her brief respite in Laurens, the remaining months of the school year passed all too fast until it was soon time for commencement. The final coup she was to execute for Jones School was in persuading Dr. Henry N. Snyder, President of Wofford College, to speak at the commencement exercises. Dr. Snyder was a gifted speaker Wil Lou knew from experience because he was a frequent visitor in the Gray home and a close friend of her father. However, it took all of Wil Lou's powers of persuasion to convince this busy man to make the fifty-five-mile trip from Spartanburg. She arranged for Coke to meet his train at Laurens and bring him by horse-and-buggy to her school, then drive him back to Laurens where he could board a train to return him to Spartanburg. Most people find it difficult to say no to Wil Lou when she has her mind set on a certain goal. Dr. Snyder was no exception so he agreed to be there.

Dr. Snyder's brilliant commencement address ended a year for Wil Lou that had been memorable. Despite the fact that her salary was only thirty-five dollars a month, with one-third of this spent on her room and board, she always remembers this year as one of her most rewarding experiences. Later in her career she was to yearn for the interested students and concerned parents such as she had encountered at Jones School, but this was not often the case.

The entire community thought she had done an excellent job teaching and begged her to remain with them, but Wil Lou had another plan in mind. As the following letter attests, Dr. Jones recommended her highly when she decided to go elsewhere.

Jones, South Carolina
July 12, '04

Miss Wil Lou Gray taught the Jones School the past session and gave perfect satisfaction to patrons and pupils. She is amiable, ambitious, energetic, has a tact for winning and retaining the love of her pupils, is in the enjoyment of good health, is a graduate of the Columbia Female College, and is in my opinion, destined to achieve an enviable reputation in teaching. I take great pleasure in cordially commending her to any school in need of a good teacher.

M.T. Jones
Chairman of Trustees

REFERENCES

Gray, Wil Lou. Columbia, South Carolina. Interview, 20 July 1975.

CHAPTER IV

Work at Wallace Lodge

A teacher affects eternity; she can never tell
where her influence stops.
Henry Brooks Adams

(Since Wil Lou Gray celebrated her twenty-first birthday on August 29, 1904, she will now be referred to as "Miss Gray.")

Miss Gray's uncle, John Gray, was chairman of the Board of Trustees for Wallace Lodge School. Both he and another uncle, Will Harris, each had a family of nine children and had long been most concerned about their children's education. As all members of the Gray clan were fervent believers in a good education, they too wanted their children to be well prepared for future college attendance. Uncle John and Uncle Will had encouraged and promoted a tax bond so the community could establish a public school. However, many residents were quite backward and felt that these men were seeking to serve only their self-interests; therefore, each time the bond issue arose, it was soundly defeated, although as the largest landholders, these two men would have paid a lion's share of the revenue. Their solution had been to establish a private school in an old lodge about halfway between Gray Court and Woodruff. Although they bore the brunt of the expense involved, any child in the community was encouraged to attend.

Miss Gray's relatives at Gray Court pleaded with her to come to Wallace Lodge School to teach and she was invited to live with Uncle Will and Aunt Lula, who was William and John Gray's oldest sister. Since she

27

realized there was a real need for her in this community, Miss Gray decided to accept their offer.

Her new home with Uncle Will and Aunt Lula Harris was called Greystone, because of its construction. Of necessity, Greystone was a huge house to accommodate the eleven members of the immediate Harris family, their housekeeper Black and her two children, a bookkeeper, and now the niece and teacher, Miss Wil Lou.

It was a blessing that Miss Gray was a most energetic person, for her Uncle Will was a busy scientific farmer, and her Aunt Lula, a graduate of Lander College, managed the large household most efficiently with the indispensable Black's help, so there was always some activity in progress to claim the young teacher's attention when she was not engrossed in her lessons for school. She felt quite at home living with this church-going family, and although she was not accustomed to rising at such an early hour for matinal prayers before sunrise, she soon learned to take part in this custom, and along with all other family members, quoted a new Bible verse before each evening meal.

Miss Gray thought the building called Wallace Lodge was much more picturesque than Jones School, but she soon found it had many of the same inconveniences. The outer walls were constructed of unfinished, unpainted planks, with such large cracks in places that in bad weather it snowed or rained almost as much inside as it did outdoors. Seats were sawed-off slabs of logs, with the bark still clinging to the outer surface. For desks, the children used long, unpainted boards which were placed in front of the rows of seats. Again she found a homemade blackboard that made writing almost impossible. Instead of the usual black wood stove, the lodge had a beautiful stone fireplace, but it required an immense effort to keep it stoked in winter, and sometimes the room grew quite frigid. The new teacher was quite relieved to find an outhouse in back of the school so she felt her lot as a country school teacher had greatly improved. The school was located about one-and-a-half miles from Greystone and she and her many cousins usually walked there and back each day, but on rare occasions they were treated to a buggy ride— a real luxury.

When Miss Gray's first term at Wallace Lodge began, she had only nine students, for cotton was an important crop in the community and most older children were kept at home until it was harvested. Later, about

Thanksgiving after the cotton had been picked, attendance at the school surged to sixty-five. This was too much for even Miss Gray's vitality, and when she was leaving to spend the Christmas holidays with her family in Laurens, she threatened not to return unless she could have some help. Then the trustees arranged for Mrs. Wallace, who was about sixty and well-educated, to be Miss Gray's assistant.

The new assistant was not always in accord with the methods of Miss Gray. She particularly was aghast that beginning students had been taught to read by the sight word method which was just then coming into vogue, before they even knew their ABC's. She was not impressed by their excellent reading ability, but could only predict a dim scholastic future for any child not thoroughly drilled each day in phonetics.

The two were in conflict, too, with their ideas of discipline diametrically opposed. Though Miss Gray had never believed in "spoiling the child," she could almost always successfully reason with a student, and would "spare the rod" except as a last resort in extraordinary cases of misconduct for which there was no other solution. On the other hand, Mrs. Wallace was quite adept at administering frequent doses of "peachtree tea," a rural expression meaning physical punishment, with the result parents did everything possible to see that their children were placed in Miss Gray's classes.

While living with the Harris family, Miss Gray was impressed by her uncle's agricultural expertise and fascinated with the rolling acres of white, fluffy cotton which was so vital to the community's economic welfare. Because she is a great believer in the dignity of labor, and was always alert for ways of raising money for her school, she determined that she and her young charges would pick cotton at recess and in the afternoons. She made a game of it and the two captains for the day chose teammates, with both sides competing to see who could pick the most cotton. Her Uncle Will commented that she had made cotton picking fashionable, for if the schoolteacher could do it, so could anyone else. However, she never presented a fashionable appearance in the cotton patch, for she had always been plagued by an ultra-sensitivity to sunlight which meant that she had to completely cover herself with protective clothing heavy enough to screen the rays of the sun which were an anathema to her fair skin.

One day Uncle Will's bookkeeper, Mr. Dorrah, wagered a dollar that

Miss Gray was not able to pick one hundred pounds of cotton in one day, or fifty pounds in one afternoon. Her Uncle Will tempted her even further when he promised to pay her one cent a pound, which she knew was twice the usual wages at that time. The next Saturday afternoon found the bundled-up schoolteacher in the cotton fields, alongside of her cousin Madge and Black. All the long, hot autumn afternoon she picked until after the sun had set. As the evening dusk deepened and the now ghostly appearing fields were bathed in moonlight, she realized she was able to pick no more and literally dragged herself to the scales to weigh her bag of cotton. While her day's yield was only forty-nine pounds, she did not win the dollar wager, but her uncle paid her the forty-nine cents she had earned for her labor. Her reaction on this occasion is typical of her approach to life in general, for she knew that she had given her best effort and done the most it was possible for her to do; therefore, she was satisfied.

While Miss Gray taught at Wallace Lodge, she had to work with large groups having students at many levels. There were not enough hours in the day to hold classes for each grade, one through ten, in each subject. She also had to find a way to give instruction without the use of books, for the school had none! To teach language, all of the students in her group, no matter what their ages or grade placement, met together and practiced the art of making conversation, always learning proper diction and grammar at the same time. She also found a favorite way of teaching history and science. Modern educators who have learned to teach by "simulation" could have observed Miss Gray using this technique at the turn of the century. Her students delighted in acting out the feats of great men in our history, from the discovery of America by Christopher Columbus until the time of Sherman's assault on Columbia, South Carolina, during the Civil War. Needless to say, her students learned a great deal of history in the process.

During this first year at Wallace Lodge, Miss Gray sought to interest the people of the community in sending their children to college and building a public school. One of her first efforts was to invite the entire adult population of the community to a meeting at the school. She carefully planned what she was going to say and sent letters home by the children urging their parents to attend. She even made a special trip to town to buy refreshments for the large crowd she anticipated. She was disappointed and dismayed by the "large" turnout which consisted of two elderly spinsters and their bachelor brother, who were, ironically, the last people in the world to need Miss Gray's well-planned lecture.

Miss Gray is almost impossible to discourage when she thinks her cause has merit, and she continued to do everything possible to incite these people to action. Whenever her uncle had agricultural experts visit his large farm, they were invited to the school in the evening to share their knowledge in public meetings. At one time, the Secretary of Agriculture talked to her patrons after a visit with Uncle Will. Also, when Lyceum seminars were held in nearby towns, Miss Gray attended with her relatives and nearly always succeeded in persuading the speakers to come to her school, without pay, to talk with the people. When she obtained the speakers' consent, she then had to induce one of her family to be responsible for their transportation.

In addition to these incidental meetings, Miss Gray arranged to hold a lecture course at the school with excellent speakers coming from Furman, Wofford, South Carolina College, and the State Department of Education. These visitors not only promoted the cause of better education, but encouraged a higher "quality of life" for the entire community. The teacher worked diligently to advertise these meetings and all of them were well-attended, with no more embarrassing "large crowds of three."

Miss Gray was happy teaching at Wallace Lodge and enjoyed living with the Harris family, but after her first year there she resigned to do graduate work at Vanderbilt University in Nashville, Tennessee, a story which will be told later.

The fall of 1906 found Miss Gray again at Wallace Lodge after she had completed a year of study at Vanderbilt. Her relatives had pleaded with her to return, and again she acquiesced. Her cousin, Madge Harris, who had studied at Winthrop College and Columbia University in New York but had not yet earned her degree, was engaged to give her assistance. She was delighted to find that in her absence the community had finally supported the local bond issue and a new school had been built, with the name being changed to Youngs School. She felt somewhat gratified that some of her preaching had not fallen on deaf ears.

It was becoming characteristic of Miss Gray to be always on the alert

31

for any money-making schemes to improve her school. When she observed that a vacant plot of land adjoined the schoolyard, she asked her Uncle Will to contribute one bushel of a new variety of Irish potato which he had recently developed. She and her students planted the bushel of "Lookout Mountain" potatoes, which produced a yield of twelve bushels. Rather than selling this crop, it was kept for seed and planted again. This time the excellent harvest was marketed and commanded a top price, providing the means for buying many new supplies for her school.

Miss Gray wanted her students to learn to appreciate the arts, especially music, but the new school did not have one musical instrument. Her father was demolishing an old building he owned at Gray Court and he consented to give her the bricks to sell. With the $25 she obtained from their sale, she bought a used pump organ, which was the means of teaching music to her pupils for an entire year, when it was then sold for $10 more than she had paid for it.

One of Miss Gray's prime ambitions had been to form a School Improvement Association at Youngs, with parents hopefully becoming as concerned about bettering the quality of their children's education as was she. This was the year for that ambition to be realized, just in time to compete for a prize the State School Improvement Association was offering. This organization was to award ten prizes of one hundred dollars each to the schools showing the most improvement in one year. Miss Gray was so certain her school was to be one of the winners that mentally she had already calculated how best to spend the money they were to be awarded. As she assessed the situation, she determined that a worthy project was to paint the exterior of the building. Since the new two-room school had never been painted on the outside, she felt that a sparkling white coat of paint was going to be a distinct improvement. The Board of Trustees agreed with her plan and volunteered to do the work themselves, but they were procrastinating and accomplishing nothing as the deadline was fast approaching for the end of the contest. Miss Gray had already purchased paint with funds she had raised singlehandedly, but still the trustees did not act. To spur the men into action, she made a date with a professional photographer in Laurens to be at the school in two days to take a picture of the building with its new coat of paint. Now the men knew they had to keep their promise. Uncle John closed his grist mill and all of his crew became painters for a day. Most of the community came to help and the teacher and her pupils wielded paintbrushes along with them. By the end of the day, two sides were glistening with fresh, white paint and when the photographer arrived early the next morning, these were the only sides which were photographed and mailed to the contest. The deadline was met and Youngs School did win one of the prizes. As soon as the photographer had left, everyone again pitched in and soon the remaining two sides matched the appearance of the others. This incident is typical of Miss Gray and her determination to meet goals she has set for herself. Her fertile imagination has always been able to "conjure up" some means to effect desired ends.

Miss Gray yearned to help these people even more than she had done already, but felt she did not yet possess the knowledge which would equip her for this task. As the school year ended, she did not intend to return; however, Fate decreed otherwise and in 1910 she was again teaching at Youngs, this time also acting as principal. Madge Harris was still there, but Miss Gray's intended replacement had become quite ill and the trustees again prevailed upon her to finish out the year as a substitute for the ailing Miss Tarrent.

Then who could have predicted that in a few years she would once again find herself at Youngs School, playing a major role in an educational experiment for illiterate adults that was to be a beacon lighting the way for the cause of adult education throughout the state of South Carolina?

REFERENCES

Gray. Wil Lou. Columbia, South Carolina. Interview, 25 July 1975.

CHAPTER V

The Campus Calls

> A university should be a place of light, of
> liberty, and of learning.
>
> Benjamin Disraeli

Vanderbilt University

As soon as Miss Gray had definitely decided to enter graduate school, she faced another important question of which school to attend. After considering Randolph Macon and other well-known women's colleges of that day, her choice finally settled on co-educational Vanderbilt University, in Nashville, Tennessee, primarily because its chancellor, Dr. J. K. Kirkland, was a good friend of her father.

It was arranged that she was to live in the home of Dr. William Vaughan and his wife, who was known as "Miss Stella." These good people had no children of their own living at home at the time, and wanted to adopt temporarily three other girls and Wil Lou, as members of the family rather than as boarders. As the Vaughans went to the depot in Nashville to meet Miss Gray and another of their newly adopted "daughters" who were arriving on the same train, they were surprised that the girls had not found each other and already become acquainted on the train. Miss Gray explained this by telling them, "Flora traveled rich, and I traveled poor." Ever conscious of thrift, she had taken the day coach rather than the luxurious Pullman.

During the year with the Vaughans, Miss Gray basked in the warmth of their friendship and in the scholarly atmosphere which pervaded the university. Her English professor, Dr. Jones, deepened her appreciation of poetry, and she can yet quote from memory much that was studied in his classes. His course was entitled, "The Fatherhood of God and the Brotherhood of Man," and the writing of such great men as Ruskin, Arnold, Rousseau, and Tennyson was studied in depth. She was further impressed by Dr. Jones's accounts of his fascinating personal experiences, such as entertaining John Brown, the fiery abolitionist, at dinner the evening before he was to be hanged for treason. Perhaps more valuable than the lessons she learned from studying great literature in this class, was his practical philosophy which was to become part of her own; this was to be concerned about others less fortunate and to turn that concern into action. He also stressed that no one could ever wholly pay for his education but should feel an obligation to repay the debt by service to the state and community. Dr. Jones would surely be pleased if he knew his protegee has contributed donations to the Opportunity School which total more than the state of South Carolina has paid her in salary during her fifty-four years of service!

Miss Gray was rather like a sponge this entire year, absorbing ideas and knowledge at every opportunity. When a guest lecturer was on campus, she attended, even if she persuaded no one else to go with her. She went to hear Booker T. Washington and stood for the entire lecture because there were no available seats in the auditorium. She was deeply impressed by the words of this great man and often after that used his life as an example of how a person might obtain an education if he had ambition.

Participating in the World Conference of the Student Volunteer Movement at Vanderbilt counted as her most memorable and inspirational experience ever. She was placed in charge of the literature desk to distribute pamphlets and brochures about the movement, and was able to meet many attending students from around the world. She had been conversing with one of the guiding forces behind the youth movement who had stopped to examine the literature, when she happened to notice the time and casually remarked that since she was already late for class, she planned not to attend at all that day. She then received a free lecture on the exact cost of one hour of education and what it was worth to the individual. She never forgot this experience and

36

thereafter attempted to instill in her students some idea of the cost of education and its value.

The keynote speaker for the Conference was Dr. Robert E. Speer, a noted theologian, but Miss Gray had not been able to obtain a reserved seat in the auditorium. Ever resourceful, she volunteered to sing in the choir which was to sit on the stage. After hearing the forceful and inspirational theme expounded, "I shall pass through this world but once," she intoned a silent prayer to be forgiven for this small bit of deception since she knew she could not sing a note, but she felt the Lord meant for her to hear this message some way. She also was able to appreciate the full glory of the anthems since she was wise enough only to mime the words and appear to be singing.

Although she had no classes under Dr. Vaughn, for he was head of the mathematics department and she was studying only English, history, and economics, living in his home made an indelible impression on her. She remembers that Dr. Vaughan had only one leg due to an unfortunate hunting accident, and he was very sensitive about that, but the brilliance of his intellect had more than compensated for any physical incapacity.

Once as Dr. Vaughan was shelving several new volumes in his library, Miss Gray noticed that they were all written in a language foreign to her. He informed her when she inquired that they were Russian and he had taught himself to read that language so he could learn about the Russian people. He had been quite concerned about the recent Russo-Japanese War and wanted to delve into the cause of it from primary sources. She never forgot the last words he said on this occasion, "Nobody but a fool needs a teacher."

Since Miss Gray and her three new friends were treated as members of the family, they were given the responsibility of preparing Sunday evening repasts and had much fun doing this. Then it was customary for the entire group to take long weekend walks, enjoying the world of nature around them.

After residing in the Vaughan home for one year, Miss Gray carried away with her three principles to which they were committed: Be a good citizen; share whatever you have with others; take care of your body. She feels she has successfully emulated the first two, but has never had time to observe the last precept strictly. The Vaughans always rested for at least fifteen minutes after each meal in an easy chair and

37

encouraged the girls to do the same, but she has never felt she should indulge in this inactivity when there were so many interesting things to do and places to go which were yet unexplored. This curiosity and thirst for knowledge was yet to take her to two other campuses in a very short time.

Martha Washington College

After a year at Vanderbilt University and another term at Youngs School, Miss Gray applied for a position at Washington College, in Abington, Virginia, for she had yearned to teach on the college level. Now in the fall of 1907, she was to have the opportunity she longed for, teaching English literature in a women's college.

Miss Gray had been so impressed by the way Dr. Jones at Vanderbilt had taught and had learned so much from his course, that she made "The Fatherhood of God and the Brotherhood of Man" the subject of her lectures to the young ladies at Martha Washington College. One student at least found the course memorable, for many years later when Miss Gray attended a reunion at the college, she was warmly embraced by the young lady who exclaimed that she could never forget the teacher who had required her to read the short story, "The Great Stone Face."

Her roommate at the college was another faculty member who taught art. She will always be remembered in a very tangible way, for from her Miss Gray learned the art of painting china. One of her prized possessions today is the set of beautiful white china emblazoned with the gold monogram W L G, which she painted under her roommate's tutelage.

The folks in Laurens were quite proud that one of their own was a college professor. They had frequent news of her activities by way of her letters to her parents, who proudly related her news to anyone interested. In one letter, Miss Gray had written to her stepmother that Dr. Long, president of the college, had made her responsible for the vesper services for that week in the chapel. She had no problem delivering an inspirational devotional for the young ladies, but when it was time for her closing prayer, the words stuck in her throat and for the first time in her life, Wil Lou Gray was at a loss for words. She had to laugh when the next post brought her mother's quick response. Her letter contained this bit of advice: "Don't you pray any more, Wil Lou, unless Dr. Long pays you

38

extra for it!"

Since Miss Gray is a most gregarious person, she enjoyed the many social affairs faculty members were expected to attend. On the other hand, she did not enjoy sitting in the young ladies' rooms whenever they entertained company, and was most bored during this rigidly enforced chaperonage.

Although she enjoyed most aspects of her teaching at Martha Washington College, she soon discovered she was not quite as fulfilled with this kind of teaching as she had hoped to be. Then, as the end of the year approached, she was further disillusioned when she was required by the administration to give passing grades to students who had not even tried to do acceptable work. Miss Gray had never been one to compromise her ideals and she submitted her resignation at the end of that year. However, she took with her Dr. Long's sincere recommendation. He had "found her competent, careful, conscientious, thorough and industrious in the performance of her duties . . . Not only in the classroom, but out of it in association with the young ladies, she has always exerted an uplifting and Christian influence."[1]

Columbia University

After her year teaching in college, Miss Gray returned to Youngs School as substitute for the ailing teacher/principal, where she completed the year for her.

While living in her Uncle Will's home, she had seen one of his tenant farmers "make his mark" when he signed his contract for the next year, because he could not write his name, and this scene had been indelibly engraved in her mind. She had done much soul-searching ever since she discovered that there were illiterate adults all around her in the rural communities where she had taught, and finally came to the conclusion that she must seek more knowledge herself before she was to be capable of alleviating their sad condition. These were circumstances which led Miss Gray to enter Columbia University in New York City in the fall of 1910, to pursue a course of study which led to an advanced degree in political science.

At Columbia Miss Gray found that she was the only female

postgraduate at that time. There was one other lady in some of her classes, but she and her husband were retired people who were merely auditing the classes. Their presence on campus gave Miss Gray a brilliant idea. She asked why older people could not return to school, no matter what their educational background, if they wanted to improve their status. At that time. she little imagined that she was to spend half a century realizing such a dream.

When Miss Gray was planning her living accommodations at Columbia University, she suggested to five other girls who were also enrolled there, two of them her cousins, that it would be more enjoyable and economical for the six of them to live in one apartment and share expenses. She became the manager of the group, budgeting the money, for each girl had contributed twenty-five dollars toward furnishing the apartment, and assigning the household chores. Since her cousin Madge was voted the best cook, she became the chef and the others took turns lending her a hand in the kitchen.

The girls shared many new encounters outside the communal living arrangement. At one time they enjoyed a cook-out breakfast on the banks of the Hudson River. Another time they journeyed to Boston on a steamer and spent a delightful three days touring that historic city and eating alien Yankee cuisine they had only read about, such as baked beans and brown bread.

It was part of Miss Gray's course of study in political science to do field work in outlying cities. She visited Tarrytown and made political surveys of towns like Westchester and Eastside. Wherever evening happened to find her, she was usually invited to spend the night. She met many friendly people this way, despite what some people had told her to expect from "Northerners."

During her year of study at Columbia, Miss Gray felt privileged that her professors were considered among the most intellectual in the entire country. Her major subject, political science, was studied in Dr. Giddings' course, "Social Evolution of the English." She studied Victorian literature under Dr. Thorndike. Three courses were taught by Dr. James Harvey Robinson: "History of the Intellectual Class in Europe," "The Protestant Revolt," and "The French Revolution." Under Dr. Dunning she studied "American Political Philosophy." She wrote her thesis under the tutelage of Dr. Dunning and chose the topic *J. C. Hurd's*

40

Political Philosophy. Although she spent an entire year writing and researching this thesis, the subject must have been uninspiring for later she was not able to remember Mr. Hurd's significance in the field of political science. However, upon the successful completion of her year's work, she received the Master of Arts degree in Political Science, in June 1911.

Miss Gray was now on her way home to Laurens for a restful vacation before traveling to a college in Louisiana where she had agreed to teach. She was not to travel far, however, for she had lost her pocketbook (a habit that was to plague her always) on the subway going to the train station. Since it contained her ticket home and all her expense money for the trip, there had to be a slight delay while she borrowed funds for her fare home. She then blithely continued on her way.

Wil Lou as she obtained a Master's degree in political science in 1911

NOTES

[1]Wil Lou Gray, Unpublished letter, 1980.

REFERENCES

Gray, Wil Lou. Columbia, South Carolina. Interview, 15 August 1975.

CHAPTER VI

Success As Supervisor

> I will not follow where the path may lead, but I
> will go where there is no path, and I will leave a
> trail.
>
> Muriel Strode

As soon as Miss Gray returned to Laurens with her advanced degree firmly in hand, Mr. George Pitts, the County Superintendent of Education offered her the newly created position of Supervisor of Rural Schools. He knew of her previous teaching success and wanted her to do for the entire county what she had done for the school at Jones, Wallace Lodge, and Youngs. She was in a quandary because she had already agreed to teach in a college in Louisiana, but that had been before she was aware of any supervisory positions available in her home county. However, she felt her training entitled her to more than the salary of fifty dollars per month which Mr. Pitts offered her. She was assured her duties would end when the school session ended, and she would be free in the summer months to do as she pleased, although she would be paid on a twelve-month basis. Still undecided, she sought advice from her relatives. Her father encouraged her to stay and work for Laurens County, but it was Uncle Jerome Christopher who finally resolved her conflict. She had told him that she wanted to teach history in a college because she had the training and knew how to do that, rather than supervise rural schools, about which she felt she knew next to nothing. Then her uncle asked, "Wouldn't you rather *make* history here in Laurens County, than teach it somewhere else?"

And now Miss Gray was embarking upon uncharted seas, her maiden voyage as an educational pioneer. Yet this was to be only the first of many subsequent ventures into the unknown and untried, which greatly extended the educational frontiers of her native state.

Having already taught in three rural schools, Miss Gray was aware of some of the problems she must surmount as the first Rural Supervisor. She soon verified that inadequate facilities, lack of teaching aids and materials, unmotivated students, and uneducated, unconcerned parents were typical in most rural areas in Laurens County.

Miss Gray was not one to sit in an office in Laurens and supervise from a distance. She knew she must be personally involved with each of the 71 rural schools and 125 teachers in the county. With this in mind, she left her home early each Monday morning, traveling from school to school in a horse-and-buggy provided by her family, and did not return home until sometime on Saturday. Most of the time she was alone, but sometimes she was accompanied on her rounds by Mr. W. K. Tate, the State Supervisor of Rural Schools. Horses can go only so fast and the two enjoyed these hours of travel between schools, for it allowed them much time to discuss school problems and propose solutions. "Motel" was not then a family word and each night Miss Gray depended upon someone's hospitality to provide lodging. This opportunity of close personal contact was not wasted and she always tried to promote the cause of better schools. These appointments at the various schools were made by the County Superintendent so the teachers and trustees always knew she was coming, and most of them seemed delighted that someone was taking an active interest in their plight.

While Miss Gray was in the schools, she looked for the most pressing needs and tried to aid the teachers in any way possible. She helped teachers arrange their daily schedules more efficiently; she observed their work and taught demonstration lessons for them. As she traveled from school to school she observed that reading instruction was a universal problem and much of her work the first year was aimed at this problem. She had to convince the teachers that specific reading skills had to be taught, for she found that most of them merely listened to children try to read and did not know how to teach reading.

However, she found the most overwhelming problem was a total lack of uniformity in the schools. Some schools had qualified teachers; others

44

did not. A few buildings were adequate; most were not. Some communities raised tax money; others refused. Some schools were in session seven months; other terms lasted eight or nine months. To effect the uniformity which she felt would improve the school conditions on a county-wide basis, Miss Gray began to implement several innovative programs in the fall of 1912, and these were expanded and improved upon during her four-year tenure as Rural Supervisor.[1]

Always plagued by the evidence of poor attendance and the lack of a compulsory attendance law, Miss Gray determined to compile statistics which proved to administrators and the public the grave extent of the problem. In each district a letter was sent to each chairman of the board of trustees asking how many children did not attend school in 1912-1913, how many were enrolled but did not attend school forty days, and the reasons for the absences.[2] She discovered that this problem was caused in large part by parents' attitudes, and she soon came to realize that they needed to be educated before their attitudes were to be changed. In one case, one of the parents at Youngs School had become more conscientious about sending his children to school every day because he knew there was to be a visit and a lecture from Miss Gray if he did not. The students were motivated to improve their attendance by perfect attendance buttons which were awarded by the county, and by free passes to Saturday morning educational films Miss Gray had obtained from the theater manager in Laurens. An additional attempt to alleviate the poor attendance was a personal door-to-door canvass by the Rural Supervisor to obtain signatures on petitions requesting compulsory attendance laws.

In order to encourage reading, library certificates were awarded to all students reading at least five books. Schools which did not have libraries were encouraged to take advantage of the School Library Law, and School Improvement Associations were formed where needed to help raise the necessary supplementary funds.

One of Miss Gray's most popular and successful innovations was arranging to have printed a monthly publication named *The School Journal*, written and edited by the children in the rural schools. Miss Gray always read the material submitted but did no rewriting, so this was not only an excellent means of teaching language arts, but it helped disseminate educational information for the whole county. In a very short time, there was a list of more than one thousand subscribers to attest to the popularity of the periodical.

To give further publicity to the county schools, the editor of the *Laurens Herald* contributed space for regular feature articles concerning education. Also, the *Laurens Advertiser* was persuaded to publish an educational issue of its paper in April, in conjunction with the promotion of the Laurens County School Fair.[3]

Under Miss Gray's supervision the School Fair became another successful enterprise. This was a competitive event for county school children, with red, yellow, and blue ribbons awarded for winners in reading, spelling, arithmetic, composition, history, sewing, declamation, and both elementary and high school athletics. Miss Gray felt that this had been a "great means of standardizing the schools," for when the five hundred students competed for the prizes offered for various events, it was easily evident that the school which had made the greatest improvement also won most of the awards. It was a source of pride for students and teachers alike that the rural schools were becoming known for their improvement and achievement and were no longer considered distinctly inferior to the city schools.[4]

In visiting the school district, Miss Gray always encouraged the formation of a School Improvement Association if there were none at that time. The Annual Report for 1915-16 declared that there were 44 School Improvement Associations in Laurens County. A total of 602 members atttended 185 meetings and contributed $2,791.93 to the schools. The extent of Miss Gray's personal effort was evident when the Executive Committee of the School Improvement Association published data from the Fourth Congressional District which credited her with the formation of 27 associations, with 532 members attending 162 meetings and raising $1,563.13 in funds. In a very tangible way, these schools had received aid from Miss Gray which led to their improvement.[5]

This same Executive Committee had commended Miss Gray for making of the rural schools a community social center. When classes were over for the day, she often made use of the school building for public meetings. Early in her career as Rural Supervisor, she had raised the necessary money for purchasing a stereopticon lantern. She showed slides from places she had visited; other slides she had depicted foreign countries; and some she had obtained from Mr. Tate to demonstrate improvements that had been accomplished in other counties. This gained the attention of those who had gathered for the meeting in progress. If taxes needed to be increased or initiated, the income and expenditures of the school in question were placed on the blackboard, and sometimes the amount of taxes paid by each member of the community![6] More often, the highest amount of taxes paid and the lowest were placed on the board, but without names, so patrons could mentally compare and decide if they should not be doing more for the education of their children. In one such meeting a farmer interrupted Miss Gray's fervent pleas for a much-needed tax increase by asking her what *she* was getting out of the higher taxes. Rather taken aback, she pointed to the blisters on her small feet that were a result of trudging across many plowed fields that week to visit homes, as she replied, "These blisters, and better schools for *your* children!" The farmer must have been impressed for he was one of the first in line to sign the petition.

From the first, Miss Gray recognized that many of the rural teachers did not approach their work with a professional attitude. To promote a sense of professionalism, she immediately reactivated the Teachers' Association which had expired two years before from lack of interest. At the first meeting she called, it was decided that the one dollar annual dues were to be spent on lecture programs and books for a teachers' library, with the names of those teachers attending five meetings and reading three professional books placed on the Superintendent's "Honor Roll."

That these rural teachers might be better prepared for their work, Miss Gray originated the practice of holding training sessions called "institutes," on a regular basis in Laurens. On the scheduled Friday afternoon teachers began arriving from outlying districts and the good citizens of Laurens provided them with a place to stay during the three-day affair. The Rural Supervisor always managed to have interesting speakers, and she and other supervisory personnel from the State Department of Education discussed specific educational aims for that year, and then in round-table discussions, teachers planned how to effect the desired objectives.[7]

In order to further foster the professionalism she advocated, Miss Gray urged her teachers to join county, state, and national teachers' organizations. One year she organized an educational sightseeing trip for her rural teachers who were members of the National Education Association. Seventy-five teachers attended the national convention in Washington, D.C., then went on to tour New York City and Philadelphia. Because Miss Gray was even then a financial wizard, the total cost per teacher was only sixty dollars. This was such a rewarding venture that she frequently arranged such tours in later years, and always referred to them as "pilgrimages," a term she coined to denote educational excursions.

Remembering some of the unpleasantness and inconvenience of her first year of teaching, Miss Gray was vitally concerned about sanitation and the appearance of the schools and grounds in Laurens County. She quickly instituted a "Clean-Up Day" which soon became traditional. In a letter to trustees prior to the opening of a new school term, they were informed as follows:

> Just at this season the appearance of the schoolhouse and yards suggests a Clean-Up Day. No good housekeeper would welcome a guest in untidy surroundings. Surely the teachers demand the respect of a visitor. If so, call a meeting of the patrons to celebrate Clean-Up Day the week before school opens. On that day yards and outhouses should be cleaned, lime scattered, wells drained, floors scoured, windows washed, stove polished, desks nailed to strips of planks, and chalk and other teaching apparatus supplied. A day's work by the people will be a saving of school money and children's time, as well as a substantial welcome to the teacher.[8]

Another major problem encountered by Miss Gray was the typical overcrowding of classes in the one- and two-teacher schools. She knew that her previous teaching had become more effective when she had some assistance, and she always strived to reduce the class loads for her teachers. The following figures suggest that she did somewhat alleviate this problem during her tenure, for in 1912 there were 71 schools with 125 teachers, but in 1916 there were 68 schools with 154 teachers.[9]

Another area of standardization that was sorely needed and can be attributed to Miss Gray's sole effort concerned the county-wide seventh-grade examinations. It was required that students in Laurens County pass an examination with a certain score before being allowed secondary school admittance. Up until 1912, each teacher was responsible for the content of the examination for his own students, and of course, Miss

48

Gray discovered great discrepancies among the examinations. She frequently found test questions written on the board which even she was not able to answer, with an emphasis on unimportant dates and details that proved nothing about how a child reasoned. She appointed a committee of teachers to make an outline of basic information and skills which students were to have mastered before entering high school, and from this came a uniform set of questions which were given early in the year to all seventh-grade students who wanted to enter high school. All students who successfully passed the examination at the end of the year, after it was graded by the County Superintendent and Miss Gray, were honored in a public ceremony in Laurens, and a certificate of achievement was awarded. The direct result of this much-needed improvement was a significant reduction of seventh-grade dropouts, for the students were now receiving recognition of their successful achievement in school and were being motivated to continue their education.

Not only did Laurens County Schools improve because of changed attitudes of teachers and students, but Miss Gray knew the power wielded by the trustees of each school, and she was able to enlist their wholehearted cooperation. During the summer of 1915 at a "Conference for Common Good" held in Laurens, the County Trustees' Association formulated objectives which they knew were important to Miss Gray, and these indicated that prospects were promising for even more successful schools in the future. The trustees' primary objectives were the following: that each school shall receive a visit from a trustee each week; that teachers are urged to become active members of the County Teachers' Association and to attend the Teachers' Institute; acceptance of the School Attendance Law in every district; and establishment of night schools for adults throughout the county.[10]

It is evident that Miss Gray was able to accomplish much in improving the schools for the rural children, but everywhere she traveled she was haunted by the specter of adult illiteracy. She realized that before optimal change was to take place in the schools, the uneducated and uncaring parents must be reached and taught also.

The Federal Census of 1910 revealed that 25.7 percent of South Carolina's population above the age of 10 was illiterate. At this time South Carolina had a population of 1,515,400. Of these, 90,707 were illiterate males 21 years of age or over. Among this number were 17,599 native whites and 72,857 Negroes, but only 206 foreign-born whites. This census further revealed that only Louisiana ranked higher than South Carolina in the number of illiterate adult citizens. Furthermore, with 10.3 percent of its native white population 10 years of age and over illiterate, the state of South Carolina was exceeded in percentage of illiteracy in this category by only 6 other states. Moreover, only Alabama and Louisiana had more Negro illiterates than South Carolina.[11]

In her home county of Laurens, Miss Gray was curious about the number of illiterates so she researched the Democratic roll of registered voters. Of the 4,525 voters, 608 had to "make a mark."[12] Her dream of adult education for the mass of unlettered citizens of her native state was first conceived when she witnessed her uncle's tenant farmer make his mark a decade before,[13] and now she felt the time was ripe for her dream to begin flowering into reality.

Miss Gray enlisted the help of Mr. James H. Sullivan, who had been the County Superintendent of Schools for the past three years, in establishing night schools for adults on an experimental basis. This project became Miss Gray's chief claim to fame while she was Rural Supervisor, and Youngs School has been cited as a historical landmark in South Carolina because of her work begun there in 1915. Because of its significance, this night school experiment is presented in detail.

These adult night schools were to be held in seven locations in Youngs Township. Miss Gray felt she knew the area quite well, and while it contained a higher percentage of illiterates than any other area in Laurens County, it also consisted largely of a white population of landowners and tenants who might have a more positive reaction to the novel idea of adult education.[14]

In a community meeting in each of the seven schools selected for the experiment, after a showing of stereopticon pictures of Yellowstone Park, the question of an adult night school was presented to the people of the community. Miss Gray had personally made a house-to-house canvass to promote participation in the project. The first response she received to her query, "Would you take advantage of a chance to learn to read and write?" inspired her, for she was assured, "I would give half I expect to make this year to learn to read and write."[15] With the help of teachers and trustees, as many as possible illiterate persons in the community were given a personal invitation to participate.

The schools met three nights a week for one month, from seven until nine o'clock. Miss Gray planned to be present once a week at each of the seven schools.

With slight variations to meet the needs of individual schools, the following schedule was planned:

7:00 - 7:15 Opening exercises

7:15 - 7:45 Writing

7:45 - 8:15 Arithmetic

8:15 - 8:45 Language, spelling or reading

8:45 - 9:00 Agriculture or civics

The opening exercises were considered to be very important. A devotional was always given first, led by class members, followed by singing. Then the teacher presented a reading, such as Dr. Clinkscales' "How Zack Came to College."[16] To vary the routine and promote interest and participation, newspaper articles were often discussed.

Next the students went to their respective groups — beginner, intermediate, or advanced. Those who had received some education were invited to participate in the experiment in order that the totally illiterate not be embarrassed.

For the writing class, the Palmer Company had donated the materials for teaching the Palmer method of penmanship. The beginners were given copies of their names, a simple sentence, or the alphabet to practice at home.

The State Department of Education had supplied Tate's *Farm Arithmetic for South Carolina*. Advanced students learned how to estimate the cost per pound of cotton and corn, to keep accounts, to mix fertilizer, and to figure interest. Beginners learned to write numbers, add, multiply, and subtract.

Advanced and intermediate students in language class studied business letters and orders, the principal parts of verbs, and common errors of usage. While these students were instructed in language, the non-readers were learning reading skills. Reading instruction was eclectic, with teachers using the complete sentence, sight word, and phonic methods. These students quickly mastered the first sentence presented, "I am a farmer."

Spelling was not neglected. Each class session students received twenty-five common words to learn. They looked forward all term to the spelling competition which was to be held at the close of their session.

In the last fifteen minutes of class time, the students studied agriculture, civics, or current events. At this time Clemson College agricultural bulletins were read and discussed. In addition, the classes received instruction concerning the duties of their various county and state officials and their own basic civic responsibilities as well.[17]

When Miss Gray arranged for prominent speakers to visit, the meetings were open to the public so the entire community benefited. Visitors during this first session of adult night school included the following: the State Superintendent of Education, J.E. Swearingen; Miss Eva Hite, President of the South Carolina Improvement Association; W.H. Hill, Assistant Corn Club Demonstrator for the South; W.H. Barton, Assistant State Farm Demonstration Agent; and James H. Sullivan, County Superintendent of Education.

It was to become a custom that these schools would close with a public spelling match and a free oyster supper. By this ploy, Miss Gray knew she would have the entire community in attendance, for the rural folk of Laurens County considered this coastal delicacy an exotic delight.[18]

The interest in this type of school was best indicated by the fact that 137 men and 7 women, ranging in age from 19 to 63, were enrolled in the schools. Average attendance was 64 percent despite incessant rain. Some of the men wanted to show their gratitude for this chance to become better educated by offering to reimburse the teachers who were receiving no additional salary for their efforts.

Teachers reported at the end of the first session that 33 beginners had learned to write their names and to read a little, and all had made remarkable progress in primary arithmetic. The teachers' interest and cooperative spirit were evident when 12 of the 13 participating in the experiment promised to return the next year and teach both day school for the children and night school for the adults in the community.[19]

The interest of the night school adults directly led to an improved situation in the day schools, for two districts immediately voted for compulsory education and petitions were circulated in another three districts. Moreover, the children were more interested in learning when their parents came to realize the worth of an education and encouraged

52

them in educational pursuits.[20]

However, the best example of the night adults' fervent enthusiasm for their opportunity to learn was demonstrated for all of Laurens County to see at the School Fair in the spring. The *Laurens Advertiser* reported:

> . . . the school parade was the crowning feature of the day. The line was formed at the grade school building and the march made to the public square, the children marching four abreast. While all of the schools deserve credit for their appearance, . . . the two schools representing extremes in age commanded most attention. These were the kindergarten pupils of the Laurens Mill . . . and the night school 'boys' of Young's Township. Not content with merely marching in the parade, these enthusiastic night schoolers gave full vent to their spirit of youth and vied with the leather-throated youngsters in cheering and rooting for their schools in the following words:
> 'Day School, Day School,
> Take a back seat.
> Night School, Night School,
> Got 'em far beat!'[21]

As a result of this brief experiment, Miss Gray drew some important conclusions:

1. The experiment demonstrates that the night school will be patronized and appreciated by those who need it most.

2. Night schools should become a part of the school system, for to educate the adult citizenship would improve the state materially, politically, socially, and religiously.

3. The minimum term of three months should be taught by the teachers employed in the day school, who eventually ought to be paid at least one dollar per night. Until established by the state, progressive teachers will give their services for a limited time.

4. The session should be held during the months of December, January, and February, when the farmers are not busy. Bad roads and cold weather are better than tired bodies.

5. At first it will be best to attempt the work in a limited area, so one person can supervise it.

6. The school should be a community school, offering something to all, both men and women, and should be patronized by the educated as well as the uneducated, so that the illiterates will not feel conspicuous.

7. Before undertaking the work, a thorough school census should be taken, preferably in an unobtrusive manner. The teachers should visit and become friends of prospective students, especially the illiterates.

8. The press, the clergy, and all public-spirited citizens are delighted to assist in this work. Before attempting the work their support should be enlisted.

9. Some special literature should be published for use in these schools — a simple reader adapted for grown-ups in the country; one pamphlet containing elementary lessons on civil government, geography, and history; and a simple bulletin on agriculture. Aside from the combination of numbers which every teacher uses, Tate's *Farm Arithmetic for South Carolina* will supply the arithmetic.[22]

The State Superintendent of Schools, Mr. Swearingen, concluded that as a result of the experiment, "Miss Wil Lou Gray and the women teachers of Youngs Township have pointed the way for the practical removal of illiteracy from our white population by 1920."[23] He further commented in his Annual Report of 1915:

> . . . The atmosphere in these schools was the best I have ever observed, because adult pupils were earnestly striving to learn, and because teachers were bringing them, without money and without price, the best they were able to offer.
>
> Such work would prove helpful in hundreds of rural communities. Pulpit, press and school might well join in a State-wide campaign to teach every adult how to read and write. Such a movement would help to remove the necessity for any man to sign his name with a mark.
>
> Already night schools have been organized in many other counties. Teachers are willing and able to do the work. It helps to bring a better chance to many neglected and forgotten men. Such work is worthy of support and endorsement at the hands of the lawmakers.[24]

The success of this experiment led to an expansion of the adult education movement the following year when 10 schools participated. There were 335 pupils and average attendance rose to 73 percent. One hundred pupils earned perfect attendance awards. These schools again continued for one month, meeting three times per week. Thirty teachers instructed voluntarily without financial compensation.[25]

Some weeks before the new term of night school was to open, Miss Gray was planning meticulously to ensure further success in the program, and she sent this letter to all teachers involved:

> The Night Schools will begin Monday night, January 17. There are in Laurens County over 500 men who can neither read nor write. If every teacher would teach four, Laurens County would have no illiteracy among the men. Won't you become enthusiastic in this work? Enlist the interest of your Trustees, School Improvement Association and Pastor. Spend the next two weeks preparing to open your school. Arrange for lighting the school. By community visiting, especially the illiterate, create an enthusiasm which will cause your school to be the best in the county. Believe in the work and others will.
>
> Miss Wil Lou Gray,
Supervising Teacher[26]

Again for this second term Miss Gray compiled and circulated a list of suggestions for the benefit of the cooperating teachers. Contained in these helpful hints is much useful information concerning the earliest adult rural schools, and they also illustrate Miss Gray's master planning, for she did not believe in results being left to chance.

> First Night: Arrange for the building to be well heated and lighted. Begin promptly. Have work thoroughly planned. Ask your pastor or some influential citizen to conduct the devotional exercises. If your people enjoy music spend a few minutes singing old familiar songs. In a few words explain the purpose of the school — a school where everybody in the community can come together and interchange ideas. State that you are willing to teach what the pupils feel they most need to know. Announce that a Perfect Attendance Button will be given to those who earn it. Tell of the prizes offered and urge students to help their school win. After these exercises, ask all pupils who have been to school more than a year to go to one part of the room. Later you can tactfully subdivide classes. Read for ten minutes every night some interesting book or article. Last year "How Zack Came to College" was enjoyed.
>
> Writing: Teach writing just as you do to the children. If students wish a book, Manual V of the Practical Writing System will be found helpful. Give the illiterates their names as the first night's writing lesson.
>
> Arithmetic: Section I. Teach the writing of numbers, simple addition, multiplication, division and subtraction. The circle device will be found helpful. Explain thoroughly enumeration. Teach multiplication

55

tables. For Section II use the Farm Supplement found in Milne's *Arithmetic*. If class is not prepared for this work, spend time on combination of numbers and fractions. Section III can use *Farm Supplement* interestingly. All students will enjoy arithmetic matches.

Reading: For Sections I and II use *Country Life Readers* which can be purchased from the Powe Drug Store. These books are especially adapted for such work, containing not only the reading matter but spelling copies for written work. I am persuaded that all three sections would enjoy reading the books, for while very simple, the subject matter will be interesting to advanced pupils, and will serve as a basis for civics discussions.

Agriculture: Get some successful farmer to take the lead in these discussions. The best textbook for use would be "Agriculture for Farm and School," R.L. Bryan, Columbia, price ten cents. If you do not care to purchase this, the following bulletins may be obtained from the Superintendent of Education's office: "Agricultural Success in a Nutshell," and "Cotton Catechism." Both are excellent, being prepared by W.H. Barton, Clemson College.

Civics: The *Advertiser* and the *Herald* will publish weekly under the caption "Night School Lessons" some articles which can be used in this department. During this recitation consolidate all of the classes. Encourage students to have free discussions and then teach a higher conception of citizenship.

Some time during this month have a social meeting and oyster supper. After twelve nights of school arrange for a public spelling match, arithmetic match and debates among the advanced students.[27]

Miss Gray and some few other educators knew that the night school concept for illiterate adults was potentially a powerful weapon for waging war on illiteracy, but she also knew ". . . these schools will never reach a high plane of usefulness until put by the State upon the business basis of some remuneration for the teacher with an extension of the term."[28] But since she had not been able to elicit such support, she regretfully resigned as Supervisor of Rural Schools.

As Rural Supervisor, Miss Gray had accomplished much during her four-year tenure, but she is the first to credit others with her success, for undoubtedly without the support and spirit of cooperation of her teachers and patrons, her labors would have been fruitless. When it became known that she was to leave Laurens County to return to Columbia University, the following excerpts from letters her teachers wrote demonstrate how they felt about her:

> You were such a help to me when I was beginning and felt so discouraged.

> I have made the changes in my work you suggested and can see an improvement already. I only wish you had visited my school sooner.

> I shall never forget the few words of advice you gave me in Laurens some few days past and assure you that I shall exert every effort to eradicate those criticisms.

> Knowing you has meant much to me. If you had not come to me while I was down at Belfast, fighting to keep my head above water and improve that school just a little bit, I don't know what would have happened to me. If someone with my ideals had not come along just then to bolster me up, I'm afraid I should have despaired of doing anything. I enjoyed every bit of my work in your county and my heart goes back to Laurens yet.

> Thank you for your help in planning our school fair. I'm so much more optimistic about it . . . you were such a help and comfort. . .

> We appreciate what you did for Mt. Olive this session. You may not realize this fact, but you have a great influence there.

> I regret very much having to give you up as our supervising teacher . . . I shall try to be successful and always abide by that good and noble example which you have set before me.

> I'm afraid it will be hard for Laurens County to find another who possesses to such a degree the rare faculty of harmonizing different opinions.

Not only did Miss Gray leave behind a legacy of love and respect in Laurens County, but largely because of her untiring efforts, Governor Manning and the General Assembly granted Superintendent Swearingen's request for $5,000 for night schools. Actually, the General Assembly appropriated only $1,000 at this time, but it authorized the State Superintendent of Education to augment this appropriation up to $5,000 with the unexpended balance from a special one-mill state school tax levied in 1913. Teachers were now to be paid one dollar for each night of teaching.[29] Ironically, the action was too little and too late, for Miss Gray had already left for another year of graduate study.

After Miss Gray's resignation, the Superintendent's Annual Report for the school year 1915-16 included the following summary of that year's night school work throughout the state:

Number of schools established	71
Number of nights taught	3,263
Number of pupils enrolled	5,013
Number of teachers employed	215
Estimated number taught to read and write	2,000 [30]

Nevertheless, Miss Gray was not impressed by these figures, for to her they indicated merely a token effort to combat the problem of adult illiteracy in South Carolina. Impatient with legislators and state leaders who feared educating the masses, especially the Negro population, Miss Gray returned to Columbia University in the autumn of 1916. She was still convinced that somehow she could acquire the knowledge which would enable her to overcome both the public and legislative indifference which was holding thousands of South Carolinians literally in bondage — enslaved by poverty, ignorance, dirt, and disease.

Youngs School is now a historical landmark in S.C.

NOTES

[1]Wil Lou Gray, *Annual Report to the Superintendent* (Columbia: State Department of Education, 1912-13), p. 134.

[2]Wil Lou Gray, unpublished questionnaire, 1913.

[3]Wil Lou Gray, *Annual Report to the Superintendent* (Columbia: State Department of Education, 1914-15), p. 131.

[4]Ibid., p. 132.

[5]Wil Lou Gray, Annual Report to the Superintendent (Columbia: State Department of Education, 1915-16), p. 57.

[6]*Forty-eighth Annual Report of the Superintendent of Education* (Columbia: State Department of Education, 1916), p. 60.

[7]Ibid., pp. 54-55.

[8]Wil Lou Gray, circular letter to trustees, n.d.

[9]Superintendent's *Annual Report*, 1916, p. 61.

[10]*Forty-seventh Annual Report of the Superintendent of Education* (Columbia: State Department of Education, 1915), pp. 133-34.

[11]Wil Lou Gray, *A Night School Experiment in Laurens County, South Carolina* (Columbia: State Department of Education, 1915), pp. 5-6.

[12]Ibid., p. 6.

[13]Wil Lou Gray, letter to May Madden, April 18, 1938.

[14]Wil Lou Gray, *A Night School Experiment*, p. 9.

[15]Ibid., p. 10.

[16]Dr. Clinkscales was a good friend of Miss Gray's father and one of her former college professors.

[17]Wil Lou Gray, *A Night School Experiment*, pp. 11-13.

[18]Ibid., p. 13.

[19]Ibid., pp. 15-17.

[20]Ibid., p. 18.

[21]Ibid., pp. 28-29.

[22]Ibid., pp. 29-30.

[23]Ibid., p. 38.

59

[24]Superintendent's *Annual Report*, 1915, pp. 30-31.

[25]Superintendent's *Annual Report*, 1916, p. 56.

[26]Wil Lou Gray, from the office of James H. Sullivan, County Superintendent of Education, Laurens, South Carolina, 1916.

[27]Wil Lou Gray, circular letter to teachers, December 1916.

[28]Wil Lou Gray, *Annual Report to the Superintendent*, 1915-16, pp. 56-57.

[29]Wil Lou Gray, "Evolution of Adult Elementary Education in South Carolina," *Adult Elementary Education Interstate Bulletin*, Vol. II, No. 5, May 1927, p. 3.

[30]Superintendent's *Annual Report*, 1916, p. 62.

REFERENCES

Forty-fifth Annual Report of the Superintendent of Education. Columbia: State Department of Education, 1913.

Forty-sixth Annual Report of the Superintendent of Education. Columbia: State Department of Education, 1914.

Forty-seventh Annual Report of the Superintendent of Education. Columbia: State Department of Education, 1915.

Forty-eighth Annual Report of the Superintendent of Education. Columbia: State Department of Education, 1916.

Gray, Wil Lou. *A Night School Experiment in Laurens County, South Carolina.* Columbia: State Department of Education, 1915.

Gray, Wil Lou. *Annual Report to the Superintendent.* Columbia: State Department of Education, 1912-13.

Gray, Wil Lou. "Evolution of Adult Elementary Education in South Carolina." *Interstate Bulletin on Adult Education,* May 1927.

CHAPTER VII

A Mission in Maryland

Go, and do thou likewise.
St. Luke

After the completion of further graduate study, Miss Gray was preparing to return to her home in Laurens when she was offered a position in Montgomery County, Maryland, by the County Superintendent of Schools, Mr. Broome. She had been highly recommended to him by Columbia University and Mr. W. K. Tate, who had supervised her work as Rural Supervisor of Laurens County. She was offered an annual salary which was excellent for a female in that day, and since the position sounded challenging, she accepted Mr. Broome's offer in the fall of 1917.

Miss Gray traveled by train to Rockville, Maryland, and found an apartment in a private home. It was a place where she felt she could be very comfortable, for on every hand she saw lovely china, crystal, and silver in rooms furnished with valuable heirlooms. Her landlady, Mrs. Luckett, claimed to be a descendant of the Indian princess Pocahontas, and her English husband, John Rolfe. Mrs. Luckett was now a widow but had been married to the headmaster of an exclusive private school in Rockville so she was somewhat supercilious toward anyone involved in public education, for she considered such work demeaning. Miss Gray has always had the courage of her convictions, however, so she did not let Mrs. Luckett's attitude bother her. She was very sorry when her landlady became quite ill and she had to seek other accommodations in another home in the winter of 1917.

This year was another milestone in Miss Gray's life, for her pioneer spirit again asserted itself when she became one of the first female drivers of an automobile in the city of Rockville. At that time a driver's license was not required in most states so she did not have to demonstrate any proficiency before she went out to tour the roads of Rockville in her brand-new Dodge. Indeed, she remembers being quite afraid of her vehicle, a cumbersome monster whose reverse gear location forever remained a secret to her. Driving along the dusty or muddy back roads of rural Montgomery County, when she reached the point where she had to turn around to return home, she was compelled to sit there until she flagged down some good Samaritan and asked him to turn her car around for her.

While she was residing in Rockville, Miss Gray followed her lifelong practice of attending both Sunday School and church services each Sabbath. She did not remember when she did not teach a Sunday School class in Laurens, and she felt this was an ideal time to retire from teaching on Sunday, for she did so much on the other six days of the week that she felt she deserved one day of rest. Seeking out the nearest Methodist church in Rockville, Miss Gray was looking forward to being taught, rather than teaching, as she located the adult class where she introduced herself as the new Supervisor of Rural Schools. That news traveled quickly, and she had scarcely seated herself when the Sunday School superintendent rushed into the room and declared that she must be the heaven-sent answer to his prayers. It seemed that there was a class of young boys in their early teens who were so incorrigible that no teacher dared remain with them for more than one Sunday, and they were even at that moment heard wreaking havoc in the next room with no adult supervision. Down deep in her heart Miss Gray did not really want to, but she cannot help responding to any kind of a challenge, so she let herself be persuaded into teaching the class, but she declared in no uncertain terms that it was to be for that one day only. In only a few moments she, the experienced master teacher, had the boys completely enthralled by her unorthodox approach to teaching Sunday School, for she could tell Bible stories so vividly she seemed to be on a first-name basis with Jesus and his Disciples. By the end of that first session she was totally captivated by the young people, too, and remained their teacher for the year she was in Maryland. It so happened that the class of boys became a godsend to her, also, for they "adopted" Miss Gray and usually one or more of them accompanied her when she had to travel the deserted roads of her rural school districts at night. More than once they escorted her home safely after her cantankerous car had refused to go any further.

As Miss Gray began to travel to her various schools to become acquainted, she was somewhat disappointed in what she found. Montgomery County was reputed to have the most progressive school system in all of Maryland, but after several visits she decided that the schools were no better than the ones in Laurens County, and moreover, the people in the communities were not as cooperative or hospitable as her own "home folks." She also found some of the patrons to be more tradition-bound and resistant to change.

In one school Miss Gray had found what she thought was an excellent teacher. She had set up a store with cans and cartons and had issued play money to the children so they could practice arithmetic skills and learn about the value of currency in a very vital way. The new Supervisor complimented the young lady on her progressive approach and could scarcely wait to tell the Board of Trustees about that wonderful teacher with her imaginative methods. Unhappily, the chairman of the trustees, a stern, sober judge, was not favorably impressed, and he embarrassed Miss Gray mightily by intoning his judgment to the entire board, "Children go to school not to play, but to learn."

Miss Gray thought it was shameful that these people lived so close to our nation's capital, but none of the parents or teachers had ever attempted to take groups of children there to see at firsthand their American heritage of a democratic government in operation. It did not take her long to remedy what she considered a sin of omission as she organized one of her famous "pilgrimages." Singlehandedly, she took a group of forty children to Washington, D.C., despite Mrs. Luckett's grim prediction that no human being could survive such an ordeal! She remembers it was a most rewarding experience for all concerned, but at least once during the tour she felt exactly like a mother hen with too many chicks. After leaving the halls of the Library of Congress, the group stood on the steps outside while Miss Gray tried to impress upon the children the power of the written word and the historical significance of this monumental edifice which had been established more than a century before. Unfortunately, the point of her lecture was lost upon the group for at that instant an airplane flew directly overhead at a very low altitude, and the excited children, squealing with delight or crying out in fright, scattered to the four winds as some of them even tried to chase the shadow of this strange contraption. This was only one of many novel and unique experiences they encountered. Surely those children still remembered that trip and the educator who made it possible for the rest of their lives.

During her year in Maryland, Miss Gray planned and conducted her work along the same guidelines she had followed in Laurens County, with one important, timely exception. Since America had become involved in World War I on April 6, 1917, as Supervisor of Rural Schools, Miss Gray determined that "the schools might be made centers from which information could be disseminated in regard to the war aims of the nation, and that the pupils might take part in the work of the day."[1] Students and patrons alike were encouraged by Miss Gray to participate in the war effort, and her teachers cooperated in helping to form Junior Red Cross organizations in all of the county schools. Miss Gray planned programs to raise funds, purchased and dispensed materials necessary for making garments and bandages for the armed services, and encouraged the purchase of War Savings Stamps and Liberty Bonds.

Miss Gray's overall objectives for the year, their revisions and the results of her plans follow:

1. To spend four days a week visiting the schools, one-half day to each of forty-one schools every five weeks.

During these visits she observed the work of the teachers, made friends with and encouraged the students, and tried to make constructive suggestions for improvement. As in Laurens County, she found reading to be the most poorly taught and neglected subject. She observed the scarcity of suitable reading material in the classrooms and determined to do something to remedy that situation. As a temporary measure, she ordered a traveling library and circulated the books as she made her rounds from school to school. Teachers were urged to use the lessons in *Community Life*, a monthly periodical, for teaching current events, and as a basis for teaching reading, spelling, arithmetic, history, and geography.

At the end of the year Miss Gray reported that she had been able to make only 175 personal visits to the schools due to impossible weather conditions in December and January. This factor led to a change in another of her goals which had been to spend one day each week in preparation, with Saturday mornings reserved for teacher conferences and correspondence. As her work progressed, she found this plan most impractical, so she reserved such tasks for days when travel to the outlying districts was not possible.

2. To establish a library in each school and encourage its use by students and teachers alike.

She was able to persuade 25 schools to take advantage of the State Library Law which allowed $20 for the purchase of books. In one school she found the library books suitable for adults rather than children, and they were too difficult for anyone below the fifth grade; yet in the entire school there were only two students above the fourth grade. The following are some of the books she found there: *The First Violin, Civilization in Europe, Life of Clay, The Scarlet Letter, Burns' Poetical Works, The Hunchback of Notre Dame, The Autocrat of the Breakfast Table,* and *Faust.* She was quick to point out her own unfortunate choice of reading materials, due to her inexperience, when she had ordered her first library, but even that would not convince the trustees to order new books, for they insisted that they had purchased a set of fine books and no one had read them. Yet most of the schools were cooperative and at the end of the year teachers reported that 1590 books had been read and 287 certificates were awarded by Superintendent Broome to students who had read more than 5 books. Finally, all concerned were very pleased with the progress made in teaching reading which was evident when Miss Gray organized an Educational Rally Day for Montgomery County Schools, and county students, in competition with the city pupils, won 7 of the 23 ribbons awarded in reading.

3. To organize at least ten School Improvement Associations, whose aim shall be to develop the community.

This was a new concept to the people in Montgomery County, and only 6 organizations were formed. However, in all, 35 night community meetings were held, with the ubiquitous Miss Gray always in attendance with her stereopticon lantern. In these meetings problems relative to the war effort and the schools were discussed and courses of action were determined. Moreover, more than 100 entertainments were held in the schools, promoting their use as a community center while raising $992.51 for the Red Cross, libraries, and other improvements.

To promote community involvement, Miss Gray urged teachers to visit homes and parents to visit schools. As a result 974 parents visited schools and 706 teachers went into the homes. On the last day of school "Community Day" was observed, and more than 2,000 parents attended these closing exercises.

4. With the Superintendent's aid to edit a section in the county newspapers, devoted to school news and the work done by the children.

When contacted by Miss Gray, the newspaper medium was most gracious and consented to print an educational feature weekly. All school matters of general interest were published, as well as classroom articles by the children. This service was valuable in two ways, for it kept the public informed, and was motivational for the students in learning composition.

5. To establish a model school near Rockville where bi-monthly conferences can be held and the actual work of the rural teacher can be observed, leading to discussions of instructional methods and materials.

Bailey School was selected as the site for this experimental model. The teacher was most cooperative and at the first meeting demonstrated her instruction for two hours. After lunch, the Supervisor and her visiting teachers participated in discussions of how to improve their work. Although Miss Gray had aimed for several meetings of this type during the year, inclement weather and other emergencies had precluded all but one such meeting. At least that one trial had proved the idea to be both beneficial and practical.

6. To hold a monthly afternoon conference with teachers in each section of the county.

Miss Gray had introduced the concept of standardized testing to her county teachers during these conferences. When they saw for the first time how their students' performance could be compared to other norm groups, they were inspired to try to do a better job. At the same time, Miss Gray always urged her teachers to vitalize their subject matter so their teaching would produce thought rather than being merely the acquisition of facts.

Due to weather conditions and numerous other interruptions, only two such conferences were held; however, bi-monthly meetings were held regularly in Rockville.

7. To assist the teachers to grow professionally.

When Miss Gray first arrived in Montgomery County, she had found very few inspired, dedicated, professional teachers. She immediately formed a voluntary reading circle course, for which study teachers were awarded credit by the Superintendent. Moreover, the teachers were urged to join professional organizations on all levels, and to subscribe to and use professional magazines.

Whenever teachers visited Miss Gray's busy office, they found exhibits of worksheets in different subject areas they could reproduce for their classes, samples of books that children enjoy, plus a bulletin board and a sand table with suggestions for each month's work. Then there was a large bulletin board devoted exclusively to examples of work done by the county students.

When Miss Gray later conducted a survey among the teachers in the 41 schools, she found that 20 teachers subscribed to 28 professional magazines; 23 had read 59 professional books; 20 reported they were conscious of professional growth; 100 percent belonged to state and county teachers' associations; 75 percent attended a state convention in Baltimore; 14 teachers belonged to the study group. Miss Gray concluded that these changes were not spectacular, but she was quite satisfied with the results since she realized that any drastic changes would be made over a matter of years, rather than a few short months.[2]

At the close of the school year Miss Gray concluded her annual report to Superintendent Broome, "My work in Maryland was made pleasant by many courtesies from the school folk of Montgomery County, for which I am deeply grateful. I count this year most valuable to me professionally."[3]

Mr. Broome was more than pleased with Miss Gray's performance and the improvement that was becoming evident in the rural schools. Miss Gray still felt challenged by the work and had high hopes for making much more progress the following year as she renewed her contract.

However, when she returned to South Carolina for her summer vacation, she was approached by Dr. Patterson Wardlaw, the Chairman of the South Carolina Illiteracy Commission, who asked her to return to South Carolina and work with him. When he assured her it would not be dishonorable for her to ask to be released from her contract with Montgomery County, or at least to ask for a year's leave of absence to give the work a trial, she agreed to return to Maryland to discuss the matter with her superiors. In the ensuing conference the State Superintendent advised her she was relinquishing a position that was the best opportunity for a female educator in the entire United States. However, both he and Mr. Broome agreed to release her from the contract if she were positive that was what she should do, but they stipulated that they would consider it as a year's leave of absence if she would only agree to return.

Miss Gray had enjoyed working with Mr. Broome and thought him a wonderful friend and a dedicated educator, but already she was anticipating the gigantic task which lay before her in her native state. She rejoiced that she had been given the opportunity for further service to her beloved South Carolina and that hopefully a way was being found for her to realize her dream of freeing those shackled by the bonds of illiteracy. Thus it was with mixed emotions that she read the farewell letter from her State Supervisor, Mr. W.J. Holloway:

> My Dear Miss Gray:
>
> I cannot add anything to the regret I expressed at the possibility of your leaving Montgomery County . . . I do feel we are losing one of our best supervisors. I consider that you belong in the upper fourth group in a rating of Maryland supervisors.[4]

NOTES

[1]Wil Lou Gray, letter to Montgomery County Board of Education, Spring 1918.

[2]Wil Lou Gray, unpublished report to superintendent, Montgomery County, Maryland, 1917-18, pp. 1-12.

[3]Ibid., p. 12.

[4]W.J. Holloway, letter to Wil Lou Gray, September 12, 1918.

REFERENCES

Columbia, South Carolina. Caroliniana Library. Wil Lou Gray Collection.

Gray, Wil Lou. Columbia, South Carolina. Interview, 15 August 1975.

CHAPTER VIII

The Illiteracy Commission

> . . . monuments that stand alone in a sea of illiteracy.
>
> John Kenneth Galbraith

The birth of the first active South Carolina Illiteracy Commission with which Miss Gray was so closely associated for many years, followed an abortive first effort conceived by state leaders in the Federation of Women's Clubs in 1917. Perhaps as in the case of some human confinements, the labor was premature, for the public and many state political leaders were not yet willing to make a concerted sacrificial effort to deliver South Carolina from its blight of illiteracy.

The story behind the organization of this first ill-fated Illiteracy Commission is reported by Miss Mabel Montgomery, who was later to become the secretary of the first active illiteracy organization:

> The first public gathering in the interest of eliminating adult illiteracy from South Carolina was held at the Jefferson Hotel, January 10, 1917, in Columbia. The creation of an Illiteracy Commission, following the example of other states with the same problem, had originated with Mrs. J.L. Coker, president of the South Carolina Federation of Women's Clubs, and Mrs. Walter Duncan, Chairman of Education. The annual executive board meeting drew near; that was deemed an auspicious time to feel public opinion on this subject. Therefore, Mrs. Coker sent out a call to the heads of many organizations and to public-spirited men and women of Columbia to meet with the club women and discuss measures to

70

Illiteracy in South Carolina - 1910

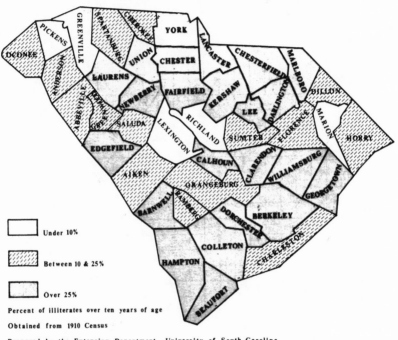

Under 10%

Between 10 & 25%

Over 25%

Percent of illiterates over ten years of age

Obtained from 1910 Census

Prepared by the Extension Department, University of South Carolina.

*Copied by F. Ayres, from the original drawn by L. Glen

combat illiteracy. On the afternoon of January 10, this meeting took place at the Jefferson Hotel, Mrs. Coker presiding. Speeches favoring immediate steps were made by Superintendent John E. Swearingen, Reverend K.G. Finlay, Miss Annie Bonham, Mr. A.S. Johnstone of the State Board of Charities and Corrections, and others.

It was the most enthusiastic opinion of this gathering that Governor Manning be asked to appoint an Illiteracy Commission to deal with the situation. This was done. Governor Manning gladly agreed. The following personnel of the first Commission were appointed in March, 1917: L.O. Patterson of Greenville; George Brown of Columbia; Wil Lou Gray of Laurens; Mrs. Walter Duncan of Aiken; State Superintendent Swearingen; and Professor J.G. Clinkscales of Wofford College, Chairman. All the members save Mrs. Duncan declined to serve. They deemed the job too huge to be undertaken.[1]

It was on March 23, 1917, that Mrs. Vivian G. Coker wrote to Miss Gray, confirming her appointment by Governor Manning and inviting her to serve on the first South Carolina Illiteracy Commission.[2] Miss Gray had first been recommended for this service by Mabel Montgomery of Marion, because their fathers had attended the same college and were

Wil Lou Gray (center front) with the first active S.C. Illiteracy Commission in 1918. Other members left to right: Mrs. J.L. Coker, J.E. Swearingen, Dr. S.H. Edmunds, Wil Lou Gray, Dr. Patterson Wardlaw, Dr. R.C. Burts, Miss Mabel Montgomery, and W.A. Shealy.

close friends. Naturally, Miss Montgomery was cognizant of Miss Gray's intense interest in adult education and her successful supervision of the rural schools in Laurens County.

Miss Gray regretfully declined this appointment, for at that time she was engaged in further graduate study at Teachers College, Columbia University. Before she could return to South Carolina, the prospective commission had expired due to lack of interest. The other appointees who also declined to serve can scarcely be blamed. They were to receive no remuneration for this onerous task and there were no funds appropriated for the establishment and maintenance of such a program.

The second Illiteracy Commission was more easily born; however, its development as a viable organization was beset with complications. This group, commissioned on December 24, 1917, was most fortunate in having Dr. Patterson Wardlaw, Professor of Education at the University of South Carolina, as its chairman. Other members appointed were: Dr. S.H. Edmunds, Superintendent of Schools at Sumter; Mrs. J.L. Coker of Hartsville, President of the State Federation of Women's Clubs; J.E. Swearingen, State Superintendent of Education; Dr. C.E. Burts, Columbia, Pastor of First Baptist Church; Miss Mabel Montgomery, Marion, Education Director of the Women's Clubs, as Secretary; W.A. Shealy, Columbia, Supervisor of Mill Schools. These active members were to be commended for they toiled without pay and voluntarily met all of their personal expenses entailed by Commission meetings and activities.[3]

Dr. Wardlaw, in assuming the chairmanship of this pioneer Commission, faced a challenge which would have defeated most persons. That he must have had great persistence and determination is indicated by the fact that he first corresponded with Commission members in early February to arrange an inaugural meeting, but it was not until June 22, 1918, that the meeting took place, after a veritable barrage of correspondence.[4]

At this first meeting the Commission formulated the following goals:

1. The Commission is to work under the leadership of the State Department of Education and as auxiliary to it.

2. It purposes to do all in its power to cooperate with, encourage and aid all persons, organizations and other agencies that are striving for the eradication of illiteracy from the state.

72

3. It will endeavor to work for such legislation as is necessary for the success of the cause; to use all legitimate means of propaganda and agitation; to become a center for the gathering and exchange of information and for correlation of all agencies in the state working toward the same end; to assist, as far as possible, in actual execution; to raise the money that may be necessary for the above-named ends.[5]

The Commission's second meeting was held on July 10, 1918. Undoubtedly, the most historic decision of its career was made when, "The Chair was authorized to communicate with Miss Wil Lou Gray in order to ascertain whether she would accept the position of field worker."[6] Therefore, Dr. Wardlaw contacted Miss Gray as she was vacationing in Laurens.

The details involved in the wooing of Miss Gray to return to her first love, her native state, are interestingly revealed in the following correspondence and from the minutes of the Illiteracy Commission meetings:

August 2, 1918, to Miss Wil Lou Gray from Patterson Wardlaw:

> We hope that we shall raise enough money to pay a good salary for the whole year, and this hope has been greatly strengthened by the appropriation of $1,000 by the Council of Defense. But we have not yet got that much money in hand. I am sure, however, that we can do this— pay $140 a month to the end of 1918, and promise the remainder of $1,600 and expenses, raising it if it has not all come in yet . . . I know this does not seem as attractive as could be desired, but think of the splendid opportunity if we can carry it through—and I think we can! Please give us just a little more time.

August 5, 1918, to Patterson Wardlaw from Superintendent Swearingen:

> . . . Again renewing my suggestion made at Winthrop for the employment of Miss Gray. I endorse without qualification your proposed salary of $150 a month with traveling expenses. These expenses will certainly exceed $500 per year. The field agent cannot live for less than $3 a day plus transportation charges. If she should be in the field half her time, her traveling would require about $900.

August 7, 1918, to Patterson Wardlaw from Mabel Montgomery:

> Am heartily in favor of securing Miss Gray at almost any

price, for she is the logical person for this position . . .

August 10, 1918, to Illiteracy Commission members from Patterson Wardlaw:

I have had today a very full and frank interview with Miss Gray. She is greatly interested, but, of course, there are difficulties to her accepting.

She is to write me after her return to Maryland, so that we shall probably hear in about two weeks. She will tell us then whether she can be released from Maryland, and if so, what salary will bring her. She is of the opinion now, however, that she will want $2,000 and she estimates her expenses would be less than $800.

Both items are larger than we figured on, but neither is unreasonable. The salary in her present place is to be increased by $200 a year, and her tenure is practically secure, as contrasted with an uncertainty here. As to expenses, Mr. Swearingen had already written me that $500 was certainly too small.

Now if we can reach the $2,800, I am in favor of giving it. In this work, the best is the cheapest.

August 21, 1918, to Patterson Wardlaw from Miss Wil Lou Gray:

I talked yesterday afternoon with my superintendent and returned this afternoon from a conference with the State Supervisor of Rural Schools. They both are willing to release me provided I wish to go. Mr. Broome very generously offered to give me a year's leave of absence in which to try out the work. If I leave, I shall not accept his offer but come with a determination to try to make the work be permanent.

In regard to salary, I am in line of promotion for a $2,000 salary and should receive $1,800 next year, including expenses. I should regret to give up the present work for less than $2,000 but if that sum is impossible, I will come for $1,800 and expenses provided I shall in no way be responsible for soliciting my own salary. I am willing to work for funds for the teachers.

There are wonderful possibilities for real service in the work and I shall be delighted to have a part with you and the other members of the Commission in lifting the burden of ignorance from our people, provided you still want me and nothing further develops here.

The third meeting of the Commission was held on September 3, 1918. The Commission wired Miss Gray as follows:

74

Proposition enthusiastically accepted. Salary $1,800
and expenses, with hope of early increase. Come
immediately.

September 6, 1918, to Patterson Wardlaw from Mabel
Montgomery:

Only the fervent 'deelighted' of one T. Roosevelt
expresses my joy over knowing Wil Lou Gray has
accepted.

September 13, 1918, to Commission members from Patterson
Wardlaw:

We can exchange congratulations on the acceptance of
Miss Gray.[7]

Returning to her native state and reporting to her new assignment,
Wil Lou Gray assumed the title of Field Worker for the Illiteracy
Commission of South Carolina on October 1, 1918. She was
relinquishing the certainty of a well-paying job for a position which she
knew could be dissolved if, in the next legislative session, the General
Assembly did not appropriate sufficient funds for the Illiteracy
Commission's work. In fact, her supervisors in Maryland had inferred at
great length that she must be slightly demented to surrender a position
which they felt for a female in that day was the best opportunity in the
entire nation, for the uncertainty of the Illiteracy Commission's offer.

In 1916 the General Assembly had appropriated $5,000 to carry on
the work begun by volunteers, but in 1917 this was reduced to $2,500.
Then in 1918, $10,000 was appropriated but it was not available until
March, too late for a spring campaign to be launched. But more
importantly, there was no supervisor available to organize the work.
Then late in 1918, after the timely arrival of their field marshal, when the
Illiteracy Commission requested a $25,000 appropriation, a conservative
estimate of the amount necessary for waging a state-wide battle, the
request was denied because the previous appropriation had not been
entirely expended.[8] This was a typical example of state politicians' lack
of insight into the funding necessary to reduce illiteracy with which Miss
Gray had to contend throughout her career.

The initial funds for the Commission's work had come in 1916 from
the generous donations of several public-spirited citizens who hoped
that if an immediate attack were launched, time would permit public
opinion to be swayed in favor of the work, and legislators might be

75

convinced that a speedy appropriation was mandatory if the battlefront were to be extended throughout the state.[9] Only then might there be a successful conclusion to the war which was being waged on illiteracy.

Additionally, the Council on Defense contributed $1,000 to the Commission. Since the draft had recently disclosed that 49.5 percent of South Carolina's young men called on to serve were unacceptable because of illiteracy, the Council considered the work as a valuable service to the war effort. Even later, when manpower needs lessened this restriction on draftees, the Assistant Personnel Adjutant at Camp Jackson in Columbia, South Carolina, reported in July of 1918 that 30 percent of the men from South Carolina were illiterate. Still later, the *New York Times* of February 18, 1919, bore the following headline: "ILLITERACY AMAZES ARMY." A sub-caption went on to read: "South Carolina worst. Percentage there 49.5 against 16.6 in New York with its large foreign element."[10] Those disgraceful figures, and the additional fact that 25 percent of all South Carolinians above the age of ten were illiterate, could partially be attributed to the following reasons: In 1916 South Carolina ranked lowest in per capita expenditure for education; annual expenditure per pupil was lowest in the nation; average salary for teachers was lowest; school term (usually seven months) was shortest; average daily attendance was next to lowest in the entire nation.[11]

Further conditions which were contributing factors to South Carolina's disgraceful amount of illiteracy have been cited previously. In the older generation, the Civil War prevented thousands from completing their education. Since there was no compulsory education law, others did not send their children to school, but kept them at home to work on the farm or in the cotton mills.

Furthermore, illiteracy was rampant because of South Carolina's large Negro population. There were too many powerful state leaders such as "Pitchfork Ben" Tillman and Cole Blease who favored denying Negro citizens a basic elementary education for fear they might "forget their place."

What a challenge to present to Miss Gray! What a superhuman effort was about to be exerted by this indomitable person!

The members of the Federation of Women's Clubs throughout the state were well aware of the successful night schools for adults Miss Gray had pioneered in Laurens County, and it was their promise to stand solidly behind her and to work staunchly beside her that prompted her to accept this new position of Field Worker for the Illiteracy Commission. Miss Gray had always been a member of this organization since she first reached adulthood, even during her year in Maryland, and she well knew what a powerful influence for good it could be.

Miss Gray was due to arrive in Columbia on October 1, but little did those Columbians awaiting her know that but for the hand of Providence she would never have reached her destination. The train on which she was a passenger had a terrifying accident in the vicinity of Baltimore late at night. Miss Gray firmly believes that Fate intervened to ensure her safe arrival in Columbia, for miraculously neither she nor any other of the passengers were injured.

Then when her train was making a stop in Camden, who should board but Superintendent Swearingen. Of course, Miss Gray had to call to him because he was blind. This dear friend was distressed when he learned that Miss Gray had no place to stay until she could find a permanent home. She had planned to stay temporarily at the Wade Hampton Hotel, but Mr. Swearingen told her it would be completely booked by the weekend military personnel from Camp Jackson. He invited her to stay with him and his wife, but she was then in the hospital with a new little son, and Miss Gray would not impose at such a time. However, when she finally arrived in Columbia she was met and welcomed by Mr. Gunter, who was a high school inspector for the State Department of Education. He insisted she stay with his family until she could find permanent lodging.

Approaching this new work with her characteristic energetic drive and boundless faith, Miss Gray was undeterred by the foibles of humanity and the quirks of nature. She was able to make steady and continuous progress in spite of public indifference in many cases, difficulties with transportation and communication, and health hazards of epidemic proportions.

Marshaling her forces as the supreme commander leading an "insurrection against ignorance" with her characteristic sense of organization, and demonstrating a knowledge of strategy worthy of a military general and a proficiency in the art of propaganda, Miss Gray submitted the following "battle plan" to the Illiteracy Commission:

1. To ask the County Superintendent and teachers to take a school census of their community and to give widespread publicity to the data collected. This information will be tabulated in the office of the Illiteracy Commission, turned over to the State Department, and disseminated throughout all public channels possible over the state.

2. The following organizations will be requested to have a program on "Illiteracy and How To Remove It": Chambers of Commerce, Teachers' Associations, Women's Clubs, and all secret and fraternal orders. Literature will be furnished, giving facts as a basis for discussion. In order to get legislative support, each organization will be requested to draw up resolutions asking for a $25,000 appropriation for the elimination of illiteracy and also to appoint a committee which will personally present these resolutions to the county delegation.

3. To request the ministers of all denominations to preach an illiteracy sermon on some Sunday designated by the Governor as "Illiteracy Sunday."

4. To assist in organizing night schools. Work will be concentrated on typical counties to demonstrate what can be accomplished. However, an effort will be made to organize a few schools in every county.

5. To hold in Columbia sometime in December, an Institute for night school teachers. The program will consist of discussions on organization, course of study, method of teaching and demonstration lessons.

6. To assist the teachers in the selection of textbooks and in arranging a course of study suitable to the conditions.

7. To encourage schools to open any time occasion demands, but to make a state-wide drive for the opening of rural schools during January and February and mill schools during December, January and February. Schools will be opened three nights a week for one and one-half or two hours. No pupil will be admitted to school who is under the compulsory age limit (fourteen years) without special permit. The state will pay the teachers one dollar per night, provided at least ten pupils are enrolled. The counties will be asked to add one dollar per night to this salary. During July and August lay-by schools will be opened for those unable to attend during the winter, and for those who prefer to continue the work.

78

8. To provide programs for a Community Session to be held every other Friday night when the entire community will assemble for an evening of civic instruction, followed by miscellaneous talks on current events. This program will be most instructive for the community and will make the illiterate feel that there is no disgrace in his attending school if his more fortunate neighbor finds it helpful to attend occasionally.

9. To encourage individuals to pledge themselves to teach one illiterate to read and write. All pupils thus taught will be asked to send their names to the Commission.

10. To attend all meetings where an invitation can be secured, provided the attendance and interest is likely to justify the expense.

11. To do anything which the State Department of Education or the Illiteracy Commission might request for the furtherance of the work.[12]

In her first year as Field Worker, Miss Gray would have liked to be in the field constantly, but of necessity she spent some time each week in her office, where her activity was prolific and varied. The office space had been provided by Dr. Wardlaw adjacent to his own.

Miss Gray has always been a firm believer in the power of the press. Thus, one of her first tasks was to write articles and letters and send them to every newspaper in the state. To stimulate interest in the summer campaign, in June 1919, *The State*, *The Columbia Record*, and *The News and Courier* devoted one complete page to the work of adult schools. Two letters were sent to each legislator urging his financial support. The president of every Federated Women's Club was written to ask her support and a pamphlet, "How Club Women Can Help Remove Illiteracy" was included. Every college president was given a plan whereby his students could participate in giving aid to the fight against illiteracy. In detail, each county superintendent was instructed in gaining the cooperation of his personnel. Not only was a multitude of circular letters sent to all teachers of adults, with helpful suggestions for their work, but hundreds of personal replies to individual teachers with problems were written. Additionally, bulletins were prepared and distributed to teachers concerning organization of classes, textbooks to be used, and curricula to be followed. All literature published by the Illiteracy Commission was distributed throughout the state. Finally, results from 330 schools sending in reports were tabulated.[13]

These office activities were illustrative of the first year's work. As the illiteracy movement mushroomed, more teachers and students became involved each week. This entailed more correspondence, more bulletins, more circular letters, more newspaper articles and speeches to compose, more institutes to organize, more statistics to tabulate, and more publicity to disseminate. Later Miss Gray compiled and edited several publications, *The Lay-By School Messenger*, *The Night School Messenger*, and *The Adult School Messenger*. Moreover, she had to cope single-handedly with most of these office duties, for it was not until her office was moved from the campus of the University of South Carolina to the State Department of Education that her budget could afford any but rare, part-time secretarial assistance.

In personal visitations throughout the state, Miss Gray was quite handicapped by reliance on trains and buses for transportation since she did not purchase a second automobile until July of 1922. She does not remember the make or model, but she does recall that it was somewhat classier than the monstrous Dodge of 1917.

Usually the Field Worker traveled to a county by invitation and first conferred with the superintendent, the supervising teacher, or organizer. She discussed the county's organizational plan; tried to interest those in the community who might be helpful; conferred with individual teachers; visited with the teachers the homes of the illiterates, in order to explain the movement and encourage their attendance; held public meetings at night or visited night schools in session.

The following extract from Miss Gray's diary is a typical week in the field for her:

March 10. Spent afternoon in Clinton. Had conference with Mr. Daniel who reported night school work in Clinton Mill in good condition, then went to see Mrs. Sloan, one of the teachers. Found forty-seven students were enrolled with an average attendance of forty. The pupils themselves had fitted out a classroom. Went to Lydia Mill to see Mrs. Oxner who had just taken a census for illiteracy. She promised to start a new school if new building could be made ready. At night went to Watts Mill, but found no school as transfer failed to come for teachers and pupils left after thirty minutes' wait.

March 11. Went to Greenville. Visited the vocational textile

80

evening class of Sampson Mill, organized under the supervision of Mr. Charles S. Doggett, State Supervisor of Trade and Industrial Education. Two teachers with nine to twelve students respectively. Students appeared to be interested. They were studying from second to fourth grade math.

March 12. Conference with Miss Perry. Mr. Barton, Miss Perry and I went to Reedy River at night — the only rural night school in Greenville County. Found excellent audience. Miss Cook, the teacher, had enrolled fifteen students with average attendance of eleven.

March 13. Conference with Mr. Greer of Woodside Mill and Mr. Jolly of Mills Mill. Both reported night work discouraging due to too many sections and too little time on the part of teachers in working it up. Talked before Thursday Morning Club and Thursday Afternoon Club. Went to Monoghan Mill at night. Found about twenty students present — six teachers. This is a night school conducted on the plan of a day school. Had conference with teachers after school was dismissed.

March 14. Interviewed foreigners. Found twelve who wanted to study. Went to Easley in the afternoon. Had conference with Mr. Hagood and Mr. Greer, presidents of the two mills. Also interviewed the teachers of each mill and arranged to start schools at once. Mr. Greer is supplementing the teacher's salary and at his will the class will be organized for adult illiterates only.

March 15. Talked to Greenville County Teachers' Association, then went to see Mr. Holmes of the Y.M.C.A. to ask him to take charge of foreign class. He was not a bit enthusiastic.

Other excerpts which depict some of the problems and rewards involved in Miss Gray's field work follow:

August 2. Walked one and one-half miles over mountains after car lights went out.

August 3. At Pickens one elderly lady and her daughter attended night school. The husband said he would whip her if she went, but she was there and enjoying it immensely.

August 4. Visited Mountain View. Went way up into mountains and to Robinson School where we found a summer school, very poor in equipment, in session. After driving for some time we found one of the trustees who said he could read but could not write, while his wife told us she didn't know 'nary' letter.

November 9. Went to Winnsboro to confer with the Service Manager of Winnsboro Mill. In the office I met a man who had been one of Mrs. Ida Brown's best students. A few years ago he could barely add up his weekly grocery bill and was earning $6.50 for 60 hours work. Due to night study he now has a position which pays him $13.60 per day.

November 16. Spent day in Spartanburg attending the D.A.R. conference. Made a talk on behalf of Tamassee after which $1400 for school was pledged.

November 25. Worked this Saturday all day in office getting up copy for a multiplication table bulletin which the Southeastern Life Insurance Company was publishing for us.

December 9. Visited Great Falls to see Mr. Hall about Miss Pittman's salary which had not been paid. Late in the afternoon my car skidded and I walked from five until eight thirty before finding help, for this is a section of country where there were practically no people. Finally reached Wateree where family of power plant manager treated me hospitably. Arrived in Columbia on Sunday afternoon.

March 5. Assisted in organizing a foreign class. Mr. Hand did not want to heat the high school so the Washington Street Methodist Church was asked for use of its Sunday School building. Miss Lessie Tiller and Miss Williams are teachers.

March 29. On Thursday afternoon went with Governor McLeod to Great Falls . . . attended commencement of Baldwin, Springstein, and Eureka schools . . . we returned to Columbia over Fairfield roads and were pleased that we came home in one piece.

As Miss Gray was directing the initial salvos which heralded the onset of an epic struggle against illiteracy in South Carolina, she "had many irons in the fire" simultaneously. Only an organizational genius could have coordinated so many activities and personnel, and only a person with the constitution of an Amazon could have had the strength to prevail. Her major efforts were directed toward organizing night schools, which followed the identical format previously successful in Laurens County, lay-by schools, opportunity schools, and "Write-Your-Name" campaigns. Her accomplishments in the latter three areas will be presented in-depth in later chapters.

On a smaller scale, Miss Gray cooperated with the military in organizing classes for the servicemen stationed at Camp Jackson who were classed as functional illiterates. She also visited restaurants and fruit stands in Columbia and enticed Russian, Greek, and Italian immigrants into classes held at the Y.M.C.A., and Olympia and New Brookland schools, where simple lessons in American citizenship were presented. These classes continued for eight consecutive weeks. The teachers received one dollar per hour if their classes had ten students.

In a similar manner, Miss Gray organized classes at the penitentiary in Columbia, for she believed it was immoral and economically unsound to spend tax dollars on illiterate inmates who, for a fraction of the cost of their incarceration, could be taught to read and write. She reasoned that if someone cared enough to educate these unfortunate members of society, they would have a better chance of rehabilitation. She was quite gratified as time passed that very few of those learning to read and write became recidivists.

All of these various types of instruction meant recruiting and training teachers on a grand scale. Luckily, Miss Gray had an instinct for placing the right teacher at the right place and in persuading those with talent to serve. Furthermore, she believed in teachers being prepared for their work and her early training courses, called institutes, held at the University of South Carolina and Winthrop College, were later extended to include Negro teachers whom she instructed at Allen University and Benedict College.

Miss Gray was always very concerned about the plight of the Negro in South Carolina. She was impressed by the fact that in her state, while white illiteracy was reduced 3 percent between 1900 and 1910, the Negroes had reduced their illiteracy 14 percent.[14] As far as she was concerned, the Negroes had proved their patriotism in World War I and should no longer be treated as second-class citizens. As she traveled over the state, she was touched by the appreciation that they showed for their opportunity to learn. Nowhere did she find a more conscientious group of students and teachers alike than in the Negro schools.

As Miss Gray engaged in all of her varied activities, she was constantly in touch with influential citizens and legislators, lobbying to obtain the needed laws for carrying on the illiteracy program. At one point State Senator J.H. Hammond declared she was "a nuisance to everybody in the legislature and was worse than chewing gum in your hair in her persistence for support of her work . . . the small appropriation given her department was given mostly to get rid of her. But she plugged on and on, trying to make us do the thing we should do — educate the underprivileged in order to improve our citizenship . . ." Her persistent clamor for a compulsory attendance law brought action in 1919 when that act was successfully passed. However, she was thwarted in 1918 when the General Assembly failed to pass the $25,000 appropriation bill which the Illiteracy Commission sought.[15] That must have been a demoralizing time for her since the news of the bill's failure to pass reached her as she lay in the Baptist Hospital very ill with influenza.

When the General Assembly had failed to appropriate funds for broadening the scope of the illiteracy movement to include the entire state, Superintendent Swearingen included in his education budget $25,000 for promoting the work of adult education. He established a Department of Adult Education, one of two in the entire United States which has rendered continuous service to the present, and also appointed Miss Gray as Supervisor of Adult Schools, working in cooperation with the Illiteracy Commission. However, this was merely a change in title and no policy alterations were necessary, but it did mean that now Miss Gray's salary would be paid by the state.[16]

As Miss Gray summarized her work after laboring for five months as Field Worker, she reported to the Illiteracy Commission that despite the ravages of the great influenza epidemic which afflicted 548,000 Americans and killed more of them than had the German army, there had been 80 schools established, with an enrollment of 2,793 adult students. Of these 687 had never attended school before. Moreover, by the end of 1919 she reported that 330 schools had been organized with 5,069 pupils, ranging in age from 14 to 80 years.[17]

But more graphic and rewarding than cold statistics to her were the warm expressions of gratitude she received from myriad adult students throughout the state, such as the following:

Smoaks, S.C.
September 15, 1919

To the Illiteracy Commission:

I have learned to read and write. My name is Barnie Linder. I am 34 years old.

Teacher: William   O.   Goodwin,   student   at   Wofford
College

Pickens, S.C.
September 1st 1919

Miss Gray I am writing you a letter to show you I have
learned to write a little since you was at Salem
I am thirty three years old and this is my first letter I will
not have to make my mark eny more

Yours truly

G.W. Blackston

Arkwright Mills

Arkwright Mills
Spartanburg, S.C.

March 21, 1919

Dear Miss Gray,

When I started to night school I could not make the letters.
When I was a boy I had no chance to go to school. Now
that I can go at night I do not want to miss a night.

Sincerely,

Walter McGraw
Age 36 years

The gratitude these students felt for Miss Gray was reciprocated by her, for because of their combined efforts, the census in 1920 reported that South Carolina had reduced its level of illiteracy more than any other state in the Union.[18]

The Illiteracy Commission continued to function under the able leadership of Dr. Wardlaw until his resignation in 1926, due to the heavy demands of his university duties. Alex Long then became chairman, and continued to cooperate wholeheartedly with Miss Gray and the Adult Division of the State Department of Education.[19]

85

Before he tendered his resignation, Dr. Wardlaw suggested a renaming of the Illiteracy Commission. He and Miss Gray had long felt that there were negative connotations implied in its present name. On September 6, 1925, the minutes reveal that it was recommended and resolved that "the name of our organization be changed from Illiteracy Commission to Committee on Literacy." It was further resolved that this body would promote a compulsory school attendance law, a goal that had long been in Miss Gray's plans. The Committee and Miss Gray envisioned such an attendance law not as a police force but as a social agency to give help. At the time they did not foresee that twelve years of hard work were to be required to bring about a workable school attendance law.

Through the years each governor has been asked by the State Department of Education to continue the Committee on Literacy. In 1943 when Governor Olin Johnston reorganized this agency, it became known as the State Advisory Committee on Adult Education, and Miss Gray was named an ex officio member.[20]

Although Miss Gray was intensely occupied in organizing and supervising the work of the Illiteracy Commission, she was never too busy to stay abreast of national events and trends, especially in the political arena. She had been impressed with Woodrow Wilson since hearing him speak in New Jersey, while attending Columbia College. She had especially approved of his endorsement of prohibition and the passage of the Eighteenth Amendment. Toward the end of his presidency it distressed Miss Gray that he was rapidly losing favor with the American people because of his support for the League of Nations.

Shortly after Miss Gray had arrived in Columbia to assume her new position, the Armistice was signed ending World War I. She still remembers vividly how Columbians reacted to the welcome news. Those fortunate enough to own an automobile formed a cavalcade downtown and paraded up and down Main Street, honking horns and otherwise celebrating for hours.

Miss Gray has always been an extremely patriotic American, and she did not grumble because of wartime restrictions such as sugar rationing, dark bread, the coal shortage, postal censorship, or government regulation of the railroads. She encouraged her teachers and their students to purchase Liberty Bonds and Stamps and helped organize

86

benefits for the Red Cross and Overseas Relief.

Miss Gray joined many others in this country in decrying what they thought was a new enemy — Bolshevism — after the Armistice. She did not condone the rash of anti-Red riots which became commonplace, but the fear of communistic doctrines added fuel to her fiery arguments against illiteracy. In an Illiteracy Commission leaflet of 1920 she wrote: "The State now faces the question of either providing sufficient funds for the education of the illiterate . . . or run the risk of having doctrines similar to the I.W.W. (Industrial Workers of the World) permeate a large percent of our people. Is it not expedient to prevent an evil rather than to permit it to develop?"[21]

Now that her country had successfully concluded its battle against the Kaiser, Miss Gray was able to concentrate all of her energy and enthusiasm in an attempt to defeat South Carolina's foremost foe — illiteracy.

James H. Hope, State Superintendent of Schools from 1922 to 1946, a loyal advocate of Miss Gray's fight against illiteracy

NOTES

[1]Mabel Montgomery, Illiteracy Commission Collection, Caroliniana Library, Columbia, South Carolina.

[2]Mrs. Vivian G. Coker, Illiteracy Commission Collection, Caroliniana Library, Columbia, South Carolina.

[3]Wardlaw Collection, Caroliniana Library, Columbia, South Carolina.

[4]Ibid.

[5]Wil Lou Gray, *Fifty-first Annual Report of the Superintendent of Education* (Columbia: State Department of Education, 1919), pp. 186-87.

[6]Dr. Patterson Wardlaw, Illiteracy Commission Collection, Caroliniana Library, Columbia, South Carolina.

[7]Illiteracy Commission Collection, Caroliniana Library, Columbia, South Carolina.

[8]Gray, *Fifty-first Annual Report*, p. 186.

[9]"The following public-spirited men and women demonstrated their faith in the cause by making generous contributions: Julia Selden, Mr. and Mrs. J.L. Coker, Mr. and Mrs. Horace Tilghman, Sadie Goggans, J.J. Lawton, J.W. Norwood, J.M. Geer, A.L. Easterling, J.E. Mills and Verd Peterson." Wil Lou Gray, "Report of State Supervisor of Adult Schools," (Columbia, South Carolina Illiteracy Commission, 1920), p. 10.

[10]Gray, *Fifty-first Annual Report*, p. 182.

[11]Ibid., p. 183.

[12]Wil Lou Gray, unpublished paper, October 1918.

[13]Gray, *Fifty-first Annual Report*, pp. 198-200.

[14]Wil Lou Gray, *Fifty-second Annual Report of the Superintendent of Education* (Columbia: State Department of Education, 1920), p. 260.

[15]Wil Lou Gray, *Fifty-fourth Annual Report of the Superintendent of Education* (Columbia: State Department of Education, 1922), p. 238.

[16]Ibid.

[17]Wil Lou Gray, *Fifty-third Annual Report of the Superintendent of Education* (Columbia: State Department of Education, 1921), p. 255.

[18]Wil Lou Gray, *Fifty-fourth Annual Report*, p. 240.

[19]Illiteracy Commission Collection, Caroliniana Library, Columbia, South Carolina.

[20]Ibid.

²¹Wil Lou Gray, "Report of State Supervisor of Adult Schools," (Columbia: South Carolina Illiteracy Commission, 1920), pp. 8-9.

REFERENCES

Columbia, South Carolina. Caroliniana Library. Illiteracy Commission Collection.

Columbia, South Carolina. Caroliniana Library. Wardlaw Collection.

Fifty-first Annual Report of the Superintendent of Education. Columbia: State Department of Education, 1919.

Fifty-second Annual Report of the Superintendent of Education. Columbia: State Department of Education, 1920.

Fifty-third Annual Report of the Superintendent of Education. Columbia: State Department of Education, 1921.

Fifty-fourth Annual Report of the Superintendent of Education. Columbia: State Department of Education, 1922.

Gray, Wil Lou. "Report of the State Supervisor of Adult Schools." Columbia: South Carolina Illiteracy Commission, 1920.

Gray, Wil Lou. Columbia, South Carolina. Interview, 20 September 1975.

Gray, Wil Lou. Columbia, South Carolina. Interview, 21 September 1975.

Gray, Wil Lou. Columbia, South Carolina. Interview, 1 October 1975.

CHAPTER IX

The Write-Your-Name Crusade

> ...they are free to think, speak,
> and write . . .
> Thomas Jefferson

During the early formative years of the anti-illiteracy movement in South Carolina, Miss Gray conceived an ingenious plan which drastically decreased the number of illiterates in the state. She felt an all-out concentrated crusade against illiteracy was imperative, for her sense of state pride was outraged by the disgraceful statistics reported by the Census of 1920. There were yet in South Carolina 38,742 Caucasian and 181,422 Negro illiterates, all above ten years of age.[1]

An initial "Write-Your-Name" pilot program which took place in Horry County in February and March of 1922 had proved practical and yielded good results. This was followed by a more concentrated campaign launched in August of 1923 in York County, singled out for special attention for several reasons. (1)York was one of fourteen counties reporting more than one thousand white inhabitants who could not read or write. (2)Despite the number of illiterates, it was considered one of the most progressive counties. (3)Miss Gray had the utmost respect for the York County Organizer, Mary Eva Hite, as a teacher and leader, for the two were close friends and had often worked together.[2]

The detailed planning and wise use of human and economic resources involved in the York County campaign, which later were multiplied across the state, again depict Miss Gray as a master strategist.

Work was begun in York on July 14, 1923, when she called a meeting of a small group of interested men and women and outlined the basic plan. Four days later a mass meeting with 200 enthusiastic participants convened, and inspiring messages were delivered by several state and county educational leaders, including Miss Gray, Miss Hite, and the new Superintendent of Schools, J.H. Hope.

Before beginning any active recruitment or teaching, county leaders consulted the Democratic Club roll and census figures to find that York County had 1,130 white and 5,420 Negro illiterates, with a total of 17.8 percent. By studying the books on file in the County Clerk's office, a list was made of every person who registered to vote with a mark, and it was discovered that of the 6,177 persons enrolled, 810, or 13.1 percent had made their marks.[3] Armed with this information, the following letter was sent to every school trustee in York County:

> The Anti-Illiteracy Campaign is now in full swing in York County. As a closing job, we want the 810 voters who signed the Club roll of this county with an X-mark in 1922 to sign it now in their own handwriting. We are calling August 19 to 25th, "Sign-Your-Own-Name" week in York County.
>
> We are sending a letter to each voter who signed the roll with an X-mark asking him to go to his schoolhouse Monday night, August 20th, at 7:30 to sign his own name if he can, and if he can't, to be taught to sign it. (Evidently it was hoped that if a recipient of this letter could not read, he would find someone to read it to him.)
>
> We are enclosing a list of the names of the X-marked voters from the precinct where you vote. Look over it and see who lives in your district. Those are the ones who are to be taught at your school.
>
> There are five things we are asking all the trustees in York County to do. They are these:
>
> 1. Advertise a "Sign-Your-Name" meeting at your schoolhouse for Monday night, August 20th, at 7:30. Get it announced at church and Sunday School on Sunday. If there is preaching service at the community church, get the preacher to touch on the subject in his sermon.
>
> 2. Give your X-marked voters personal invitations to be present Monday night.
>
> 3. Get one or two competent people to act as teachers. Give them the enclosed teaching instruction sheet. If they will follow that, they will have no trouble.
>
> 4. Open the schoolhouse Monday night, and have good lights.

91

5. Report the work done.

We are sending you a sheet copied from the Club roll books. If an X-marked voter can write his name, get him to sign this sheet Monday night. If he can't do it then, get him to do it as soon as he can write.

If some of those voters simply will not come to the school, would it be possible to go to their homes to teach them, rather than leave them making their X?

When all have signed, please forward the sheet to this office AT ONCE. Who will be the first? That is an honor to be desired.

Please impress on everyone the great importance of having every voter write his own name in 1924. Let's have York the first county in South Carolina to have a Club roll without an X. What do you say?

Let our slogan be, "I'LL WRITE MY OWN NAME."

Cordially yours,

John E. Carroll, County Superintendent
Mary Eva Hite, Organizer, York County
Anti-Illiteracy Campaign[4]

Without exception all of the trustees contacted labored long and hard. One of them even drove eighteen miles in a buggy into town to find out how he could be more helpful.

Prospective teachers were given these directions for teaching the illiterate:

It takes three nights - or three lessons - for a person to learn to sign the Club roll.

Lesson No. 1:   Give copy—all letters separate. Example: J o h n   D a v i d   W r e n n — 45 — F a r m e r — Y o r k, S. C.

Lesson No. 2:   Give copy - all letters joined. Example: John David Wrenn, 45 — York, S.C.

Lesson No. 3:   Practice writing above lesson from memory.

Don't fail to give plenty of copies for practice out of class. Remember, the Club roll must be signed with pen and ink.[5]

These teachers who volunteered their time and effort without thought of payment, either taught groups at the school or individually. If they found a person who was too timid to approach a class, many times they would walk for miles through the August heat to the illiterate's home.

As an incentive offered to motivate the unlearned to come to school to learn to write their names, ages, occupations, and addresses, the banks in York County deposited one dollar and opened an account for each new signee. Every person claiming this prize had to present a certificate signed by the person who did the teaching and the dates of the lessons.

The press was most cooperative and the *Yorkville Inquirer* in an editorial stated that "Teaching an adult illiterate to write his name is a great service and teaching him or her to read is almost like saving a soul." The ministers in York County must have agreed with the writer, for they labored diligently and were untiring in their encouragement.

During the three-day campaign 200 men and women were taught to write their names. The oldest pupil in the county, James Madison Cook, a Confederate veteran, at the age of 83 was delighted to have this delayed opportunity to learn to write.[6]

The determination of the teachers was exemplified by one volunteer who told this story.

> I tried to get a man who could neither read nor write, but every time he had a good excuse. One day as he was passing my boarding place on his way to the mill, I went out and had a little chat with him. I carried my tablet and pencil along for I was determined to give him one lesson even if he sat on his horse while I gave it. He sat there while I proceeded to give him his first copy. At last he said, 'If you are just going to teach me anyway, I guess I better git off this sack of corn and come in.' So he came in and finished his first lesson. The next day he returned at the same hour. Since that time he has been coming to the schoolhouse and is one of my star pupils.[7]

Then Miss Hite told of one influential man in the county who procrastinated several times after he had promised to come to the school, until she and the local volunteer teacher paid him a personal visit. They had taken their papers and pencils with them and proceeded to give him a lesson in writing his name on the spot. With tears in his eyes he told them he had thought he was too old to learn, but now he knew he could. That same afternoon he was at the school eager for his second lesson and became one of the best pupils in the group. Moreover, he was such a dedicated convert to the cause of literacy that in trying to persuade others to come learn to write he related that he would not take three hundred dollars for what he had learned in the three days he had attended school.[8]

93

Later that year, in November and December of 1923, Miss Gray launched the first intensive state-wide "Write-Your-Name" campaign. She called a state organizational meeting in October, where it was planned that county mass meetings would be held on November 3, local district meetings on November 9, three-day classes would meet on the week of November 10 through 15, and prizes would be awarded on November 17. The campaign was to continue through December 10, with local communities to change the suggested dates to meet their needs.

As in York County, the over-all purpose of the campaign was "to teach in three days every person in the local district to write his name, so that never again will a man or woman in South Carolina be forced to make his mark." Additionally, each illiterate was to learn to write his age, occupation, and address. A further goal not stressed in York County was to communicate to these pupils new ideas pertaining to education and thrift. For this purpose, special editions of the *Lay-By School Messenger*, prepared by Miss Gray, were to be published with articles illustrated and written in simple language for the novice learners. The publication of this classroom newspaper was the most generous contribution of Mr. Ambrose E. Gonzales, the founder of the *State* newspaper in Columbia.[9]

To increase participation, many prizes were offered by public-spirited citizens and institutions. Mr. Gonzales, who already had contributed so generously, donated $5,000, unsolicited, to the campaign and distributed to each pupil who learned to write his name, an easy, revised copy of *Aesop's Fables*. The Illiteracy Commission donated $10 to each of three schools which taught the largest number to write names, with the money to be spent for library books for the school. Further, the Commission gave $25 to each of the two teachers who taught the largest number of illiterates to write their names, provided they taught more than twelve. Finally, a Certificate of Appreciation was presented by the Governor to every person who taught at least one person to write his name.

The Federation of Women's Clubs had participated under their own auspices since 1919, in their own campaign to decrease illiteracy, and had been awarding beautiful silver prizes donated by Sylvan Brothers to club women teaching the most illiterates in one year. They were more than eager to join Miss Gray in her crusade for she had become their Chairman of Education in 1922.[10]

94

To demonstrate the efficacy of Miss Gray's appeals to any organization or institution which could render service to the cause of stamping out illiteracy, the following account of her appearance before the South Carolina Bankers' Association banquet, in June 1923, is recounted. Miss Gray's speech can be found in its entirety in the published *Report of Proceedings* of the Bankers' Twenty-third Annual Convention, but the gist of her inspirational and persuasive message concerned the extent of the illiteracy problem in our state, the cost of this economic liability in dollars and cents, and heart-warming human interest stories of what learning had meant to those who had never before had an opportunity to attend school. As she concluded, Miss Gray was enthusiastically applauded and several influential men rose to their feet to offer whole-hearted personal endorsements of the "Write-Your-Name" campaign she proposed to activate. Then the group resolved unanimously to contribute one dollar to the account of any person who learned to write his name in the upcoming state-wide campaign. The opinion of Colonel D.A. Spivey of Conway must have been a consensus among the group of bankers. He commented, "I wish to unqualifiedly give my endorsement . . . When Miss Gray enters your office, ask her what she wants, and give it to her . . . You need not enter into any competition with her argument . . . Simply ask her what she wants and give her a check for it. Do just exactly what she asks you to do and I guarantee you will do the right thing."[11]

The most significant outcome of the "Write-Your-Name" campaign was the fact that so many illiterates who had never before been exposed to any type of learning, found they were successful and this created for them a desire to seek more knowledge. Wanting to learn to read was the next logical step for thousands of these illiterate adults who had just learned to write their names. They had been starving for knowledge, and now had an enticing taste of it. Consequently, Miss Gray had to find a way to provide the sustenance for which they were clamoring.

These "Write-Your-Name" and later very similar "Stamp-Out-Illiteracy" campaigns were conducted throughout South Carolina for some years, with Miss Gray actively involved in them until 1939. Their outstanding success in large measure can be attributed to Miss Gray's organizational ability and leadership, admired in a Horry County newspaper which referred to her as a "little Napoleon."[12]

NOTES

[1]J.H. Hope and Wil Lou Gray, *Night and Adult Schools* (Columbia: South Carolina Illiteracy Commission, 1923), p. 14.

[2]*Write-Your-Name Bulletin* (Columbia: South Carolina Illiteracy Commission, 1923), p. 6.

[3]Ibid.

[4]Ibid., p. 7.

[5]Ibid., p. 8.

[6]Ibid., pp. 8-10.

[7]Ibid., p. 15.

[8]Ibid.

[9]Ibid., pp. 1-4.

[10]Ibid., pp. 3-4.

[11](Miss Gray conveyed the message she intended, despite the fact that she was introduced as "Lula" Gray.) *Report of Proceedings of the Twenty-third Annual Convention of the South Carolina Bankers' Association* (Richmond: Virginia Stationery Co., 1923) p. 143.

[12]Wil Lou Gray Collection, Caroliniana Library, Columbia, South Carolina.

REFERENCES

Columbia, South Carolina. Caroliniana Library. Wil Lou Gray Collection.

Hope, J.H. and Gray, Wil Lou. *Write-Your-Name Bulletin*. Columbia: South Carolina Illiteracy Commission, 1923.

South Carolina Bankers' Association. *Proceedings of the Twenty-third Annual Convention*. Greenville, South Carolina, 1923.

CHAPTER X

Lay-by Schools

> The harvest truly is plenteous, but the labourers are few.
>
> St. Matthew

Merely supervising the night schools throughout the state would have been a full-time job for most ordinary mortals, but as the newly appointed Supervisor of Adult Schools, Miss Gray soon inaugurated another major educational innovation for uneducated adults, in the fall of 1919. Since cotton was South Carolina's chief crop, the month of August was the farmers' vacation month, after their fields had been "laid by" awaiting maturity and harvest. She therefore felt this would be the best time to establish schools in rural areas for those with little or no previous education. The timing was strategic for another reason since the most qualified teachers were available during their summer vacation. There had been one attempt at such an undertaking in 1913 in Spartanburg County when Julia Selden organized night schools in mill villages in which the teachers were paid one dollar per night by the mill owners.[1] However, the scope of Miss Gray's plan was much broader and the organization more complex.

Counties were urged to employ an organizer who was able to devote her entire time to the work for that month. Organizers were "to plan the method of work, to select teachers and with them attend the State Institute at Winthrop College, to create public sentiment by writing articles and talking at public meetings, to select centers for work, to assist teachers with organization, classification, selection of textbooks and method of instruction, to visit schools and give suggestions, and to see that reports were properly filed." They were also asked to see that schools were clean and prepared for students. It was suggested they contact missionary society groups and Sunday School classes to donate refreshments. Trustees were asked to help organizers take a census in each school district by visiting each home personally to determine who were the illiterates. Miss Gray suggested a tactful way for the organizers or trustees to get this information would be to ask something like, "Did you have good school advantages when you were young?" Organizers were urged to contact all illiterates, invite them to come to classes and emphasize to them that no one would be attending the classes who could read or write much, or who were under fourteen years of age. Sessions were to last from twelve to twenty-four days and times were determined by the needs of the students.[2]

As Supervisor for all adult work, Miss Gray felt that only the highest qualified, experienced, and dedicated teachers could motivate adult illiterates to attend school and learn to love learning. She suggested that county organizers who did the actual hiring of lay-by teachers make the following stipulations: Teachers must hold first-grade certificates and have successful teaching experience, vivid personality and organizing ability. No married woman living in the community may be employed for the reason that she cannot give the minimum requirement of ten hours a day necessary to make the work a success. Teachers must board in the community where they teach and remain there during weekends. Teachers must attend the Winthrop Institute unless enrolled in another summer school.[3]

Many of the lay-by teachers went to the various communities to live and immediately identified themselves with all community activities. They visited the homes of all who needed to come to school, often giving individual lessons until the student's confidence was gained and he was willing to enter a class. Some made their circuit on horseback and held babies while the mothers read and recited their lessons. In these cases, home students could receive perfect attendance awards and attend commencement exercises after they had received twelve lessons. These teachers received one dollar per hour, provided ten students were enrolled and an average attendance of five was maintained. Most of the

98

teachers taught more than one class a day.

Miss Gray stipulated that teachers in lay-by schools were to attend the one-week training session provided for them through the courtesy of Winthrop College. There the month's work was planned in an intensive Teachers' Institute. These training sessions emphasized the importance of meeting the individual needs of adult students.

There were five primary objectives which Miss Gray emphasized to teachers of lay-by schools: (1) encourage students to create more wholesome home atmospheres, (2) create a desire to read more and better literature, (3) promote the beautification and modernization of homes, (4) organize a community club, (5) establish a circulating bulletin library. Teachers were taught to always stress the practical, such as how to care properly for babies, what to feed the family, how taxes are spent, and how to prevent spreading germs.[4]

In their training sessions, teachers were provided with a suggested class schedule:

Opening Exercise	10 minutes
Reading - Beginners	35 minutes
English - Those with slight training	
Phonics - Beginners	20 minutes
Spelling - Others	
Writing - Beginners	20 minutes
Letter writing - Others	
Arithmetic	25 minutes
General Topics	10 minutes

Opening exercises were to consist of a reading from the Bible, singing, and the reading of some inspirational story of achievement. Each night of the session one verse of the twenty-third Psalm was to be written on the board in script, and then read in the Bible to teach the relationship between manuscript and cursive writing. At the close of each opening exercise, students were to spend a few moments memorizing a famous poem or quotation.

The principal text used for teaching beginning reading was *The Lay-by School Messenger*. In addition, the newspaper was used as a teaching tool. It is thought that Miss Gray was one of the first educators in the nation to use the newspaper in the classroom as a text for teaching reading skills. This unique teaching tool had been graciously donated by Ambrose E. Gonzales, the public-spirited founder of *The State* newspaper previously mentioned, and was published weekly during the month of August and distributed to lay-by students.[5] A typical issue contained pictures and human interest stories of adult students, and reproductions of their writing. Copies of letters pupils wrote to Miss Gray were included. As Adult Education Supervisor and editor, Miss Gray wrote inspirational editorials and "pep talks" to encourage the new learners. There were usually two pages of simple mottos, such as, "We learn to read that we may read to learn!" There were simple poems, a calendar of the month, extremely simplified articles about civic responsibilities, health rules, map studies for teaching geography, grammatical exercises, anecdotes, word games, and recipes. With this single periodical written in simple language, instructors could teach any elementary subject. Included in its pages were lessons from one of the few textbooks which were available for adult students who had little or no previous learning, *The Country Life Reader*, which could be purchased from R.L. Bryan Company for thirty cents. A typical lesson on taxes reads:

Taxes for Progress

I shall pay my taxes.
I pay a tax on my home.
I pay a tax on my land.
I pay a tax on my cattle.
I pay a tax on my money.
I pay a tax on many other things.
Where does the money go?
It goes to keep up the schools.
It goes to keep up the roads.
It goes to keep down crime.
It goes to keep down disease.
I am glad I have something to pay taxes on![6]

Teachers of today will especially be interested in how reading was taught sixty years ago to adult students in South Carolina schools.

Write and print on the board the words to be taught.
Drill thoroughly on these words until students can recognize them in the book, on the board, or on cards.
(Every teacher should make her own perception cards.)
Read for the students the first sentence. Have students

100

read sentence as a whole. Discourage from the first simply calling of words. Continue the lesson in the same manner. After the students have read in turn, let one student read the entire lesson. Assign next lesson at the close of reading period, which assignment consists of a drill on the new words, and the teacher's reading the new lesson to the students. With this detailed assignment, the students can study at home. Call attention the first night to capitals and method of punctuation. Urge students to discuss the subject matter, because each lesson contains a thought which should be made their own. REVIEW EVERY NIGHT. Teach students to read the calendar.

Teachers were cautioned not to attempt to teach spelling to beginners, but to concentrate on phonics with that group, constantly teaching the sound value of letters as pupils read. Spelling was taught to those students who had some slight education. Teachers chose words from "One thousand Words Commonly Misspelled," found in the back of Arnold's *Mastery of Words*. They were urged to have written as well as oral spelling, to give definitions of unusual words, and to use them in sentences. Words misspelled in students' writing assignments were to be put on the board and discussed.

As adult students were shown how to write their names, the letters were written the first time with spaces between the letters, and in ensuing lessons students were shown how to join letters to form their complete names. When Miss Gray recommended to the lay-by teachers to use a thorn or hairpin to trace letters on copy papers prepared so students could practice at home, she may well have been the first proponent of the "kinesthetic" method of teaching reading and writing, which is a multi-sensory approach. It is really amazing how many so-called "new" techniques of teaching were used by Miss Gray some sixty years ago. Today, teachers are trained to stress "configuration" to beginning readers, whereas Miss Gray taught her teachers to "point out differences in the height and shape of various letters."[7]

More advanced students were taught how to write good letters, both personal and business. Many elderly adults were able to correspond with family members long absent for the first time after they had attended lay-by classes. They were so grateful to their teacher and the Supervisor who had made it all possible, that usually their first letter to be mailed was addressed to Miss Gray.

101

In the arithmetic classes, beginning students were taught to write to one hundred. They were drilled on multiplication, subtraction, addition, and division. Examples of their problems were supposed to be based on real-life situations which were meaningful to them in the work which they did. The more advanced students covered the same material, only the work was more difficult. At the conclusion of each session, teachers and students were to discuss any interesting topics which were of concern to the class or about which they wanted information.[8]

No discussion of the teaching methods and materials employed in the earliest adult schools in South Carolina is complete without recounting the story behind another "brain child" the *Bible Story Reader*. From the onset of her work with adults, Miss Gray perceived a desperate need for simplified texts which would be appealing and motivational for her students. The older ones especially had one primary reason for attending classes — they had been yearning to be able to read their Bibles. Even though they might be absolutely terrified of the idea of entering school, Miss Gray reasoned that they would learn to read even more quickly if they had an extremely simplified version of the Scriptures. Her family had always been extraordinarily supportive, and she felt no compunction about asking her stepmother Mary, and Mrs. Emily Meng Jones, a close friend of the family, for assistance. Both "Mamie" and Emily had been excellent teachers and they agreed to attempt such a project "if Wil Lou would promise to help." The result of this talented trio's team effort was the *Bible Story Reader*, which immediately created quite a stir in educational circles, not only in South Carolina, but throughout the Union.

The text of this elementary reader for adults included both Old and New Testament stories, the Ten Commandments, and a few favorite hymns. Attractive, artistic illustrations by Tissot added to the book's appeal. When the manuscript was submitted to the Johnson Publishing Company of Richmond, Virginia, it was accepted for publication at once, becoming a source of delight for thousands of adult primary students who never before had been able to read a story from the Bible. The State Federation of Women's Clubs donated a *Bible Story Reader* to each adult student.[9]

Another cooperative member of the Gray-Dial clan played an important supporting role in Miss Gray's dramatic struggle to combat illiteracy throughout the state. When she had decided that a play dealing with the illiteracy issue would be a most effective medium for conveying her message to the masses, Miss Gray discussed this idea with her cousin, Rebecca Dial. The play *Sand* was the outgrowth of this conversation. In her play, Miss Dial depicted the conditions arising from illiteracy. In the course of the drama a home whose family members are illiterate is marvelously converted through a little learning because members of the family have attended night school. In the final scene a typical night school commencement is enacted, with one graduate carrying her infant as she received her certificate, as often happened in real-life adult schools. *Sand* was presented by amateurs, who were often adult students themselves. The play was sponsored by local club women so its entire proceeds could go to further the anti-illiteracy crusade being waged. It was performed throughout the state during the twenties and thirties.[10]

The September report from the first lay-by teachers after their inaugural session in 1919 indicated:

Number of schools	250
Number of teachers	294
Total enrollment	4,943
Average attendance	70%
First grade students	2,886
Students taught to read	2,214
Students taught to write	2,322
Average age of illiterates	31[11]

However, the above numbers do not tell the human interest stories which are the most important product of the anti-illiteracy movement, such as 98-year-old Harriett Linder of near Clifton, who registered in the Cowpens school in 1923 and was a successful student, and one family in York County who enrolled three generations at the same time, men aged 76, 45, and 20.[12]

As a result of her year's work in 1919, Miss Gray concluded, "The people of the state are behind the movement as demonstrated by the cooperation given the Supervisor in the counties in which I worked. If the legislature will provide sufficient appropriation, and if the counties will finance an Organizer, there will be no illiteracy problem in South Carolina in five years." Unfortunately, the General Assembly was not always so inclined, and in 1922 when there was a decrease of $8,000 in

103

appropriation funds, by the month of September Miss Gray foresaw that all of their allocation would have been spent, and she was forced to cancel all lay-by school work for that autumn.[13]

The lay-by schools continued throughout the years, culminating in the 1929 campaign which enrolled in one month 8,405 students. The teacher institutes which Miss Gray had inaugurated in the fall of 1919 were one decade later responsible for a week of intensive training for 200 teachers and 15 organizers at Winthrop College.

This tremendous 1929 campaign was climaxed by a State Commencement at Clemson College. Some 700 teachers and students from 20 counties converged at Clemson in an educational pilgrimage which Miss Gray considers to be one of the highlights of her career. She felt that most of her adult charges experienced a "sense of state pride and county consciousness" they had never before known, because of their participation in such an impressive ceremony. Certainly their lives had been tremendously enriched because they had dared to accept Miss Gray's challenge — "You are never too old to learn!"[14]

Unfortunately, again due to curtailed state appropriations for adult education, lay-by schools in South Carolina were discontinued in 1929. It was not until 1936 that Miss Gray could continue to cultivate this potentially productive crop of eager learners and some classes of this type were in session until 1941.[15]

NOTES

[1]Wil Lou Gray, "Evolution of Adult Elementary Education in South Carolina," *Interstate Bulletin on Adult Education* II, (May 1927), p. 3.

[2]Ibid., p. 4.

[3]Wil Lou Gray, unpublished circular letter, 1929.

[4]Gray, "Evolution of Adult Education," p. 4.

[5]*Fifty-second Annual Report of the Superintendent of Education* (Columbia: State Department of Education, 1920), p. 208.

[6]Cora Wilson Stewart, *Country Life Reader* (Richmond: B.F. Johnson Publishing Company), quoted in *The Lay-by School Messenger*, 18 August 1923.

[7]*A Midsummer Drive against Adult Illiteracy in South Carolina* (Columbia: South Carolina Illiteracy Commission, 1920), p. 9.

[8]Ibid., pp. 5-10.

[9]Harriet Gray Blackwell, *A Candle for All Time* (Richmond: The Dietz Press, Inc., 1959), p. 269.

[10]Rebecca Dial, *Sand* (Columbia: The State Company, 1920).

[11]Wil Lou Gray, *Report of the State Supervisor of Adult Schools* (Columbia: State Department of Education, 1920), p. 24.

[12]Ibid.

[13]J.H. Hope and Wil Lou Gray, *Night and Adult Schools* (Columbia: The Illiteracy Commission, 1923), p. 16.

[14]Wil Lou Gray, "South Carolina's Program for Belated Learners," *Journal of American Association of University Women* 23, (January 1930), p. 83.

[15]*Sixty-first Annual Report of the Superintendent of Education* (Columbia: State Department of Education, 1929), p. 38.

REFERENCES

A Midsummer Drive against Adult Illiteracy in South Carolina. Columbia: South Carolina Illiteracy Commission, 1920.

Blackwell, Harriet Gray. *A Candle for All Time.* Richmond: The Dietz Press, Inc., 1959.

Dial, Rebecca. *Sand.* Columbia: The State Company, 1920.

Fifty-second Annual Report of the Superintendent of Education. Columbia: State Department of Education, 1920.

Fifty-third Annual Report of the Superintendent of Education. Columbia: State Department of Education, 1921.

Fifty-fourth Annual Report of the Superintendent of Education. Columbia: State Department of Education, 1922.

Fifty-fifth Annual Report of the Superintendent of Education. Columbia: State Department of Education, 1923.

Fifty-sixth Annual Report of the Superintendent of Education. Columbia: State Department of Education, 1924.

Fifty-seventh Annual Report of the Superintendent of Education. Columbia: State Department of Education, 1925.

Fifty-eighth Annual Report of the Superintendent of Education. Columbia: State Department of Education, 1926.

Fifty-ninth Annual Report of the Superintendent of Education. Columbia: State Department of Education, 1927.

Gray, Wil Lou. "Evolution of Adult Elementary Education in South Carolina." *Interstate Bulletin on Adult Education* II (May 1927): 3-5.

Gray, Wil Lou. *Report of the State Supervisor of Adult Schools.* Columbia: State Department of Education, 1920.

Gray, Wil Lou. "South Carolina's Program for Belated Learners." *Journal of American Association of University Women* 23 (January 1930): 82-85.

Gray, Wil Lou; Gray, Mary Dunklin; and Jones, Emily. *Bible Story Reader.* Richmond: B.F. Johnson Publishing Company, 1920.

Hope, J.H. and Gray, Wil Lou. *Night and Adult Schools.* Columbia: The South Carolina Illiteracy Commission, 1923.

Sixtieth Annual Report of the Superintendent of Education. Columbia: State Department of Education, 1928.

Sixty-first Annual Report of the Superintendent of Education. Columbia: State Department of Education, 1929.

Sixty-second Annual Report of the Superintendent of Education. Columbia: State Department of Education, 1930.

Stewart, Cora Wilson. *Country Life Reader.* Richmond: B.F. Johnson Publishing Company, n.d.

The Lay-by School Messenger. 18 August 1923.

CHAPTER XI

Perennial Pilgrimages

Give me . . .
My staff of faith to walk upon . . .
And thus I'll take my pilgrimage.
Sir Walter Raleigh

In the summer of 1913, Miss Gray, accompanied by her cousin, Madge Harris, spent one entire summer vacation traveling in Europe, primarily visiting Switzerland and Italy. Since that time, she has been a great believer in the educational value of travel. She feels that everyone ought to travel regularly, even if it is necessary to borrow the funds to indulge this inclination, because "life is measured by one's ability to respond to his environment, and no activity enlarges one's environment more than reading and travel." Accordingly, she annually arranged tours for her adult students, calling them "pilgrimages."

From the time Miss Gray took a group of teachers from rural Laurens County to the National Education Association convention in Washington, D. C., because they could not afford to travel individually on their small salaries, until she retired as Director of the South Carolina Opportunity School in 1957, she delighted in arranging each year at least one low-cost, educational sight-seeing tour for her adult students from all over the state. Miss Gray has always felt that a personal visit to a historic location was the most effective method of learning history and at the same time, encouraged a sense of state and national pride.

Most of these adult students had little money and as a result, most had never been more than a few miles from their doorsteps. It was in meeting the challenge of arranging travel details of the pilgrimages which might involve thousands of students that Miss Gray proved her financial wizardry and organizational genius. On reflection, she herself is amazed that she was able to afford so many valuable learning experiences and impart so much pleasure to so many people for so little money.

To ensure that maximum educational benefit resulted from each pilgrimage, plans were made throughout the year. Whenever a destination had been decided, a course of study based upon the city was developed for the students and written with a controlled vocabulary for easy reading. This motivational material was distributed through county organizers to individual teachers and students. As a result, by the time a group arrived in a city, they were already familiar with its landmarks and other significant features. Moreover, they were also learning about other areas they would traverse en route. Just as important as the history and geography they learned, was the social growth promoted by assembling a travel wardrobe, planning for food and lodging expenses, practicing thrift to save for the trip, and learning travel etiquette.

The first time that Miss Gray planned a trip of any consequence for her adult students was in conjunction with a state contest she arranged in 1922. That year 82 students and 9 teachers from 14 mill schools and 7 rural night schools assembled in Columbia on a warm, spring Friday afternoon. Thanks to their Supervisor who had made careful preparations to see that they received royal treatment, they were entertained at a luncheon by the University of South Carolina. That evening they were guests of the Masons of Columbia, who sponsored a declamation contest for them, followed by addresses by the Governor and other important persons. After they had competed in the three basic skills — reading, writing, and arithmetic — they were taken on an educational tour of Columbia. From this first small group of "pilgrims," Miss Gray envisioned the tremendous educational potential of such outings. Consequently, she decided that an annual pilgrimage was to become a vital feature of her adult education program, beginning in 1923.[1]

108

The pilgrimages had a variety of destinations, but the favorite with the adult students and their teachers was the tour of historic Columbia, their state capital. Miss Gray really did not know what to expect when she planned the first pilgrimage to Columbia for one Sunday in April 1923, but she was almost overwhelmed by the tremendous response of the students from all over the state. Thousands, from the rolling hills of the Piedmont to the low-country Atlantic coast, poured into Columbia. Transportation of all types had been arranged for them and they arrived in cars, school buses, and flat-bed trucks containing improvised seats. One excited group even disembarked from a large furniture van that had been borrowed for the occasion.

It had been arranged for University students to serve as volunteer guides when the pilgrimage group toured the State House. It was their task to convey to the group the historic aspects of each portrait, statue, and relic. In addition, the Governor had agreed to be in his office to shake hands with each participant, which was a thrill they were always to remember. As soon as the tour of the State House ended, after the group had eaten picnic lunches they had packed for the day, the State Highway Patrol provided escort vehicles to ensure the safety of the group as they traveled throughout the city.

Native Columbians who had volunteered to help "Miss Wil Lou" were rather amazed when they discovered the visiting students knew more about the city than they did. As Trinity Church was pointed out, before the guide began to relate its historic significance, one student instantly reminded the group that "Henry Timrod, the poet who wrote 'Carolina' was buried there." As the group approached the First Baptist Church, the guide was pre-empted again by students who recited that, "The Secession Convention was held there just before the War between the States," and "The Yankees meant to burn it, but by mistake they burned another church instead." This scene was re-enacted all over the city as the adult students visited the locations they had been learning about in their classes at home.

It became traditional for the adult students to troop into Township Auditorium at sunset for the climax of the day's activities. The students usually produced some sort of colorful historical pageant, with the help of the talented Miss Erin Kohn, Miss Gray's co-worker and friend. For instance, one year the students honored Governor and Mrs. Olin

Johnston as county representatives brought gifts produced in their particular region and amassed around the state's First Family an impressive array of South Carolina's abundance.[2]

On another occasion, the pilgrimage of 1936, 8,000 adult students and teachers arrived in Columbia to celebrate the Sesquicentennial. This was a special treat for Miss Gray and her students, for they were spectators rather than participants when the Sesquicentennial Commission entertained the group with a special performance of "The Spirit of Columbia," which depicted the highlights of the capital city for 150 years since its founding in 1786.[3]

Then after the patriotic fervor aroused by the pomp and pageantry, it was customary for the pilgrimage to draw to a reluctant close on a solemn note with vesper services in various churches. For many years it was traditional for this service to be held in Trinity churchyard under the majestic water oak planted by Wade Hampton, with Bishop Finlay presiding over the services.

Encouraged by the tremendous success of the first few pilgrimages, each year Miss Gray planned some type of educational travel, and each year the number of participants mushroomed. One of the most successful years for pilgrimages was in 1935 when in three successive April weekends, Miss Gray made all of the arrangements for 10,000 adult students to visit Columbia and Charleston. The first Sunday 5,000 white students made the journey to Columbia and the following Sunday 4,000 Negro students congregated there. This first state-wide Negro pilgrimage enjoyed "Vanguards of Our Race," a pageant depicting the Negro's contributions to poetry, science, literature, and music. On the next Sunday, approximately 1,000 students from the Piedmont region were taken to Charleston for their first view of the Atlantic Ocean and that picturesque historical city.[4]

Miss Gray particularly remembers that Charleston pilgrimage because of the problems involved in finding overnight accommodations for her students. The city was overflowing with tourists visiting the famous gardens which were at the peak of their glory that weekend. Although Miss Gray had found enough cots for the lady travelers in her group, the men had to sleep on pallets in a large hall. And the tireless Supervisor, after she had seen that all of her "boys and girls" were bedded down for the night, retired to her automobile and slept there.

110

However, no one seemed to mind the Spartan sleeping arrangements because they were all so elated with what they had seen and done on that memorable day. In fact, as the occasion was drawing to a close, one "pilgrim" remarked, "Miss Gray, didn't we all have a good time, and not one soul had even one drink!" But what was miraculous about the outing was that 1,000 adults traveled from the extreme northern parts of the state to the port of Charleston, were supplied with a night's lodging, four meals, a boat ride, morning service in historic St. Philip's Church, and admission to Magnolia Gardens, at a cost of $3.

These pilgrimages continued through the years with groups venturing farther and farther away from home, with Miss Gray forever seeking to enlarge the horizons of her adult students' learning environment. In 1927 and 1932, pilgrimage groups ventured as far as Washington, D.C., after assembling in Columbia to board a train. With the Supervisor's careful budgeting, a student was able to enjoy a full weekend in Washington for the nominal cost of $25, which was not bad for the priceless memories the students carried home. Yet even more venturesome was the pilgrimage in 1939 when the students entrained for a week's visit to the New York City World Fair, after a tour of the nation's capital.

On rare occasions Miss Gray became discouraged when attempting to arrange the thousand and one details entailed in planning a pilgrimage for thousands of people who were involved in the adult education program in South Carolina, for it did require Herculean effort. Sometimes it seemed that as soon as one perplexing problem was resolved, two others sprang forth, Hydra-like, to take its place. In her personal diary in 1938, in a rare pessimistic mood she wrote:

> The difficulties encountered with such an undertaking are innumerable and each time I promise myself never to attempt another such trip, but . . . such pilgrimages cement the year's work as nothing else could do.

Such disclosures as this remind us that after all, Miss Gray is a very human person, a mere mortal who never presumed to be a miracle worker. As such, she was more than discouraged, she was heartbroken when a group of her students were denied entrance to a public beach in Charleston because of the color of their skin.

However, these infrequent moments of despair were temporarily forgotten when she received letters from grateful students such as the following:

May 5, 1938

Dear Miss Gray,

I know I am late, but I want to thank you for making it possible for us to go to Charleston. I never enjoyed a trip so much in my life. Just to think of seeing those gardens, the Brookgreen, and the others. I enjoyed them all and then the nice fish supper and the boat ride and the church service at St. Phillips Church. We went out in the cemetery and found the Calhoun monument. I enjoyed the things we saw in the museum and to tell the truth I enjoyed everything from the time I left home till I got back, for we went one way and came back another, and everything was new. I never get to go anywhere for I have to work. I have been left a widow twice so you see I have no chance to go. I just thought what a wonderful world God made for us. We just find Blessings everywhere we go. My mind is on everything so till I can't hardly write but anyway I want to thank you. I know now that God blesses us with Beauty full things and you made it possible for us to see some of them. No one else would of thought of such a thing. Everyone in our party said they enjoyed it so much. Mrs. Keith said she enjoyed it more than any trip she had ever made. I sometimes think of it as a thrill and some times it is a sad thought to think we may never see you again but let's hope to. I will always remember you waving goodby as we left the Middleton Gardens. I hope you and Miss Major will have a nice vacation. I learned to love you both. Ernest don't know I am writing or he would send his best regards for he is always talking about Miss Gray. I want to thank you for what you have done for Ernest. I had to take him out of school and put him to work to help me make a living for the family as he is the oldest of four. I hope you will pardon me for being so late but it was still on my mind and heart so, I just thought I would tell you. I hope you will excuse this sorry writing for I never did go to school much. Back 52 years ago things were not like they are now. I will tell you how old I am if I don't mind. With love and best wishes to you Miss Gray and also to Miss Major.

Sincerely yours,

Mrs. Annie Holcombe
104 Cemetery Street
Pickens, S.C.

NOTES

[1] James H. Hope and Wil Lou Gray, *Adult and Night School Bulletin* (Columbia: State Department of Education, 1923), p. 25.

[2] *Education F E R A* (Columbia: State Department of Education, 1934-35), p. 6.

[3] *Sixty-ninth Annual Report of Superintendent of Education* (Columbia: State Department of Education, 1937), p. 58.

[4] *Seventy-fourth Annual Report of Superintendent of Education* (Columbia: State Department of Education, 1942), pp. 43-44.

REFERENCES

Education F E R A. Columbia: State Department of Education, 1934-35.

Hope, James H. and Gray, Wil Lou. *Adult and Night School Bulletin.* Columbia: State Department of Education, 1923.

Seventy-fourth Annual Report of Superintendent of Education. Columbia: State Department of Education, 1942.

Sixty-ninth Annual Report of Superintendent of Education. Columbia: State Department of Education, 1937.

113

CHAPTER XII

A Quarter Century of Progress

(1921 - 1946)

For age is opportunity no less
Than youth itself.
Henry Wadsworth Longfellow

Tamassee - The Cornerstone Was Faith

August 2, 1921, was an auspicious day for Miss Gray as State Supervisor of Adult Education. It was on this day that an "Opportunity School" was organized as an experiment in adult education, with Miss Gray as originator, developer, active supervisor, and generally the guiding light for another educational "first."

At some time during her studies at Columbia University's Teachers College, she had read of the "folk schools" in Denmark, and a similar attempt at developing an adult educational program in Denver, Colorado. These two concepts had fused in her mind, and a unique idea evolved into a vacation boarding school on an elementary level for girls over fourteen and women, the first such "opportunity school" in the United States. Its primary purpose was to provide a chance for summer study to those girls and women in the textile mills who had not been able to obtain a complete education.

The idea was born, and now Miss Gray had to find the proper environment and nourishment for its development. As she had discussed

114

her thoughts concerning such a school with her family, her brother Dial, who was engaged in the wholesale grocery business at that time, enthusiastically commended her plan and became the first donor to the cause when he contributed a barrel of flour for the school. He took it for granted that there was to be such a school if his sister had her heart set on it. Today, Miss Gray laughingly recalls that her first Opportunity School was founded with no more assets than her own faith and the barrel of flour from Dial.

Miss Gray then set out to find the proper surroundings for her pioneer school. She had criss-crossed the entire state many times in her travels as State Supervisor, and Tamassee, a secluded spot among the rolling Blue Ridge foothills of Oconee County, had always charmed her. Tamassee, an Indian word meaning "the sunlight of God," had been part of a land grant to General Andrew Pickens for service during the Revolutionary War. In 1921 it belonged to the Daughters of the American Revolution, who had established a school for neglected children in the rustic hills. Tamassee was twelve miles from the nearest railroad at Walhalla and almost inaccessible. In later years Miss Gray was to quip that she had deliberately chosen such a secluded spot for her experimental school so that in case it had failed, no one would have been the wiser.

Miss Gray felt that Tamassee was the perfect spot to introduce females from poverty-stricken homes to standards of living they had never before experienced. She had long known that South Carolinians who were culturally, economically, and educationally disadvantaged could not become better citizens, or better parents and homemakers, as long as they had no higher standard of living than the one to which they were inured. Though the idyll at Tamassee would be only a brief respite from the drudgery of their lives, she envisioned that whatever these students experienced in the Opportunity School could transform and enrich their lives when they returned to their homes.

When Miss Gray went to the Tryon home of Mrs. Frank Cain, the regent of the South Carolina Daughters of the American Revolution, not only was her wish to borrow Tamassee's facilities fulfilled, but a contribution was also donated for the girls' board while living there. Of course, it was helpful that Miss Gray was a member of the D. A. R. and was on the Board of Directors that operated the school.

At first it was planned to charge a small amount for each girl's living expenses, but when the Supervisor visited homes in the country and in mill villages where prospective students lived, she soon realized that they would be fortunate to collect the one dollar book fee. Although Miss Gray has never asked favors for herself, she has absolutely no qualms about soliciting aid for others when she can do no more for them independently. As her powers of persuasion were employed, the Illiteracy Commission contributed one hundred dollars, ministers appealed to their congregations, merchants in Seneca and other nearby towns gave generously, and people in the community and enrolling students brought produce from their farms amd gardens to add to Dial's barrel of flour. At the end of the four-week term, account books revealed that the board had cost five dollars for each student, and they had actually gained weight!

After Miss Gray had questioned day-school teachers about likely prospective students, she personally recruited almost all of the eligible girls and women who most needed help and who were most receptive. To be eligible, students could not be younger than fourteen, could not attend public school, or could not have progressed beyond the fifth grade. Seventeen girls and women registered as boarders in the day school, but Miss Gray had been beseeched by so many males for an equal chance that a session was added at night for those living in the area. At the community meeting announcing the opening of the school, nineteen men and one woman eagerly enrolled in the night class.[1]

Although the ages of the female students ranged fron sixteen to thirty-five, they were always referred to by Miss Gray as "my girls." When she went to Walhalla to meet the train that was bringing the students selected for Tamassee, Miss Gray noticed among this group a young widow who seemed so superior to the others that it did not seem possible she fell into the eligible category. However, she soon had to change her mind when the woman told how she had first gone to work in a textile mill at the age of nine, had seldom gone to school, and had married at sixteen. Her husband died at an early age and left her with three small children. She returned to the mill, the only work she knew how to do, but when she found she could not feed her children and care for them properly on her small wages, she was forced to place them in an orphanage. Now that they were adolescent, and upon visiting her, they had commented that

116

their mother did not talk the way their teachers did. These comments hurt her terribly because she had always done her very best. She knew immediately when she heard of the school at Tamassee that here was a golden opportunity to attain her greatest goal in life at the moment — "Miss Gray, I aim to talk proper."

A father who brought his two daughters to the school said they had to go to work in the mills at a tender age because the family was so poor. Then later they were ashamed to return to school because they were so much older than the other students. The Opportunity School was an answer to his prayers that some way could be found to educate his daughters.

Another very pretty, obviously intelligent girl recounted how she had been forced to labor in the mill because of her family's poverty when she should have been attending school. She could recall gazing out the window of the mill as she sat at her machine, enviously watching the children who were going to and from school each day.

Miss Gray chose Miss Mary (Mamie) McLees as the teacher. She was to hold classes for the girls and ladies in the mornings from nine to twelve o'clock, while her night class met from seven until nine. Since the first session was to continue for four weeks, Miss Gray soon saw that Miss McLees must have an assistant to enable her to give more individualized instruction to those on a primary level. Her sister, Miss Lucia McLees, volunteered to serve without pay, and she taught any students who were above a fourth-grade ability level. There were also two other volunteer teachers and several visiting instructors from Winthrop College and the community. Miss Gray also arranged for state home demonstration agents to offer instruction in sewing, handwork, and arts and crafts.

The curriculum at Tamassee offered the basic tools of learning, the traditional 3 R's, supplemented by an emphasis on health habits, good manners, civics, domestic science, and arts and crafts. The work was so planned that every act of the day was educational.

The day at Tamassee began at 6:30 and breakfast was served at 8:00. There were four rotating groups of students performing all of the household chores. After students had been in classes from 9:00 until 12:00, they began to prepare the noon meal and lunch was served promptly at 2:00. These meals were carefully planned so that they could be attended by the girls while lessons were continuing. In the early

117

afternoon they studied hygiene and citizenship, and late afternoon hours were reserved for recreation and arts and crafts, followed by supper at 6:30. Following this schedule the girls and women all had an equal chance to be trained in cooking, table-setting, good manners, hygiene, and generally how to live cooperatively in a group. Their mealtimes were protracted affairs when correct speech and manners were stressed. The students did not feel this to be an ordeal they must endure, but rather they looked forward to these times with much pleasure, for all of them begged to be taught correct table manners and diction. Above all else, these girls and women aspired to become "ladies."

On Sunday afternoons the group walked to the home of some night school students who had volunteered to entertain the group; then they would enjoy a time of fellowship in the community "sing-along." Miss Gray was certain she had made a wise choice of teacher when she heard how Miss McLees had ordered one young man to hand over his gun when a long-smoldering family feud erupted in the midst of one of these Sunday afternoon social affairs, and the young man meekly complied.

The facilities at the rustic Tamassee camp were quite limited, but Miss Gray personally saw to it that the girls received lessons in personal hygiene, for most of them confessed they had never seen a bathtub nor used a toothbrush. Since there was no indoor plumbing, a water detail was sent to the mountainside spring each day so baths could be taken in a galvanized washtub each evening before bedtime. Again Miss Gray was thankful to find the traditional rural outhouse out back, and with her students protesting that she let them perform such a menial task, she was the first to scrub that facility in order to teach an early lesson in sanitation.

These students also experienced a world of fashion for the first time. Although they had worked in textile mills most of their lives, they did not know how to make clothing for themselves or do any type of handwork. The young widow who aspired to "talk proper," was taught by a visiting teacher from Winthrop College to make millinery. She became so talented in the art that she was able to leave the mill when she returned home and support herself by making hats for discriminating women. Later, all three of her children became college graduates, largely due to their mother's influence. There is no doubt that only four weeks at Tamassee Opportunity School had changed her life, and the lives of many others, in a profound way.

However, the most amazing outcome of the Tamassee experiment in adult education was the revelation that such an undertaking, with the exception of the Supervisor's salary, could be financed on a shoestring at a total cost to the state of South Carolina of a mere $100 for Miss McLees' salary.[2]

At the close of the first session at Tamassee, the experiment had proved such an overwhelming success that Miss Gray realized larger, better, and more accessible facilities must be found to provide an equal chance for the thousands who deserved to improve their lives through education. It had always disturbed Miss Gray that although the state distributed some educational appropriations on a per capita basis, a lion's share of the funds went to state-supported secondary schools and colleges. This meant that the thousands who had been forced to drop out of elementary school were not going to have an opportunity to complete their education, and it was this group that concerned Miss Gray as State Supervisor of Adult Education. She agonized as well over how to educate the older citizens who had never been to school at all.

Furthermore, it had always seemed to Miss Gray an extravagant waste for colleges and universities to close their doors during the summer months when college enrollment did not warrant a year-round program. Miss Gray felt that these facilities could just as well be made available during the summer months to the uneducated adult citizens of the state who wanted to begin or continue an education. A college campus with its aura of culture and learning would be the most motivational atmosphere possible for her adult students, and she was determined to find such a location for her next opportunity school in the summer of 1922.

Tamassee, the site of the first Opportunity School in S.C.

NOTES

[1]Wil Lou Gray, *Adult and Night School Bulletin* (Columbia: State Department of Education, 1923), p. 21.

[2]Ibid., pp. 18-22.

REFERENCES

Gray, Wil Lou. Columbia, South Carolina. Interview, 11 October 1975.

Gray, Wil Lou. *Adult and Night School Bulletin.* Columbia: State Department of Education, 1923.

120

Opportunity Schools at Lander, Erskine, and Anderson

As a lifelong Methodist, Miss Gray was sure that a church-supported institution of higher learning would most probably react favorably to her plea for summertime use of its campus. She appeared before an educational committee of the Upper South Carolina Methodist Conference meeting in Lancaster and stated her case. One of the committee members was Dr. John O. Wilson, minister and president of Lander College, a school for young women in Greenwood. Fortunately, Dr. Wilson's Christian commitment and concern extended to illiterate adults, and he readily acquiesced to her request, stating: "Lander College was founded to serve the womanhood of South Carolina — a different group, it's true, from the one Miss Gray represents. If Lander College is needed now, by a different group, her doors stand open to Miss Gray's students." [1]

Now that the first impediment was removed, a multitude of logistical arrangements had to be organized. It was to become the Supervisor's practice to move her office to the site of each opportunity school before the opening of each summer session. Even months before opening, Miss Gray was at work recruiting students and teachers, finding resource personnel, planning curricula, acquiring materials, making arrangements for room and board, equipping a library with appropriate reading material, and attending to other details to ensure a successful session. In an extensive publicity campaign, letters were sent out by the Chairman of the Board of Education and Lander College to prominent ministers. Miss Gray followed this with a letter to mill executives, social workers, teachers, missionary leaders, and club women. She realized that only through the personal influence of these people could the message concerning the Opportunity School reach those who most needed and wanted it. Not trusting to just the written word, Miss Gray personally visited mills and drove miles into the country seeking prospective students.

The cooperation of the mill executives was exemplified by Mr. J. P. Gossett, a mill owner from Anderson, who sent in reservations for twenty girls, four from each of his mill villages. He wrote, "The money invested in these schools is the best investment we have ever made." Alexander Long sent one employee from each of his mills and made loans to others

121

wanting to attend. The president of Judson Mills, B.E. Geer, was very cooperative because he believed his employees attending the Opportunity School would return to the job as better workers and better citizens.[2]

Upon registration, a copy of the Lander Opportunity School Bulletin was mailed immediately to each girl with a personal note from the college and one from the State Department of Education. This was only one effort to make the girls feel that a genuine welcome awaited them at Lander.

There were no academic requirements to attend the Lander Opportunity School. Miss Gray wanted the school to be open to any girl and woman with a good mind and healthy body who had not completed the sixth grade, who was over the age of fourteen, and who was unable to attend a public school. These students were grouped according to ability and enrolled only in classes that would be meaningful and useful. No classes were above a sixth-grade level of difficulty. Moreover, the classes were kept quite small so students had more individual attention and progressed as rapidly as their ability permitted.

When the first session of the Lander Opportunity School opened on Monday, July 24, 1922, Miss Gray had scored another triumph, for Lander was the first college in this nation to open its doors to females for the purpose of teaching the mastery of basic reading and writing skills, in an environment that enlarged personal horizons and awakened latent ambitions. In this first session 89 "girls" enrolled, ranging in age from 14 to 51, from all over the state and from all walks of life. There were housewives, mill workers, and farmers' wives and daughters. They came from 13 counties, with 30 pupils coming from Anderson, 13 from Greenwood, and 10 from Richland. There were 2 who lived in a town, 9 lived in rural areas, and 78 resided in mill villages. They had three things in common: (1)They had all been deprived of an education. (2)They were all wage-earners. (3)They all wanted to learn. The average number of years of school was three, but there were classes for ability levels from the first through the fifth grades.

The girls assisted with the work of the school so their living expenses were only $12.50 for the month. Every household chore was actually a class session with the housekeeper giving the students valuable and enjoyable instruction. By 7:30 each morning they were ready to begin

122

another day of learning. For five hours each day they attended classes in reading, writing, arithmetic, spelling, English, civics, and history. After dinner each evening they met in the chapel for discussions and demonstration lessons on table manners, preparation of food, planning and serving meals, and selection of clothes. Late afternoons were reserved for recreation, and evenings were spent preparing their work for the next day or enjoying movies.

Their classes were extremely practical, for they learned how to plan household purchases, to keep household accounts, to prepare nutritious and balanced diets, to plan family needs, and to set a table. The culmination of this learning experience was a commencement ceremony when each pupil participated in a school pageant and modeled a garment she had made in class. The instructor announced the garment's cost, usually ranging from $.59 to $3, with the gingham fabric coming from mills where the students worked.

Miss Gray had chosen her faculty from teachers who had already been successful in adult teaching. They were employed to teach only five hours per day, but they literally taught day and night. Many times their most valuable teaching was not in the classroom, but while chatting, walking, or participating in recreation periods with the students after classes were over. There were four teachers in addition to Miss Lessie Tiller, who acted as dean for the school.

The Methodist Conference paid the salaries of the housekeeper and cooks, while the State Department of Education provided the salaries of the teachers. In addition to the faculty members, each week Miss Gray arranged for other resource personnel from various state agencies to give instruction, such as home demonstration agents, the Anti-tuberculosis Association, and professional nurses.

The Lander Opportunity School became an outstanding success largely because of the mill presidents and superintendents who paid the expenses of the students enrolling from their plants. In addition, Sunday School classes, missionary societies, businesses, clubs, and individuals donated scholarships. The American Legion and its auxiliary groups frequently contributed funds. The few students who were not awarded scholarships borrowed the money or withdrew from savings accounts to pay their own way. The majority of those who came for the first time vowed to Miss Gray that they planned to return home, work even harder, and save whatever they could in order to return for more learning.[3]

In writing of the school's success, Dr. Wilson said:

> I had the good fortune to witness the Opportunity School of 1922 at Lander College. My interest was great before it opened, but it grew day by day to the end. The faculty was so capable and entered into everything in such good spirits that they deserved the success which was realized. They were teaching and helping all day long and much of the night sometimes. The students were so full of their opportunity that it is wonderful what success they achieved. They had only to learn and they made marvelous progress in that.[4]

This was to be the sole Opportunity School session Dr. Wilson witnessed, for his death that same year was mourned by Methodists, alumnae, and educators throughout the South.

At the conclusion of the first term at Lander, Miss Gray was touched by the students' warm expression of gratitude. She counted their newly acquired social graces and ability to cope with problems of daily living just as important as the measurement in years and months of gains in scholastic achievement. One young lady from a mill village in Spartanburg said:

> I have learned many things this month that have been my greatest desire to know all my life. And that is good table manners, and to learn to cook, and to learn to speak correctly. And one good habit I have learned is to brush my teeth three times every day. And how to improve my health. I feel I have learned more than I can express. And my greatest desire is to continue my studies when I go home. I can never thank the one who told me about this school and Mr. Swearingen and Miss Gray, and others who have helped make this school a success enough. Only by showing my country what it has meant to me and letting it show what I have gained by making the most of the opportunity which I once refused.[5]

A bright attractive girl who left school as a young child because illness and misfortune struck her family stated:

> I can't express what I have got out of this month. First I learned table manners, something I wish every girl could learn. Next I learned to take care of my teeth and what to do to prevent T.B. I have studied hard and enjoyed my studies. I know I have improved in many ways and I am

124

going to continue my studies when I leave and show the people in my community what this month has meant to me. I can't express my thanks to Dr. and Mrs. Wilson and Miss Gray and the ones who made it possible for us to be here. I thank the teachers who have tried so hard to make this month a success.[6]

A grandmother who had never before been to school looked upon her opportunity to attend Lander as an answer to her prayers that she might learn to read her Bible and be able to communicate with her absent daughter in a distant state. She wrote:

I thought I would try to say something about the opertunity school for if it hadent been for you all I could not ever riten. I would not never forget you all for being so nice to me. My daughter is visiting me now — she said she was so thankful to you for your kindness.

Two friends who enrolled together wrote:

Edna and I have worked every day since we came home and I hope to get to work on so I can save my money to go back to Lander next summer. Edna said she thought about Lander in the day time and dreamed about it at night. I do to.

From Lexington County, a mother wrote:

The reason I am here at school is this, I have a little boy seven years old, to whom I want to give an education if I possibly can. I knew there was so much that I could learn at this school that would help me, so that I thought that I would be able to do more for him. I can say this school at Lander College has been a great help to me. If I can possible do so I want to come back next summer. It is my earnest hope that I can get others to come with me who I know need it so much.[7]

Lander College continued to provide this educational opportunity for all female adults who had not completed elementary school for three years. One more session was held at Tamassee as well, in 1923.

While Miss Gray was inaugurating the distaff program at Lander College, she had not neglected the men of the state who also needed an opportunity to begin or complete an elementary education. Heartened by her success in acquiring Lander's facilities for her girls, Miss Gray approached the Board of Education of the State Baptist Convention to plead for facilities for the men. The Baptists, too, were most cooperative and provided their Academy at Gross for the men and boys who would be eligible to enroll in the same type of program that had been such an unqualified success at Lander College. Unfortunately, that institution burned to the ground before the plan could be implemented so there was no opportunity school for men in 1922.[8]

However, Miss Gray, further encouraged by an even more successful summer at Lander College, approached the trustees of Erskine College at Due West, an institution supported by the Associate Reformed Presbyterian Church. Reacting favorably to Miss Gray's presentation, the trustees opened the doors of Erskine College to men and boys over fourteen who had little or no education, in 1923, when seventy-two students enrolled.[9] However, due to doctor's orders, Miss Gray had to leave the organization of this school in the hands of her cousin and cohort, Marguerite Tolbert.

A basic curriculum identical to the format of the Lander Opportunity School was followed at Erskine College. Classes were extremely practical and related as closely as possible to knowledge which was necessary for advancement in the textile mills where most of the men and boys were employed. For instance, in their advanced arithmetic classes, the men were taught concepts involved in textile calculations in carding, spinning, and weaving. They had lessons in understanding taxes and the importance of savings and insurance programs.

The students at Erskine were extremely motivated by their need for better jobs with more pay which they knew their newly acquired skills would produce. After a hectic morning schedule of continuous classes, the men studied outdoors under the trees all afternoon, and ever thirsty for all the knowledge they could absorb in such a short time, they demanded to have additional classes at night. The dedicated Erskine faculty found themselves holding classes all hours of the day and night until bedtime, but they were overjoyed that the men were so eager to study and learn. All of this was possible because Miss Gray had carefully selected teachers who were well-trained, sympathetic, and genuinely interested in the plight of the unlettered. These teachers were determined to uphold the ideal which was presented in the first publicity bulletin issued by Miss Gray to promote the Erskine Opportunity School: "That life may be made easier, happier, and more useful for the neglected and forgotten men of the mill, the farm, and the home."[10] Their dedication was more than repaid by the good reports which were heard from employers, such as Jesse T. Crawford, the superintendent of Riverside Manufacturing Company of Anderson, South Carolina. His was a typical comment: "Of the eight young men we have sent to these schools, three have risen to the position of section men . . . while one has made night overseer since his return." James P. Gossett reaffirmed his support of adult education, by paying the expenses each summer of twenty men, in addition to the twenty female employees he sent each year from his plants. Moreover, while his male employees were attending classes at Erskine, he supported their families in their absence.[11]

The Erskine Opportunity School continued each summer through 1930. The sessions there were equally as rewarding for both faculty and students as had been the schools held at Lander. The spirited comments of enthusiastic older students were tremendously inspirational for everyone involved in the program at Erskine College. A.B. Campbell, a sixty-three-year old farmer and grandfather proudly proclaimed: ". . . I am not too old to learn. Four weeks ago I came to Erskine Opportunity School hardly knowing my ABC's but I can read and write now! The first word I learned when I came to the Opportunity School was 'God,' and I have seen Him everywhere. The first sentence in my *Bible Story Reader* was 'God made man.'" When Mr. Campbell had heard of the school at Erskine, he had left his home at three o'clock in the morning in order to be on time when the doors opened on Monday morning. When Miss Gray learned he was determined to walk this distance each day in order to receive an education, she awarded him a scholarship so he might concentrate all of his energy into learning.[12]

Another Erskine alumnus testified after his return home: "My mind recalls the vision I had at Erskine Opportunity School in 1929. It was then and there I saw for the first time what life had in store for me. I came away determined to re-enter school . . . I am certainly happy over the outcome." That student later became an ordained minister.[13]

In the meantime, since Lander College was being closed for repairs during 1925, Anderson College, a Baptist-supported school, offered its facilities during the summer to Miss Gray for her "girls." This godsend was gratefully accepted. Summer sessions were offered at Anderson until once again a remodeling program necessitated a move. Therefore, the facilities at Women's College in Due West were provided for the years 1928, 1929, and 1930, when for the first time opportunity schools were held for both men and women in the same community.[14] The convenience of this was a great relief to Miss Gray, who was used to coordinating the programs in two schools in different locations in the state at the same time. She was happy to print publicity bulletins for the two schools which read, "Go Due West, young man" and "Go Due West, young women."

To illustrate the daily activities and interests of typical adult students at Due West, the only Opportunity School annual to be published, *The Open Door* of 1929, included a daily journal entitled "Erskine Calendar of Startling Events."

Sunday
June 8

Nobody was due to come, but about forty arrived in time for one of Mrs. Pressley's good chicken dinners. Three cars came up from Columbia and brought ten students. Among them were some girls. Everybody ate at Erskine on Sunday. At seven p.m. we had a short devotional service at the Woman's College, where we were introduced by counties and told the ideals of the school. At eight o'clock we all went across the street to evening worship with the A.R.P.'s.

Monday
June 9

Everybody else arrived and met everybody else. The old timers almost kissed one another, they were so glad to be together again. There was some scrambling to find enough beds and cots to go around, and over telling Director Evans from Student Evans, they were both so tall and good looking and wore glasses. However, Mr. McDill prevented sleepless nights by letting us have the dormitory over the bank. They tried to put the quietest and best boys down there, and when it came to selecting them, they all claimed to be lambs. However, the goats who got down there were soon separated from the sheep and brought back where they could be under Mr. Williams' eye. Dr. Hamilton and Miss Cunningham gave us a once over, using the newest methods, counting ages by teeth, intelligence by the set of the ears, and homesickness by the amount of food consumed. Pep meeting in chapel at 7:30.

Tuesday
June 10

Work began with intelligence test. Nobody knew how many legs a fly has. Classes assigned.

Wednesday
June 11

Regular class work, hard work. Prayer meeting at 7 p.m. Dress parade at eight. Occasion, visit from GIRLS.

Thursday
June 12

No study period. Storm kindly put end to lights. Had a sing-song in the dark. Contributed five dollars to buy a wreath for Miss Thomas' aunt who passed away that morning. Did not get flowers sent, so put money in bank towards scholarship for worthy boy next summer.

128

Friday	Some boys showed signs of homesickness.
June 13	Treatment: big dose of salts. Ball game in afternoon. Beat Due West. Dress parade again.

GIRLS, STUNTS, GIRLS.

Saturday	Week-enders went home. Tacky party at Woman's
June 14	College. Boys admired girls until early bell broke up fun.

Sunday	Everybody went to Baptist Sunday School except a
June 15	few that were caught trying to pitch horseshoes.

They were — well, we had gone to Sunday School, we did not hear what was said to them. Went to church. Called on girls from 4 to 6. Lots were late to supper. Chapel at 7:30.

Monday	Strung beans for dinner. Five fine clubs organized.
June 16	Harmonica Band played. Made invitations to Alumni Banquet.

Tuesday	Shucked corn for dinner. Lecture in evening by Miss
June 17	Nell Whaley on health. Gave us all some straight posture dope. Had a good time with girls afterwards

but had to turn back at monument which gets closer and closer to the building every year.

Wednesday	Routine. Basketball game. Ice cream for dinner.
June 18	Prayer meeting led by boys.

Thursday	Musical at Woman's College. Sat with girls. Good
June 19	time.

Friday	Setting up exercises every morning or a hike.
June 20	Kangaroo Court organized. Baseball. Girls came over in evening.

Saturday	Baseball. Alumni Banquet for old pupils and friends.
June 21	Picnic for new pupils. Boys got a fill of ice cream for once in their lives. Said the banquet was a great

success. They stayed long enough and ate long enough.

Sunday	Routine Sunday. Some boys slipped off to the
June 22	swimming pool and broke the Sabbath. Something else broke on Monday. Good dinner. Dates with

peaches in the afternoon from 4 to 6. Some late to supper, as usual.

Monday	Setting up exercises, of course. Did most of week's
June 23	laundry in order to save money to buy electric ice cream freezer.

Tuesday	Routine: Rain. Mr. Lawton delivered fine talk. Gave
June 24	twenty copies of his book.

Wednesday	Beans. Another rainy day. No mock wedding.
June 25	Disappointed. Nearly wore out the phone calling up Mrs. Fleming. Boys allowed to go to swimming pool

in charge of William Latham. Prayer meeting.

129

Thursday June 26	Setting up exercises. Beans. Routine. Practice with girls. Learned our new yell, and you can just bet it was not hard to do: Rootity-toot, rootity-toot, Mrs. Giles Fleming's Institute, Powder and curls, powder and curls, GIRLS! GIRLS! GIRLS!

Friday
June 27   Helped make up exhibit for Miss Gray to take to Atlanta. Our friend, Bob Galloway, celebrated his seventieth birthday at noon. We had him to dinner at six. All the boys who had birthdays in June and July sat at the birthday table. All would have had birthdays these months if they had known it in time. Lots of fun at table. Lecture by Dr. Reed Smith of the University. Entertainment at Woman's College. All went as guests of school.

Saturday
June 28   Play practice. Last moot court. It was a scream. Those who did not plead insanity said they were in love and not responsible for dropping things on campus and such other things as they were charged with.

Sunday
June 29   Routine. Ice cream. Killed a long black snake. Saw another. Stunt night. Girls did most of stunting.

Monday
June 30   Fine meeting in chapel at seven. Beans. Wedding at girls' school. Great success. Play practice. Made commencement invitations and mailed to donors and friends. Baseball. Basketball. Girls came up.

Tuesday
July 1   Election of student body officers. Iran Gunnells elected president. Done under auspices of Good Citizenship Club. Lots of fun. Regular election stunts indulged in. Greenwood band concert. Walked with girls to monument.

Wednesday
July 2   Student body meeting to get statistics. Beans. Routine. Long practice. Five visitors from Charleston came by from American Legion meeting in Anderson. Liked boys and school. Served ice cream and cakes. Boys acted up like Chesterfields. Proud of ourselves. Clearing house in chapel for bad habits. Many promised to give up tobacco in all forms.

Thursday
July 4   Glorious Fourth made more glorious by having only two classes and the girls coming to spend day on Erskine campus. Picnic dinner, wieners, sandwiches, lemonade, fruit, ice cream, and the girls, made a real day of it. Hard play practice.

Friday
July 5   Everybody weighed a second time. Average gain, five pounds. Caught up loose ends everywhere, cleaned house, walks, gardens, back yard and everything. Practiced. Received distinguished visitors from five states. Ice cream for dinner with lots of other good things. Mr. and Mrs. Hope had supper with us. Best commencement yet. Covered ourselves with glory with acting, singing, and speech making.

Saturday	Said goodby to everybody with tears in our eyes.
July 6	Promised to meet all the old fellows again next year.
	Slogan: "Erskine or bust in 1930." Farewell till next
summer.	

C.L. Ledford, Seneca
Henry Giles, Greenville
Claude Evans, Anderson
William Lands, Spartanburg
Irby Rains, Rock Hill
Lawrence Workman, Laurens
Grover Cox, Greenwood[15]

During the years of the early opportunity schools the Baptist and Methodist faiths each continued to contribute $250 annually to the cause of adult education. This, combined with the state-supported teachers' salaries, and the scholarships provided by civic-minded individuals and organizations, permitted successful opportunity schools to be held each summer until 1946 in various locations.

Women students at Lander College

First Opportunity School for men at Erskine College in 1923

NOTES

[1] *Lander College Opportunity School Bulletin*, 1922, p. 12.

[2] *Opportunity Schools Anderson College, Erskine College Bulletin,* 1925, p. 16.

[3] *Lander Bulletin*, pp. 10-12.

[4] Ibid., p. 12.

[5] Ibid., pp. 8-9.

[6] Ibid., p. 9.

[7] Ibid.

[8] *Fifty-sixth Annual Report of the Superintendent of Education* (Columbia: State Department of Education, 1924), pp. 85-86.

[9] *Lander College, Erskine College Opportunity Schools Bulletin,* 1924, p. 13.

[10] *Erskine College Opportunity School Bulletin,* 1923, p. 4.

[11] Ibid., p. 20.

[12] Wil Lou Gray, "The Early History of the Opportunity Schools," unpublished paper, 1923.

[13] Ibid.

[14] *Sixty-third Annual Report of the Superintendent of Schools* (Columbia: State Department of Education, 1931), p. 76.

[15] Erin Kohn, Editor, *The Open Door,* Vol. I, 1929, pp. 25-27.

REFERENCES

Erskine College Opportunity School Bulletin. Due West, South Carolina. 1923.

Fifty-sixth Annual Report of the Superintendent of Education. Columbia: State Department of Education, 1924.

Gray, Wil Lou. "The Early History of the Opportunity Schools." Unpublished paper, 1923.

Kohn, Erin, editor, *The Open Door I*, 1929.

Lander College Opportunity School Bulletin. Columbia: State Department of Education, 1922.

Opportunity Schools Anderson College, Erskine College Bulletin. Columbia: State Department of Education, 1925.

Sixty-third Annual Report of the Superintendent of Education. Columbia: State Department of Education, 1931.

A Decade of Achievement

In addition to the promotion, organization, and management of the summer opportunity schools, other state-wide adult education programs entailed supervision by Miss Gray. Fortunately, the Illiteracy Commission employed a full-time office assistant in October 1921, freeing the Supervisor for more constructive work.

During the first decade of the early opportunity schools, Miss Gray continued to reach thousands of illiterate adults in the lay-by and night schools, but the most important addition to her already frantic schedule was the organization of "special schools for adults." In many mill villages there was a sufficient number of adult pupils to warrant the employment of a full-time teacher. The dedicated teachers that Miss Gray recruited for this work were paid $1200, with $750 being paid by the mill and $450 by the state, for a nine- or ten-month term. During the day these teachers visited the homes and gave instruction to uneducated mothers, while organized classes were taught at any hour convenient to students. One teacher in Clinton taught while the mill workers were laboring at their looms. Once a month the teachers held a community meeting when problems of civic interest were discussed by invited guests, and at other times, students demonstrated what they had been learning in their classes.

In their reports to Miss Gray, the teachers related how much some of these adult students had profited from their instruction.

> One of my students was very eager to read and write but was afraid her husband would laugh at her efforts. Therefore, it was kept a profound secret that she was studying. During the years, he was employed for several months at a mill in North Carolina and he was much surprised at receiving a letter from her soon after leaving home. He could hardly believe it and was so pleased and proud of her achievement that after returning to Rock Hill, he would tell all his friends how 'his old lady stole a march on him.' He then asked me to teach him some of the more difficult calculations in arithmetic needed in his own work.[1]

Another teacher reported:

> A mill employee, age thirty-three, has been living in Clinton for sixteen years. He started to night school in the first grade three years ago. He is now in the fifth grade. He won the prize for perfect attendance last year and the

133

prize for the best notebook this year.

Mary, age twenty-seven, had never been to school a day in her life. She could not come to school at night and did not have time to study in the mill, so I went to her home at noon. During her lunch she would study for thirty minutes each day before going back to the mill. She and her sister studied together at night. She can now write a letter and read the Bible. Last winter she read the *Bible Reader* and *Country Life Reader, Book I* and *Book II.*

No student's life has been so transformed as one of my students who was sixty-one years old. This splendid woman made many sacrifices to give her sons and daughters what she did not have. When the adult school came into her life, all except one son had left home for homes of their own. After a few weeks in adult school, the mother began to write to her absent children. Before the year was out, the letters she wrote to her relations compared favorably with those of educated persons much younger than she was. Soon she bought a testament, Psalms, and hymnbook. Her school book was always within easy reach. I would often see her churning on the porch and reading at seven a.m.[2]

To gain some idea of the number of adults reached throughout the state in the educational programs offered for those with little or no education, including the 713 students enrolled in the 7 "special schools" in the mills, the yearly total in 1921 was 11,250. As Miss Gray was able to expand the program throughout the years — if the legislature appropriated sufficient funds — the ranks of the illiterates were reduced, but the Supervisor reported during these years to feel like "Alice in Wonderland" who had to run constantly as hard as she could merely to stay in one place.[3]

Considering the extent of Negro illiteracy in South Carolina — in 1920, 29.3 percent over 10 years of age were so classified — and the fact that many influential political leaders who doled out state funds for education believed in "white supremacy," it is amazing that any progress at all could be reported. In 1925 Miss Gray's annual report stated that the appropriations for night school totaled $37,834, of which only $4,534 was earmarked for Negro schools. With these funds the Supervisor could provide services for 7,848 white adults, but only 2,944 Negroes.[4]

It was largely because of three factors that Negro illiteracy was somewhat reduced in South Carolina between 1920 and 1930. (1)A valuable service was rendered by Jeanes supervisors. Anna T. Jeanes, a Philadelphia Quaker, had bequeathed a sum to be used for effective supervision of Negro schools in many parts of the South. Her legacy continues today in the form of the Southern Education Foundation. (2)Further aid was given by the Rosenwald Foundation which granted $17,358 to be used in the 1929-30 pre-census campaign. This grant was not renewed after 1930; however, it established a precedent in South Carolina when it placed major emphasis on eradicating illiteracy among the Negroes. (3)Miss Gray was able to persuade many Negro teachers to serve without pay when no funds were available for salaries. These dedicated educators performed an invaluable service for their race and to the state of South Carolina.[5]

As a result of these cooperative efforts and local funding amounting to $23,074, in 1929-30 there were twice as many night schools organized for Negroes as for whites and Negro enrollment, 37,800, rose to 68.7 percent of the total enrollment of 55,036. Only two years before the Negro enrollment was 24.2 percent of the total. By this time adult work had been organized in every county except Calhoun, Fairfield, and Hampton.[6]

After 1930 there was not such a drastic inequity in state appropriations for adult basic education; however, unequal expenditures for white and Negro students unfortunately continued for another twenty years. For example, according to the State Superintendent's Sixty-third Annual Report, during the school year 1930-31, the state spent an average of $2.65 per adult student; however, the average expenditure per white student was $4.27 while Negro students received an average of $1.33.[7]

During these years, the people who worked with Miss Gray, her friends and her relatives, were always concerned about her health because she would not slow her pace. They were quite relieved when she requested a leave of absence in the fall of 1925 and asked Mary Eva Hite to assume her duties until her return. However, their relief was short-lived, for they soon discovered that the indefatigable Supervisor planned to return to Teachers College in New York with the express purpose of writing a textbook to be used in adult classes.

Miss Gray had always been plagued by the dearth of teaching materials, especially textbooks, which were appropriate for uneducated

135

adults. Such texts must, of necessity, have to be written simply, with a basic vocabulary content, but with an interest level that made them appealing, meaningful, and useful to adults.

Her advisor at Teachers College, the education branch of Columbia University, was Dr. Albert Shiels. When he found out that not one scholar had enrolled in one course he was scheduled to teach (Who would be intrigued by "How Cash Flows"?) he promised Miss Gray to spend all of that free time counseling her as she prepared the textbook of her choice for publication. That is how her book, *Elementary Studies in Civics*, was published.

Though it was a relatively small book of only eighty pages and sold for forty cents, it was quite large in the broadened conception of civic education which was presented. Miss Gray set forth the training which would "equip one to live more efficiently not only as a voting citizen, but also as members of a family, as neighbor, and as worker." The ten chapters concerned the topics "Good Manners," "Health," "Education," "Budgeting," "How to Invest Money," "Our Government," "How Our County Works for Us," "What Our State Does for Us," "What Our National Government Does for Us," and "Life or Death."[8]

Throughout the project Dr. Shiels offered invaluable, practical advice and moral support, though in one instance Miss Gray had to override his objection to one topic and included it in the book despite his disapproval. He had been astounded that Miss Gray had included in her chapter "Health," the admonition that complete baths should be taken at least twice a week, and that underwear should be changed at those times. When she assured him that thousands of South Carolinians did not practice such rules of personal cleanliness and that good citizenship should begin with pride in one's appearance, he conceded the point since she was the one who had spent a lifetime working with such people and should certainly know whereof she spoke.

Upon completion of her elementary civics textbook, Miss Gray resumed her duties as State Supervisor of Adult Education on July 1, 1926, and immediately involved herself in even more projects to help uneducated adults. For instance, she was constantly being called upon to attend conferences and to deliver speeches throughout the United States concerning adult education. She went whenever and wherever possible, many times at her own expense, for she was always eager to learn what other states were doing to combat illiteracy, and to tell of South Carolina's giant strides in providing educational opportunities for her uneducated citizens.

Not only was Miss Gray the major moving force behind the adult education program in her native state, but other agencies also called upon her as a consultant, for her expertise and innovations had become known far and wide. In 1927 she was asked to visit the state of Oklahoma and aid educators there in establishing a program of adult education similar to the one which was developing under her leadership in South Carolina. She spent several weeks touring that state, studying the conditions there, and making recommendations.

In September 1930, Miss Gray accepted an invitation that had been extended by educators in Newfoundland. Accompanied by her good friend and secretary, Miss Erin Kohn, she set sail from Boston Harbor and traveled through the land of Evangeline to Halifax. In their fifteen days in Newfoundland, the two South Carolinians became acquainted thoroughly with the people, their local customs, and the picturesque locale. In fear and trembling, they descended into an eleven-hundred-foot iron mine, two and one-half miles under the Atlantic Ocean. Since two thousand of the island's six thousand people worked in the mines, they wanted to experience their working environment personally. In the mining village they organized an adult school where eighty-three students enrolled. Forty-five of these students were totally illiterate. Another school was organized in St. John's at the Imperial Tobacco Factory. The plant manager, Mr. Patterson, was from Greer, South Carolina, and had lived in Newfoundland for nine years. Delighted to welcome fellow Sandlappers, he offered his plant as a place for the Bureau of Education to organize an adult school and was instrumental in obtaining his company's financing for the classes.

Returning home to her office in the State Department of Education after what seemed almost like a vacation to her, for she was performing only one task instead of fifty, Miss Gray immediately set her sights upon her next goal. Because of the growth in the numbers of adult citizens who were clamoring for an education, and because the Census of 1930 had ranked South Carolina as the most illiterate state in the Union, she could foresee that a larger facility must be found to accommodate the number of adults who could be recruited to attend an opportunity school. Her

137

skill as a talented "borrower" was once again evident when Clemson College agreed to lend its campus for the first Clemson Opportunity School which began on July 16, 1931.[9]

Throughout this busy decade Miss Gray observed many new national trends. She saw a period of post-war disillusionment after World War I, a new status for women, the promotion of the "Freudian gospel," the mass production of the automobile, prohibition and big city racketeers, and the public craze for radio and movies. All of these factors had combined to produce a revolution in manners and morals in our country, but Miss Gray was too involved in planning for the eventual abolition of illiteracy in South Carolina to be overly concerned.

During this period Miss Gray was aware of the drastic style changes in women's fashions, but here too, she was not concerned. Most of her adult life she has had a weight problem, and the boyish look designed for the flappers of the Roaring '20's was not for her. She has always dressed conservatively and purchased whatever she sees in the stores that she likes, if it appears to be serviceable, regardless of the latest vogue. It did not bother her in the least to be described as "dowdy" in a *Collier's* magazine article, but it upset her admirers terribly. Moreover, she had first bobbed her hair for the sake of convenience twenty years before it became the rage in America, and never stopped to consider whether or not her coiffure was stylish.

During this period Miss Gray enjoyed the radio and listened mostly to the news broadcasts. She occasionally attended the movies, but did not idolize Rudolph Valentino as did most females in America. While a graduate student at Columbia University she enjoyed several Broadway plays and recalls standing in long lines to buy tickets for performances of Galli-Curci, the great coloratura soprano. She had no time for mah jong, contract bridge, or crossword puzzles, the latest entertainment crazes during the 1920's.

Miss Gray was a Southerner, but she violently disagreed with proponents of white supremacy, segregation, and Jim Crow laws. She was aghast at the rise of the Ku Klux Klan, patterned after the organization of Reconstruction days for the purpose of persecuting mostly Negroes, but also Jews and Catholics. After the Klan had murdered a man in Laurens for no other reason than that his skin was dark, her father spoke at a meeting in front of the courthouse, vehemently

138

denouncing such an act. Miss Gray was quite proud of his courage, but she remembers the fright of her stepmother who was convinced that such a foolhardy act would bring down the Klan's wrath, with their home and businesses being burned in reprisal.

The revolution in morals during this period did not alter Miss Gray's beliefs. After the conflict between religion and science which gained international attention in the Scopes "Monkey Trial," many schools discontinued any type of religious services, but not Miss Gray. Until her retirement she continued to expect her students to attend chapel and vesper services, believing her work to be a "Christian commitment."

Again in this decade Miss Gray observed a time of political change. She saw Harding's "Age of Normalcy" make a farce of political honesty. Then the Coolidge and Hoover era led to a period of prosperity and the "Big Bull Market." It seemed to her that there was rising prosperity everywhere but in the South, where cotton was no longer "King." Finally, the stock market crash of 1929 dragged America into the "Great Depression." As a consequence, Miss Gray can remember the threat of having her water service discontinued because she was unable to pay a ten-dollar water bill.

Miss Gray and her family, including her father, were early proponents of women's suffrage when it was a most unpopular cause in this country. She recalls visiting the General Assembly in Columbia when her father was a member to hear this issue debated, and she was appalled that one of her own cousins was among the foremost opponents of this measure.

Subsequently, most Americans were looking for a political leader who could raise this country out of the Great Depression. At the same time Miss Gray was anticipating the move to Clemson College and relishing the challenge of removing South Carolina's name from the top of a list of states with the most illiterate citizens.

NOTES

[1]James H. Hope and Wil Lou Gray, *Adult and Night School Bulletin* (Columbia: State Department of Education, 1923), p. 4; *Fifty-Third Annual Report of the Superintendent of Schools* (Columbia: State Department of Education, 1921), p. 253.

[2]*Fifty-third Annual Report of Superintendent of Education* (Columbia: State Department of Education, 1921), pp. 254-55.

[3]Ibid., p. 256.

[4]*Fifty-seventh Annual Report of Superintendent of Education* (Columbia: State Department of Education, 1925), p. 83.

[5]*Sixty-second Annual Report of Superintendent of Education* (Columbia: State Department of Education, 1930), p. 31.

[6]Ibid., p. 31.

[7]*Sixty-third Annual Report of Superintendent of Education* (Columbia: State Department of Education, 1931), p. 76.

[8]Wil Lou Gray, *Elementary Studies in Civics* (Columbia: The State Company, 1927).

[9]*Sixty-third Annual Report,* p. 82.

REFERENCES

Fifty-third Annual Report of Superintendent of Education. Columbia: State Department of Education, 1921.

Fifty-fourth Annual Report of Superintendent of Education. Columbia: State Department of Education, 1922.

Fifty-fifth Annual Report of Superintendent of Education. Columbia: State Department of Education, 1923.

Fifty-sixth Annual Report of Superintendent of Education. Columbia: State Department of Education, 1924.

Fifty-seventh Annual Report of Superintendent of Education. Columbia: State Department of Education, 1925.

Fifty-eighth Annual Report of Superintendent of Education. Columbia: State Department of Education, 1926.

Fifty-ninth Annual Report of Superintendent of Education. Columbia: State Department of Education, 1927.

Gray, Wil Lou. *Elementary Studies in Civics.* Columbia: The State Company, 1927.

140

Gray, Wil Lou. Columbia, South Carolina. Interview, 5 January 1976.

Gray, Wil Lou. Columbia, South Carolina. Interview, 10 January 1976.

Hope, James H., and Gray, Wil Lou. *Adult and Night School Bulletin.* Columbia: State Department of Education, 1923.

Sixtieth Annual Report of Superintendent of Education. Columbia: State Department of Education, 1928.

Sixty-first Annual Report of Superintendent of Education. Columbia: State Department of Education, 1929.

Sixty-second Annual Report of Superintendent of Education. Columbia: State Department of Education, 1930.

Sixty-third Annual Report of Superintendent of Education. Columbia: State Department of Education, 1931.

Clemson Days

During the many years Miss Gray had been supervising the annual opportunity schools, she had lamented the fact that there had been no empirical data available to prove that the education she was promoting for those with little or no previous schooling was worthwhile. She knew for a certainty that most students' lives had been bettered and enriched, but how could she convince others that it was not too late for these educationally deprived adults, who perhaps could learn as quickly as children, if not more so.

Therefore, in the fall of 1930, it was decided to organize the first session of the Clemson Opportunity School on an experimental basis. Miss Gray was gratified that this educational venture allowed her to test two other pet theories, and, at the same time prove that adults could profitably learn. She had long maintained that men and women could be housed on the same campus, attend classes together, and profit from the experience. Moreover, she had continuously preached that South Carolina was drastically short-changing its Negro citizens by depriving

55 Negro adult students participated in the Clemson Experiment of 1931

them of their chance for equal educational opportunities. She had been observing these Negro adults in their classes for a long time. She hoped to prove that their native ability to learn, when given an equal opportunity, was not that much different from other racial groups. Therefore, she was delighted to arrange an Opportunity School for Negroes at Seneca Junior College, by courtesy of Negro Baptists, and to include them in the Clemson experiment.[1]

An application was filed with the American Association for Adult Education for a subsidy of $5,000. After favorable consideration of the proposal, the funds were granted by the Carnegie Corporation of New York. This sum provided 100 scholarships of $20 each and $1,000 each for the services of a competent psychologist and expert on tests and measurement, for instructional materials and tests, and for supervision of the experiment. Dr. William S. Gray of Chicago University accepted the directorship; Dr. J.W. Tilton of Yale University was selected as psychologist; Miss Gray continued her duties as supervisor. She then appointed Miss Erin Kohn as dean of the first Clemson Opportunity School, and carefully selected 22 faculty members, of whom 6 were unpaid volunteers.[2]

The major purposes of the Clemson experiment were the following: (1) to determine critically and objectively within certain limits the progress of adults of limited education when favorable conditions for learning are provided, and (2) to determine the limitations of the instructions given for students of differing levels of capacity and varying amounts of achievement in the fundamental tools of learning. Three levels of adult education were selected for study: (1) the initial stage in which specific effort was made to attain functional literacy; (2) the early literate period in which common needs predominate; and (3) a later stage when specialized curricula are essential.

Six specific aims were adopted to carry out the major purposes of the two experimental schools. These aims were to determine the social, economic, and educational status of the students at the time of enrollment; to measure the probable learning capacity of each student; and to classify the students into homogeneous classes in order that instruction might be adapted to their needs. Other aims concerned determining the progress and areas of weakness of students during the term in the fundamental subjects taught; studying the relationship between individual progress in such variables as age, sex, and intelligence; and observing the changes in attitudes and habits of students through informal types of training given in the dining room, during recreation periods, and in connection with auditorium programs, special lectures, concerts, and religious services.[3]

Eligibility to participate in the experiment was determined by the students' having little or no education, good health, good moral character, a desire to learn, and perseverance. A total of 233 students took part, from first grade through ninth grade levels, ranging in age from 14 to 70 years. Miss Gray had visited 17 counties to seek eligible students, had sent out hundreds of circular letters to those who might know of interested adults, and appointed key personnel throughout the state as recruiters.[4]

A testing program was implemented for the following purposes: (1) to provide objective evidence of the capacity and educational status of each group, (2) to furnish an accurate basis of classification, and (3) to give initial scores with which to compare final scores for computation of gains or progress. Before formal classes opened, students were classified into sections according to the results of the reading and intelligence test scores, with each class containing 12 to 20 students.

Although the curriculum was designed to emphasize reading, arithmetic, writing, and spelling, other areas were not neglected. Since many students were actual or potential homemakers, instruction was offered in sewing, cooking, and home furnishing and decoration. Also, a varied program of informal instruction and training provided for the social, moral, and personal needs of the students. Instructors emphasized the "wise use of leisure, the amenities of life, the value of acquiring an open mind, appreciation of the good and the beautiful, and the need for dependability, punctuality, and civic responsibility."[5]

Since one of the primary objectives of conducting the experiment was to determine if, in fact, these educationally deprived adults were capable of learning, their progress was compared to that normally made by primary-age children. During the four-week term, the average progress of the students made in reading, writing, spelling, and arithmetic in the Clemson experimental group was equivalent to the progress made by primary-age children in 3.9 school months. The average progress of the students in the Seneca group was equivalent to that made by children in 3.4 months. The average progress of the students in the Clemson intermediate group equaled that normally made by grade-school children in 7.5 months. As expected, the average progress of the Clemson advanced group in these subjects was equal to that made normally by upper-grade pupils in 9.5 months. In all cases, the norms for the Seneca groups were only fractionally lower than those for the students at Clemson. [6]

The researchers concluded from this data that many adult students who had recently attained literacy could achieve in three to four terms in an opportunity school of four weeks the norms usually reached by pupils completing the sixth grade.[7]

All of the data that was collected during the course of the experiment was treated statistically to determine implications concerning the psychology of adult learning. Age was found to be negatively correlated with speed, and with the amount learned during the month of the experiment. Moreover, age was found to be positively correlated with size of vocabulary and with a large measure of deliberation.[8]

However, the most significant conclusion reached by the research staff was what Miss Gray had long ago learned, that adults, both white and Negro, "are eager for the advantages which opportunity schools afford." Moreover, it was proved that these adults can learn in the proper educationally stimulating environment. Also, it must be noted that another of Miss Gray's intuitive assessments was correct — there was no significant difference between the amount of learning of Caucasians and Negroes.[9]

Upon completion of the Clemson and Seneca experiment, the results of the study were published in *The Opportunity Schools of South Carolina, an Experimental Study,* by William S. Gray, Wil Lou Gray, and J. W. Tilton. The program of adult education as set forth in this volume soon became a model for educators throughout the United States, and the diminutive Miss Gray attained a stature unsurpassed in the annals of adult education.

However, it was the gratitude expressed in letters written to her after her students returned home that made all of the long hours and hard work seem so worthwhile. A beginner wrote, " I want to come back next year and . . . bring my wife with me." Another student wrote, "It would be hard for me to estimate the amount of benefit school was to me. Life seems changed altogether for me. I want to go to Clemson again, but I have brothers and sisters who are due a chance too." A young mother of three wistfully stated, "I often wish I could be in an Opportunity School for a year. It would do me so much good. Here at home I have so many things to do that I do not find time to study but very little." The following letter written by an adult student to a friend at home while she was attending the 1935 Clemson session is a typical reaction to this novel learning experience. She wrote:

> Dear Mildred,
>
> Have you ever been so busy during the day that you hardly had time to think? My schedule here at the Opportunity School is so full that I scarcely have any time of my own.
>
> Our day lasts from seven in the morning until ten in the evening. After rising, we clean up our rooms and prepare for breakfast at seven-thirty. There is little time between breakfast and work time. We stay in classrooms until twelve o'clock with one short recess. At twelve we go to chapel at which time we usually hear some speaker. We leave chapel just before one o'clock and rush to our rooms to get ready for luncheon.
>
> Our afternoons are less fully occupied than our mornings. We enjoy an hour rest period, known as quiet hour, which lasts from two until three. At three most everyone has a class in handicrafts. Others go to the dairy, the poultry farms, or the gardens for lessons. Some stay in their rooms. From four to six we are free to do as we like. Most of us use these two hours for writing letters, studying, ironing, cleaning up, swimming or various kinds of ball games.
>
> Our happiest time comes at night. We always stay an hour in the dining room, enjoying the food, the songs, speeches, stunts, conversation and special features. Two nights a week we have passes to the movies. On these nights we have little time for anything else as we are required to go to our rooms at ten. On evenings on which we do not go to the Y, we play outdoor games, go to chapel for an hour or more, to vespers on the lawn and then for a hike with the teachers or a stroll about the part of the campus on which we are allowed to walk.
>
> All in all our days here are busy ones and we are usually ready for bed when the bell sounds at ten. We have such a good time, however, we don't realize how busy we are until we get into bed and the lights go out, as is happening right now.
>
> Affectionately yours,
> Helen [10]

Dr. Tilton and Dr. William S. Gray, the leaders of this experimental study, were most impressed with what had been accomplished. They planned to conduct a more sophisticated study the next year with Miss Gray's assistance. Unfortunately America was in the grip of the Depression, and funds for organizing such a study could not be secured in 1932.

The Clemson Opportunity School continued to be held for a four-week session each summer for twelve years. During this time Miss Gray was constantly improving and expanding the educational program offered to adults.

The publication of *Clemson Days,* which began as a weekly newspaper written by adult students and edited by Miss Gray and Erin Kohn, was quite motivational for recruiting new students and encouraging graduates to form alumni groups for further study. By the end of a decade at Clemson, the paper had grown from being published four times a year during the school term to an illustrated school magazine published every two months and mailed to thousands of alumni all over the state.

Miss Gray was always looking for practical instruction which would most benefit her adult students. She decided to construct and decorate a model home at a modest figure as an inspiration to students who previously lived in substandard housing. She hoped to motivate her students to save for such a future home for themselves and their families. Therefore, she persuaded Clemson College to part with a small plot of land, and businesses to donate materials — no easy task in the midst of a Depression. Because Clemson College was training Federal Emergency Relief teachers at the same time the Opportunity School was in session, it was arranged that these one thousand teachers eat with the Opportunity School students and have their meals prepared by Miss Gray's staff. By careful planning and economizing in the kitchen, and saving twenty-five cents per week for each person served in the dining room, the Opportunity School was able to accumulate $1,000.

After construction of this model home began in 1936, her dream of being able to build such a model home for $1,000 would have been realized but for one small setback. Carpenters had put on the roof with the gable pointing in the wrong direction. Thus, it had to be removed and reversed. However, Clemson College came to the rescue, and the structure was completed for another $500. While the Opportunity School was not in session, the home was rented to a Clemson professor and this rental soon repaid what Miss Gray considered a debt, the additional $500. Most of the labor was provided by students under the National Youth Administration program. These same men and boys the next year constructed beds, tables, and other furniture in the school carpentry shop,while the women and girls upholstered second-hand furniture, and made rugs, curtains, quilts, and linens. The total cost of the furnishings was $251.48. After a contest, students and Miss Gray coined the name "Opphame" for the demonstration home.[12]

Opphame had been such an inspirational and educational venture that Miss Gray determined to begin a similar project, but since many of her adult students were unable to afford even $1,500 for home construction, this house was to be even more modest. In 1940, "Opphame, Jr.," a cottage costing $849.94 was built, again on land donated by Clemson and with funds saved by economizing in the dining hall. By renting Opphame, Jr. while the Opportunity School was not in session to Clemson professors, its debt was soon repaid as well.[13]

The enrollment of the Clemson Opportunity School sessions began steadily increasing in 1933 when the Federal Emergency Relief Administration was mandated. The faculty now numbered 30 to provide for the needs of 257 adult students. Of these, 137 girls and women from 14 to 60 were attending on scholarships provided by F.E.R.A. To assist those students not eligible for these scholarships, Miss Gray arranged to place baby chicks with prospective students to raise in order to earn money to help pay their own way.

At one point in 1933, all funds had been exhausted and Miss Gray personally underwrote poultry and garden projects from her own income. Matters became even worse that year when the Clemson bank failed and some Opportunity School funds were lost.[14]

In these Clemson adult education summer sessions, the curriculum was expanded to include in addition to the basic 3 R's, spelling, history, English, geography, civics, textile arithmetic, home economics, public speaking, manual arts, art appreciation, simple psychology, letter writing, citizenship, health, manners, dramatics, band, chorus, gardening, and poultry raising. By 1942, the final year for the Opportunity School at Clemson College, the curriculum had again been expanded to include Bible, algebra, orchestra, parliamentary law, clothing, home beautification, nutrition and foods, industrial arts, home nursing, South Carolina home ownership, and choosing a vocation. When students had mastered the basic elementary subjects, they were allowed to choose from this list of elective subjects and study whatever was of interest to them.

Another unique feature of the annual opportunity schools was Miss Gray's idea of planning each summer's work around a central theme. For instance, when South Carolina was the theme, the students in one homeroom might develop a unit called "Making a Living in South Carolina." Another might study "Great South Carolinians" and yet another might pursue "Historic Spots in South Carolina."[15]

The last year at Clemson there were 40 faculty members. Due to the war effort, the enrollment had fallen to 260 students, after a record-breaking high of 382 in 1939.[16]

Miss Gray can still recall vividly the types of students who came to Clemson Opportunity School. One year Janie, age eleven, got off the bus carrying her ragged but obviously much-loved doll. Miss Gray was heartbroken to tell her at registration that she was too young to enroll, but when she learned that Janie, as the older daughter of a large family of eight, had been keeping house and cooking for the entire family while her widowed mother earned the living, she was allowed to stay. A retired teacher, more than seventy years old, came to pursue a hobby of painting. Sarah, a young widow at twenty-two, left school after the ninth grade, but when given the State High School Certification Test, ranked far above the average college freshman. Tiny Mary, fifteen, starved by a squalid environment, could only sit, almost autistic, and watch the activity of others. James was from a disadvantaged home so isolated he had never before seen an automobile. After his mother had died, he ran wild in the mountains. Sixty-three-year-old Mrs. Jones had entered a mill at age eight, later married, reared a family, and cared for an invalid mother, and could not read or write. Helen, twenty-five, left a good job to earn a high school certificate in order to become a nurse. Such individuals as these became Miss Gray's "children," and no natural mother could have been more concerned and compassionate.[17]

Moreover, no one could have been prouder than Miss Gray when she watched the first two standard high school diplomas being awarded to

149

two of her Clemson students, J.L. Corbin and C.L. Magalis, for credits they had earned while studying at the Opportunity School. Mr. Magalis later became a publisher and Mr. Corbin became a soil conservationist for the state of Georgia. It is extremely unlikely that these two men, and thousands more like them, could have achieved success in their chosen fields without the inspiration and further education they received in the opportunity schools.[18]

However, it was only after a heated battle that Miss Gray had convinced state leaders that South Carolina should award state high school equivalency certificates based on the General Equivalency Diploma Test, rather than on hours of credit in a classroom. There were many high school principals and county superintendents who objected to this progressive step, and they bitterly denounced Miss Gray for her efforts in promoting such a measure, claiming that it down-graded their programs in the state's high schools. Fortunately for her adult students, her will prevailed, and South Carolina began awarding equivalency certificates in 1942. By 1945, 14 Opportunity School students had received their certificates, and by the time Miss Gray announced her retirement in 1957, 280 certificates had been awarded to her adult students.[19]

NOTES

[1]*Sixty-third Annual Report of Superintendent of Education* (Columbia: State Department of Education, 1931), pp. 83-84.

[2]Ibid., p. 82.

[3]William S. Gray, Wil Lou Gray, and J.W. Tilton, *The Opportunity Schools of South Carolina — an Experimental Study* (New York: American Association for Adult Education, 1932), p. 15.

[4]Ibid., p. 16.

[5]Ibid., pp. 17-18.

[6]Ibid., pp. 75-76.

[7]Ibid., pp. 91-92.

[8]Ibid., pp. 108-121.

[9]Ibid., p. 127.

[10]*Seventy-fourth Annual Report of Superintendent of Education* (Columbia: State Department of Education, 1942), p. 37.

[11]Ibid., p. 25.

[12]*Seventy-third Annual Report of Superintendent of Education* (Columbia: State Department of Education, 1941), p. 45; *Sixty-ninth Annual Report of Superintendent of Education* (Columbia: State Department of Education, 1937), p. 59.

[13]*Seventy-second Annual Report of Superintendent of Education* (Columbia: State Department of Education, 1940), p. 39; *Seventy-third Annual Report of Superintendent of Education* (Columbia: State Department of Education, 1941), p. 45.

[14]*Sixty-seventh Annual Report of Superintendent of Education* (Columbia: State Department of Education, 1935), p. 51.

[15]*Seventy-third Annual Report,* p. 43; *Seventy-fourth Annual Report,* p. 31.

[16]*Seventy-first Annual Report of Superintendent of Education* (Columbia: State Department of Education, 1943), p. 25.

[17] *Seventy-fourth Annual Report,* pp. 35-37.

[18] *Seventy-third Annual Report,* p. 46.

[19] *Seventy-fourth Annual Report,* p. 30.

REFERENCES

Gray, Wil Lou. Columbia, South Carolina. Interview, 15 February 1976.

Gray, William S.; Gray, Wil Lou; and Tilton, J.W., *The Opportunity Schools of South Carolina — an Experimental Study.* New York: American Association of Adult Education, 1932.

Seventieth Annual Report of Superintendent of Education. Columbia: State Department of Education, 1938.

Seventy-first Annual Report of Superintendent of Education. Columbia: State Department of Education, 1939.

Seventy-second Annual Report of Superintendent of Education. Columbia: State Department of Education, 1940.

Seventy-third Annual Report of Superintendent of Education. Columbia: State Department of Education, 1941.

Seventy-fourth Annual Report of Superintendent of Education. Columbia: State Department of Education, 1942.

Sixty-third Annual Report of Superintendent of Education. Columbia: State Department of Education, 1931.

Sixty-fourth Annual Report of Superintendent of Education. Columbia: State Department of Education, 1932.

Sixty-fifth Annual Report of Superintendent of Education. Columbia: State Department of Education, 1933.

Sixty-sixth Annual Report of Superintendent of Education. Columbia: State Department of Education, 1934.

Sixty-seventh Annual Report of Superintendent of Education. Columbia: State Department of Education, 1935.

Sixty-eighth Annual Report of Superintendent of Education. Columbia: State Department of Education, 1936.

Sixty-ninth Annual Report of Superintendent of Education. Columbia: State Department of Education, 1937.

Federal Relief and Adult Education in South Carolina

After the Federal Emergency Relief Administration was established in 1933, South Carolina was one of the first states to accept and put to use federal aid for unemployed teachers. Miss Gray's work then became a cooperative undertaking between the State Department of Education and the Educational Division of the Work Projects Administration. Miss Gray joined forces with Elizabeth Hutto, Literacy Supervisor for the W.P.A., and held intensive one-week training sessions for new Relief teachers at the University of South Carolina, Allen University, and Benedict College. Additionally, Miss Gray attempted to unify the state and federal programs, aided in preparation and distribution of materials, and in supervision. Unification was a difficult task since the underlying programs were so different. The W.P.A. was mainly concerned with employment for those persons on relief, whereas Miss Gray's primary purpose was education for adults. She had always located schools where the need was greatest and appointed dedicated, well-trained teachers. Since only persons on relief could be hired as W.P.A. teachers, many were not really qualified to teach or did not have the desire to teach, and many were given certificates marked "Emergency W.P.A."

This government aid was available for a period of nine years but was discontinued in 1942. Miss Gray felt at times the government's Relief programs were both a bane and a blessing. The financial aid was helpful, of course, but the mountains of paper work and miles of red tape it entailed were a hindrance. More over, if funds were available that month the work continued, but frequently the money was not received promptly and classes had to be discontinued until government checks arrived. The State Supervisor, always organized and efficient, was often frustrated and outraged by such poor management of an educational program. Nevertheless, one did not criticize President Franklin Delano Roosevelt in her presence, for she was a staunch supporter of the theory behind his New Deal, and felt the fault lay with poor administration on the state level.[1]

During the Depression years Miss Gray's work load was tremendously increased because of the many state and federal relief educational programs to aid South Carolina's unemployed citizens. Fortunately, she had the able assistance of Mabel Montgomery, a good friend and co-worker from Marion, who was employed by the Federal Emergency Relief Administration as an assistant to Miss Gray.

In 1933 when the F.E.R.A. program began, 336 white and 119 Negro teachers who were in the one-week training sessions held classes for approximately 10,000 adult students. The National Youth Administration and Work Projects Administration recruited students and furnished scholarships for thousands of needy citizens. These Relief classes were organized in any location convenient to students, and by 1935, 18,746 adults were attending classes in public schools, humble homes, and churches. Teachers also went from house to house to reach mothers who could not leave home because of small children. These teachers reported some of their triumphs and disappointments to Miss Gray, for she always expressed such an interest in each individual, no matter what age, sex, race, or amount of education. One teacher taught a twenty-five-year-old father of three who had been supporting his family since age eleven and was "my most ambitious student." "A man of sixty who lived far out in the country walked to town once a week for his lesson and a new assignment." "An illiterate mother of six children learned to write to her husband who was ill at Camp Oteen." "A mother, daughter, and two sons from one family attended classes together." "Illiterate fourteen-year-old twins, slightly deaf and with a marked speech impediment, had tonsils removed on entering school. These physical defects improved and they made three grades in one year." "Mrs. B. has in two years emerged from a beginner to seventh grade."[2]

One Relief supervisor reported a case which firmly substantiated one of Miss Gray's tenacious beliefs, that an adult education program could not be measured by numbers enrolled or by average attendance, but by "changed attitudes on the part of students as reflected in finer individual living and in a keener sense of community responsibility." She wrote:

> We did not believe it possible that a simple home could make as much improvement as one of ours has. When we first went into this home the father and son were both in need of medical aid but refused it. Our teacher was not welcome, but she did not give up. She kept visiting the home until finally they consented to let the teacher take them to see a doctor, assuring them that there would be no cost. Now they are in good health. The blessed thing about it all is that they have improved the health

154

conditions and have become health-minded in many respects. This house has come under the Rehabilitation program and they have repaired the house and put a pump on the back porch. Before this they carried water one-fourth of a mile. They have put in window sashes and screens. They have four children now in public school and the father, mother and two sons are in the F.E.R.A. school. All the result of one teacher. They did not have any reading material . . . Now they take a newspaper and two magazines and read them, too. They are always glad to have the teacher visit their home and even ask her to dine with them. They visit and attend public affairs. Before they were shut-ins. They have joined the Home Demonstration Club and other community affairs. The mother and daughter were the only ones attending church. Now the whole family goes and one member of the family has joined the church."[3]

In 1935 Miss Gray became involved in yet another federal relief program when she discovered that there were 1,943 young men in the Civilian Conservation Corps camps in South Carolina who could not read or write. In fact, one Negro camp reported that one of every four workers was illiterate. Miss Gray sent seventy of her most dedicated teachers to work in pairs at the camps where the need was greatest. Primarily, these teachers were concentrating on young men who had not yet completed the fifth grade.[4] Very soon the C.C.C. counselors began to notice tremendous improvement in the attitudes of these young workers after they had learned to read and write. J. P. King wrote:

The teachers in this camp have been able to accomplish with illiterates more than I have been able in six months. I have found that the patience they have acquired through teaching adults and sympathetic understanding of the illiterate has enabled them to overcome the greatest obstacle in this type of work—an inferiority complex.

David Blackwell, a camp supervisor, reported:

. . . the work of the teachers has done wonders with the boys; the entire morale of the camp is on a higher level.

It was a disgrace that the work could not be continued in 1937 due to a lack of funds; however, later the work in C.C.C. camps was resumed until 1942 when all federal aid was discontinued.[5]

155

NOTES

[1]*Sixty-eighth Annual Report of Superintendent of Education* (Columbia: State Department of Education, 1936), pp. 59-65.

[2]*Sixty-seventh Annual Report of Superintendent of Education* (Columbia: State Department of Education, 1935), p. 47.

[3]Ibid., p. 48.

[4]*Sixty-eighth Annual Report*, pp. 62-63; *Seventy-fourth Annual Report of Superintendent of Education*, 1942), p. 29.

[5]*Seventy-fourth Annual Report*, p.30.

REFERENCES

Seventy-fourth Annual Report of Superintendent of Education. Columbia: State Department of Education, 1942.

Sixty-seventh Annual Report of Superintendent of Education. Columbia: State Department of Education, 1935.

Sixty-eighth Annual Report of Superintendent of Education. Columbia: State Department of Education, 1936.

At Last! School Attendance Legislation

Miss Gray, the State Sperintendent of Education, and the Committee on Literacy had continuously advocated throughout the years an adequate school attendance law. Finally, on July 1, 1937, the "Regular School Attendance Law" was enacted. Two other attendance laws had been legislated earlier, but the laws had no teeth in them and provided no form of supervision so neither of them was ever enforceable.[1]

However, the School Attendance Law of 1937 not only provided for attendance of all children between the ages of seven and sixteen years and the taking of a school census and enrollment of all children not already enrolled, but provided for the election of "attendance teachers," prescribed penalties for violation of the law, and appropriated $76,800 annually for salaries of attendance teachers. Because this law, too, made no provision for state coordination, Miss Gray was asked by James H. Hope, the State Superintendent of Education, to act as state coordinator. Although this area was not considered in the domain of the Adult Division, Miss Gray accepted the assignment gladly since she had long preached that the lack of a supervised compulsory attendance law was a major factor in perpetuating illiteracy.[2]

So now Miss Gray had to find time in an already overcrowded agenda to recruit these special "attendance teachers," hold state-wide meetings with them and maintain close contact with them in the field. She edited a monthly newsletter for them to help in their work and recorded and tabulated monthly reports of attendance. She was overjoyed to report at the end of 1937 that the average attendance had risen to 80 percent, the highest ever attained in South Carolina. Moreover, in the first two months of the next school year, attendance figures soared to 91 percent.[3]

These forty-six attendance teachers were *not* truant officers, but certified teachers who were trained by Miss Gray at the University of South Carolina to prepare them for a difficult task, that of locating and keeping in school all children between seven and sixteen, especially those who had never been in school or who had a history of irregular attendance. These teachers found cases of handicapped children that no one had ever known about before, and provided medical aid for them. They reported cases to the Department of Public Welfare or other civic-minded service organizations which furnished shoes, clothing, or books

157

to those children in need. They checked on those absent from school and had the authority to request warrants to be served on uncooperative parents.

County Superintendent O. M. Mullinax of Cherokee County addressed a state convention of attendance teachers. Miss Gray never forgot one case he cited.

> Believe it or not. Sixteen children in one family. None had ever attended school until the father was forced to send them by a court conviction under the attendance law. The father is supposed to be a farmer, but I suspect him to be a maker of illegal whiskey. He kept his children at home so that he could sleep in the daytime while they plowed and cut wood, even the girls. He refused to send the children although the teacher and attendance teacher used persuasion and gave him clothes and shoes for them. After the court conviction the mother thanked me with tears in her eyes. Even the children past sixteen attend school now.[4]

After Miss Gray had worked with the attendance teachers for over a year, Miss Erin Kohn assumed the position of attendance coordinator because "Miss Gray's physician has ordered her to lighten both her work and her hours." It was at this time that Miss Gray, in a state of physical and mental exhaustion, was accompanied by her cousin, Marguerite Tolbert, to the mountains of New Hampshire, where she was to rest, both physically and mentally. Although Miss Tolbert could ensure physical inactivity, she could do nothing to stop Miss Gray from worrying about her adult students and the extent of the illiteracy problem. As a result, when they reported back to work a few weeks later, Miss Gray had conceived even more plans and projects to develop the state's educational program for adults. Although she had no further responsibility for the attendance program, she did continue to train the special attendance teachers.

NOTES

[1]*Sixty-ninth Annual Report of Superintendent of Education* (Columbia: State Department of Education, 1937), pp. 56-57.

[2]Ibid.

[3]*Seventieth Annual Report of Superintendent of Education* (Columbia: State Department of Education, 1938), p. 73.

[4]Ibid.

REFERENCES

Sixty-ninth Annual Report of Superintendent of Education. Columbia: State Department of Education, 1937.

Seventieth Annual Report of Superintendent of Education. Columbia: State Department of Education, 1938.

Seventy-first Annual Report of Superintendent of Education. Columbia: State Department of Education, 1939.

Seventy-second Annual Report of Superintendent of Education. Columbia: State Department of Education, 1940.

Seventy-third Annual Report of Superintendent of Education. Columbia: State Department of Education, 1941.

159

Concern for the Neglected Negro

The results of Miss Gray's previously mentioned Clemson-Seneca Experiment added fuel to her sometimes heated discussions with politicians and educators concerning more emphasis on educating the masses of Negro illiterates in South Carolina. Census figures from 1930 had shown that there were 36,246 (5.1 percent) white and 156,065 (26.9 percent) Negro South Carolinians who were illiterate. This great discrepancy was very evident in some counties, such as Calhoun, which reported 33 white but 1,860 Negroes in 1930 who could not read or write.

Miss Gray's early efforts in adult education to a large extent had to be concentrated on the white population since the state still did not distribute its appropriations equitably between the white and Negro schools. The lack of state support for Negro adult basic education was an extension of the problem which existed in public schools in the state. For instance, in 1935 South Carolina spent an average of $42.25 per year on a white child's education, but only $8.70 on a Negro child.[1]

For years, Miss Gray had been telling legislators and educators that illiteracy was primarily a Negro problem and the Census of 1930 verified her contention. However, when she attempted to push for more funds for Negro adult education, she was warned by powerful politicians that she was endangering her total program, so "tread lightly." She knew why South Carolina had replaced Louisiana as the state with the most illiterates, for Huey Long had outspent South Carolina five dollars to one in a massive pre-census campaign aimed chiefly at Louisiana's Negro population. Although between 1920 and 1930 only three other states had improved their literacy rate any more than South Carolina, all of Miss Gray's hard work and concern was not enough to prevent her state from rising to the top of the rankings in number of illiterates.[2]

Therefore, during the 1930's, despite the threats of politicians, Miss Gray made a concentrated effort to establish more programs for Negroes and to find ways of financing such programs. In addition to the 1931 Opportunity School for Negroes at Seneca Junior College, in 1936 Miss Gray organized the first Opportunity School for Negroes at Voorhees Industrial School in Denmark, South Carolina, with 44 boarders and 60 night school students enrolling. The second school at Voorhees registered 46 boarding students and 78 additional night students, from 14 to 80 years of age. Their educational range was from beginner to seventh grade, with the average amount of schooling being third grade.

At Voorhees, as a practical instructional unit, Miss Gray arranged for the adult students to remodel a dilapidated four-room tenant house for the purpose of teaching how to make the most of materials at hand. While engaged in this project, students not only learned the 3 R's, but also thrift, economy, and sanitary living conditions, as well as the social possibilities of a home. Moreover, they were able to accomplish the remodeling project with a cash outlay of only $25.[3]

Also during the late 1930's and on into the early 1940's, there were more and more night school classes organized specifically to meet the needs of the neglected Negro population throughout the state. By 1942 there were 188 Negro teachers holding night school classes on an elementary level for those Negro adults who had not previously been able to attend school.[4]

In 1938 Miss Gray arranged for an Opportunity School for Negroes to be held at Benedict College in cooperation with the W.P.A. Education Division. This school was used as a demonstration school for training W.P.A. teachers under the direction of Mrs. Dora Daniel, W.P.A. Negro Literacy Supervisor. At this Opportunity School, 72 students from 25 counties participated.[5]

However, Miss Gray was not going to be satisfied by "stopgap" measures to educate the illiterate Negroes who were being denied an education through no fault of their own. She vowed not to rest until there could be some type of program available to the adult citizens of South Carolina, no matter what their race or educational background.

NOTES

¹*Twenty-first Annual Report of State Supervisor of Adult Education* (Columbia: State Department of Education, 1938-39), pp. 19-20; *Seventy-first Annual Report of Superintendent of Education* (Columbia: State Department of Education, 1936), p. 68.

²*Twenty-first Annual Report*, p. 19.

³*Sixty-eighth Annual Report of Superintendent of Education* (Columbia: State Department of Education, 1936), p. 65; *Sixty-ninth Annual Report of Superintendent of Education* (Columbia: State Department of Education, 1937), p. 58.

⁴*Seventy-fourth Annual Report of Superintendent of Education* (Columbia: State Department of Education, 1942), p. 27.

⁵*Seventieth Annual Report of Superintendent of Education* (Columbia: State Department of Education, 1938), p. 72.

REFERENCES

Gray, Wil Lou. "Adult Education among the Negroes in South Carolina." *American Association for Adult Education*, 1938.

Seventieth Annual Report of Superintendent of Education. Columbia: State Department of Education, 1938.

Seventy-fourth Annual Report of Superintendent of Education. Columbia: State Department of Education, 1942.

Sixty-eighth Annual Report of Superintendent of Education. Columbia: State Department of Education, 1937.

Twenty-first Annual Report of State Supervisor of Adult Education. Columbia: State Department of Education, 1938-39.

Concern for Prison Inmates

Ever since Miss Gray was first appointed the Supervisor of Adult Education, she was interested in the many illiterates who were inmates in the State Penitentiary. However, funds were seldom appropriated for the purpose of educating prisoners, and it was difficult to recruit teachers. Therefore, attempts to organize adult classes at the State Penitentiary were sporadic throughout Miss Gray's career as Supervisor.

However, some interest was displayed in this area by other than Miss Gray's Adult Division in 1932, when, at the request of the U. S. Department of the Interior, a prison school was organized in cooperation with prison authorities. Miss Gray arranged for classes to be conducted by two teachers five days a week for a term of six weeks. The program was voluntary for inmates who had less than a seventh-grade education. There were 27 beginning students participating, of whom more than half had not attended school for more than a day. The average attendance at any school for this group was 3 months, and the average age was 32. The average sentence was less than 2 years (with the exception of 4 life-termers), for it was felt that these were the ones most likely to benefit from learning basic skills because they were to soon return to the outside world where they would need job skills if they were to become law-abiding citizens.[1]

At this time Miss Gray had concluded that the state was spending $40.65 per year on the average child's education, but it was costing $211 to institutionalize a criminal. Such unwise and wasteful expenditure just never made sense to her.[2]

Miss Gray was not concerned with only the male inmates; she had earlier conducted a survey of the women prisoners and found that of 92 women, illiteracy was at least a second-generation problem. The average education of 13 white inmates was sixth grade and that of their mothers was fifth grade. Of these 13, only 4 had reached a secondary level and none had graduated. Of 79 Negro women, 50 had mothers who were totally illiterate, and the average education of the others was less than 2 years. Of the 79 female Negro inmates, 42 were illiterate and the average education of the other 37 was fourth grade.[3]

In 1939 Miss Gray reported in her annual report to the Superintendent of Education other disgraceful and shocking data. The

State Penitentiary had just released figures which indicated that of 1,259 prisoners, 417, or 34 percent were unable to read or write. Moreover, of the 149 inmates who had been electrocuted since 1912, 3 of the 29 whites and 50 of the 120 Negroes were illiterate.[4]

Miss Gray was likewise concerned about the fate of juvenile offenders. When she investigated conditions at the state educational facility at the John G. Richards Industrial School for Negro boys, she found that for the 200 boys in the reformatory, with an average age of 14 and an average education of second grade, there were practically no educational opportunities available other than vocational training. And these boys were under the sole guardianship of the state! As a matter of fact, their conditions were so deplorable that on Miss Gray's first visit, she found all of the boys already "locked up" for the night although it was only five o'clock on a warm, sunny afternoon. When she asked if she might visit their wards to talk to them and perhaps read them a story, the Superintendent refused. "Oh, Miss Gray, I can't let you do that, for these boys do not even have sheets on their beds."[5]

Later, in 1943, two members of the State Penal Board and Miss Gray visited the Federal Penitentiary in Atlanta, since it had been cited as having an excellent educational program for its inmates. They invited Atlanta's Director of Education, Dr. G. G. Killinger, to visit the South Carolina State Penitentiary and meet with the full Penal Board. Dr. Killinger came and toured the penal institutions, and he made recommendations for improving prison educational opportunities. Unfortunately, the initiation of the program was delayed until after World War II because it required a psychiatric study of each prisoner as part of the educational assessment, and such services were unavailable in wartime. Once again, Miss Gray's efforts to provide some kind of an educational program to aid in the rehabilitation of state prison inmates were stalemated.[6]

In connection with Dr. Killinger's visit, Miss Gray relates a story to prove her contention that without the unquestioning, loyal support of her friends and family, she could not have accomplished all that she did. As she was leaving a panel meeting with Dr. Killinger, members of the State Penal Board, and Governor Olin Johnston late one night, she felt the group might accomplish more for prison reform in an informal meeting. With her characteristic Southern hospitality, she invited the large group

164

to breakfast at 8:30 the next morning at her home, knowing full well that her cupboards were bare and all grocery stores were already closed. On the way home from the meeting, she stopped at her cook's house and asked Eugenia if she was able to come to work an hour earlier the next morning. When she arrived home, she made out a menu and grocery list and began calling friends, especially the ones living in her other four apartments. Then with an untroubled mind, she set the alarm for 6:30 and promptly went to sleep. When the nearest grocery store opened its doors at 7:30 the next morning, there stood her faithful cousin, Marguerite, with grocery list in hand and car idling at the curb. Meanwhile, Miss Gray was directing the cleaning of the apartment until it was immaculate, the table setting, and flower arranging. When the guests arrived promptly at 8:30, the friends had all departed. As they were enjoying a lavish repast of grapefruit, sausage, grits, and hot waffles, they marveled at the obvious efficiency of their serene hostess who could produce such a feast so early in the day and still remain unruffled!

NOTES

[1]*Sixty-fourth Annual Report of Superintendent of Education* (Columbia: State Department of Education, 1932), p. 59.

[2]Ibid.

[3]*Sixty-ninth Annual Report of Superintendent of Education* (Columbia: State Department of Education, 1937), pp. 61-62.

[4]*Seventy-first Annual Report of Superintendent of Education* (Columbia: State Department of Education, 1939), p. 43.

[5]Ibid.

[6]*Seventy-first Annual Report of Superintendent of Education* (Columbia: State Department of Education, 1943), p. 38.

REFERENCES

Gray, Wil Lou. Columbia, South Carolina. Interview, 6 June 1977.

Sixty-fourth Annual Report of Superintendent of Education. Columbia: State Department of Education, 1932.

Sixty-ninth Annual Report of Superintendent of Education. Columbia: State Department of Education, 1937.

Seventy-first Annual Report of Superintendent of Education. Columbia: State Department of Education, 1939.

Seventy-fifth Annual Report of Superintendent of Education. Columbia: State Department of Education, 1943.

A Dozen Years of Change

As world and national conditions changed throughout the 1930's and early 1940's, Miss Gray was wisely adjusting her adult educational program to meet the changing needs of South Carolina citizens. She had done her part as a Democrat to elect Franklin D. Roosevelt. She felt that his program of relief and reform had helped put the country back on its feet economically. In fact, if federal funds had not been available throughout the 1930's, there would have been no educational program at all for adults in South Carolina.

By 1940 it seemed that due to improved roads and the number of consolidated schools throughout the state, it was to be more practical to consolidate numerous isolated night schools into a program of county continuation schools.[1] These continuation schools met one night a week for ten weeks and were for any adults who could study for credit or the sheer joy of learning, regardless of previous education. This type of program was also adopted in some communities for Negro schools.

During this same period of time, Miss Gray was asked by the Commanding General of the Thirtieth Division, Henry D. Russell, to establish schools for illiterates at Fort Jackson. She therefore developed an intensive program of elementary education and agreed to provide one teacher for every twelve South Carolinians stationed there who could not read or write. She made the provision that an average attendance of eight must be maintained and that the W.P.A. furnish teachers for out-of-state soldiers. She further stipulated that the young men be released from routine drills on the two afternoons of class each week. The military was most cooperative until the war situation became quite tense after six weeks. Therefore, when field maneuvers began in May of 1940, school was out, so to speak. Nevertheless, even though the program was short-term, much had been accomplished. The teachers reported that the recruits were serious, motivated students, who were joyously writing their very first letters for Mother's Day that year. The Supervisor was also gratified to receive from General Russell a letter of commendation for her cooperation.[2]

As America engaged in another world conflict, Miss Gray felt even more personally involved than she had in World War I. Hundreds of her Opportunity School students and alumni became members of the armed

167

forces, and to many of them she was a surrogate mother. Hardly a day passed that did not bring letters from her "boys and girls," and each letter was answered promptly.

On the homefront, Miss Gray encouraged adult students to do their part for the war effort by cultivating victory gardens, investing in war bonds and stamps, and conserving natural resources and rationed goods. She always maintained that becoming educated was a vital part of being a patriotic citizen.

By 1942, conditions due to the war effort necessitated a return to the smaller night school classes, for the larger educational centers that had been holding continuation classes for adults were now devoted to intensive vocational training for war workers. Therefore, 42 white and 188 Negro teachers held night school classes, largely remedial, and primarily taught basic skills.[3]

Other changes were necessitated because for the first time since 1933 no government aid was available for adult education. Also organizations and businesses were unable to award scholarships due to the demands of the war effort. However, enrollment did not drop, and Miss Gray always managed to find some way to provide for the educational needs of the thousands who were crying for a chance to learn.

During the years Miss Gray was supervising the work at Clemson, she received three awards from the state of South Carolina in recognition of her achievement in the field of adult education. As early as 1934 Miss Gray earned state-wide recognition when she was included in *Who's Who in South Carolina*, with a lengthy list of creditable achievements. In a similar vein, one of the most treasured awards of her extensive career was bestowed in 1937 when the University of South Carolina presented the highly coveted Algernon Sydney Sullivan Medallion to "one who reached out both hands in constant helpfulness to his fellow man."[4]

In 1941 the *Anderson Daily Mail* devoted a full page to the accomplishments of "this distinguished citizen, Miss Wil Lou Gray," as a public service award. A "Scroll of Honor" was presented "in recognition of outstanding public service" and thousands more South Carolinians became acquainted with her notable achievements through the medium of the press.[5] These awards were only the first of dozens to be presented to Miss Gray in her lifetime, and all were richly deserved.

168

NOTES

[1]*Seventy-third Annual Report of Superintendent of Education* (Columbia: State Department of Education, 1941), pp. 31-32; *Seventy-fourth Annual Report of Superintendent of Education* (Columbia: State Department of Education, 1942), p. 29.

[2]*Seventy-fourth Annual Report*, p. 27.

[3]Ibid.

[4]Erin Kohn, "Wil Lou Gray," *South Carolina's Distinguished Women of Laurens County* (Columbia: Vogue Press, 1972), p. 117.

[5]*Anderson Daily Mail*, "A Scroll of Honor," 1941.

REFERENCES

Anderson Daily Mail. "A Scroll of Honor," 1941.

Kohn, Erin. "Wil Lou Gray." *South Carolina's Distinguished Women of Laurens County*. Columbia: Vogue Press, 1972.

Sixty-second Annual Report of Superintendent of Education. Columbia: State Department of Education, 1930.

Sixty-third Annual Report of Superintendent of Education. Columbia: State Department of Education, 1931.

Sixty-fourth Annual Report of Superintendent of Education. Columbia: State Department of Education, 1932.

Sixty-first Annual Report of Superintendent of Education. Columbia: State Department of Education, 1933.

Sixty-sixth Annual Report of Superintendent of Education. Columbia: State Department of Education, 1934.

Sixty-seventh Annual Report of Superintendent of Education. Columbia: State Department of Education, 1935.

Sixty-eighth Annual Report of Superintendent of Education. Columbia: State Department of Education, 1936.

Sixty-ninth Annual Report of Superintendent of Education. Columbia: State Department of Education, 1937.

Seventieth Annual Report of Superintendent of Education. Columbia: State Department of Education, 1938.

Seventy-first Annual Report of Superintendent of Education. Columbia: State Department of Education, 1939.

169

Seventy-second Annual Report of Superintendent of Education. Columbia: State Department of Education, 1940.

Seventy-third Annual Report of Superintendent of Education. Columbia: State Department of Education, 1941.

Seventy-fourth Annual Report of Superintendent of Education. Columbia: State Department of Education, 1942.

Return to Lander

After the Opportunity School session of 1942 at Clemson College, the facilities there were needed by the military. Once again Miss Gray was looking for another home for her summer program which had gained so much popularity throughout the state.

Fortunately, Lander College again offered its campus to 243 boarding students enrolling for the 1943 session, and Miss Gray was glad to return to the Opportunity School's former home which evoked so many happy memories of the earlier schools. Moreover, she was doubly happy that now her cousin, very talented and capable Marguerite Tolbert, had recently become the Assistant State Supervisor of Adult Education.[1]

There were some changes evident between the first summer session at Lander College in 1922 and the school now beginning in the summer of 1943. For one thing, the tuition had exactly doubled and was now $25 per student, or $23 in war stamps. The theme for the 1943 session was "My Part in Helping on the Home Front and Permanent Peace," so the fact that America was at that time engaged in World War II created an entirely different atmosphere on the Lander campus. In an effort to conserve rationed tires and gasoline, Miss Gray sacrificed her annual educational pilgrimages. Instead, Lander adult students hiked to various local spots of interest. Furthermore, Miss Gray cooperated with local draft boards and somehow found scholarship funds for men who had been rejected by the military because of educational deficits.[2]

Another voluntary service rendered by the State Supervisor was maintaining close personal contact with Opportunity School alumni who were now stationed all over the world. To this day she treasures the reams of correspondence which steadily flowed between her office or home and the farthest corners of the world. The following excerpts from alumni letters speak for themselves:

> I wish I could be at Opportunity School this year. I hope every single one of the student body will grab every one of the many opportunities I know will be there. I'm not a philosopher, but I'd like to say this: progress makes opportunity, opportunity is the seed of education, ambition is inspired by success.

The Opportunity School has given me a better understanding of people, the importance of education, and the value of a good memory.

I wish the Opportunity School could last longer and we could have more of them. When I went I couldn't even write a letter; now I am in military intelligence with Philippine guerrillas. I think lots more people would go to Opportunity School if they had the money, and I think the State should make it possible.

The urge to go forward which I gained at the Opportunity School has inspired me. I never did get my high school credits but I'm still on my way to college. I've saved almost $800 and I intend to pull through regardless of my handicaps.

Before my month at Lander I spent my time pitying myself because my husband was overseas. Oh, occasionally I dreamed of the home we would one day have, but those dreams were only wishful hoping, and not concrete plans for my future, or my husband's. The fact that I enrolled at the University of Georgia was due to the encouragement I received from the entire staff at Opportunity School. Now that I've joined the WAC's I've transferred to the Extension Course, and after the war I'm going back to school.

There were also changes in the curriculum at the Lander Opportunity School due to the war. There were now courses especially planned for wives of servicemen and their babies. A nursery supervised by trained nurses was available on campus so mothers of young children and infants could take courses to meet their needs. Some of the courses now offered were taught by "Dr." Mamie McLees, the very first Opportunity School teacher at Tamassee, on leave from State College in New Jersey. She had been enticed to come to Lander and teach "Simple Psychology," "Personality Development," and "Problems in Leadership."[3]

A further change was the development of a counseling service for Opportunity School alumni and other adult students who were interested in continuing their education and obtaining a high school diploma. For these students, Miss Gray had arranged for the University of South Carolina to administer a standard examination in cooperation with the State High School Division, and each school session saw more and more adult students taking advantage of this chance to earn a high school diploma, or even to become successful students in colleges and universities.[4]

Many conditions at Lander might have changed since the first session there, but there was never a change in the way Miss Gray's adult students felt about her. The student body at Lander in 1944 unveiled a "Friendship Portrait" at the annual alumni meeting. Miss Erin Kohn spoke with love and respect for her dear friend on this occasion:

> The climax of this banquet is the unveiling of your portrait, painted under your protest, and donated by hundreds of friends and students who have known, appreciated, and applauded you during the years you have labored for South Carolina. This portrait is a gift of love and devotion, of pennies and dimes and dollars! It is a gift which has been transmitted into something finer than mere canvas and pigments for it materializes love given and received; faith in your fellow man amply rewarded.

> You have earned the victor's wreath—won through months that knew not hours nor weather. You have fought a good fight and won a hard race. The wish of those celebrating this event in your honor is that you, Wil Lou Gray, may never lose your love for all of God's creatures; that your power to turn sight into insight may increase with every passing day, and that your present high point of achievement may be but tidings of greater things to come through many more happy years.[5]

This portrait was in turn presented to Miss Gray's alma mater, where it was proudly displayed in a place of honor until it was destroyed in a disastrous fire which razed much of the Columbia College campus.

NOTES

[1]*Seventy-first Annual Report of Superintendent of Education* (Columbia: State Department of Education, 1943), p. 30.

[2]Ibid., p. 32.

[3]*Seventy-sixth Annual Report of Superintendent of Education* (Columbia: State Department of Education, 1944), pp. 38-39.

[4]Ibid., p. 39.

[5]Ibid.

REFERENCES

Gray, Wil Lou, and Tolbert, Marguerite. *A Brief Manual for Adult Teachers of South Carolina*. Columbia: State Department of Education, 1943.

Seventy-first Annual Report of Superintendent of Education. Columbia: State Department of Education, 1943.

Seventy-sixth Annual Report of Superintendent of Education. Columbia: State Department of Education, 1944.

Camp Opportunity, Jr.

In 1944, Miss Gray with the help of Marguerite Tolbert, developed another highly successful innovative program to meet the educational needs of a special neglected group of South Carolinians, those adolescent boys of working mothers and perhaps absentee fathers, for whom the adult program at Lander Opportunity School was unsuitable. Many of these boys had been problem students in day school. They were primarily from industrial centers, but thanks to Roosevelt's New Deal child labor laws, they were too young to be employed in the mills during their summer vacations. Since their parents were usually employed in war industries or in the service, they were a real problem with so much unsupervised idle time, and many were headed toward a career of juvenile delinquency.

Such a problem did not really belong to the Adult Division, but Miss Gray felt that this was "a war baby which was left wailing on our doorstep. Common humanity compelled us to succor it and nurse it to health. When a suitable foster parent appears, we will hand over the child with our blessing. Until then, we are merely doing our best for this appealing war orphan."[1]

Therefore, Miss Gray and Miss Tolbert organized an educational program for 99 boys from 30 counties at Camp Opportunity School, Jr., for one month during the summer at Camp York near Kings Mountain State Park, in cooperation with the State Forestry Commission. For this innovative program, they were especially careful to select a faculty which was unusually capable and experienced.

The objectives of this camp were the following:

1. To strive for the total development of each boy, mentally, physically, socially, and spiritually.

2. To help the boys, through camping experiences, to eliminate the strains of war.

3. To keep campers healthy and fit.

4. To train campers for democratic living and leadership by delegating responsibilities and having all participate as far as possible in the government of their groups and camp.

5. To train campers in knowledge and skills essential to preservation of life and military situations. Therefore, stressing

175

swimming, hiking, lifesaving, first aid, camp cooking, weather study, learning to be happy away from home, and learning to cooperate with, and live happily with, boys their own age, developing self-reliance and resourcefulness and the ability to look after one's self.

6. To encourage campers to make their contribution to the war effort by buying stamps, salvaging tin cans and paper, avoiding waste, conserving natural resouces, keeping physically fit, and developing skillful hands in manual arts.

7. To help the boys make better adjustment to their day-school program.[2]

As eligible boys were identified, special diagnostic tests were given to discover individual differences and needs, and the classroom work included not only the necessary drill on the 3 R's, but an intensive course in letter writing, daily reading of the newspapers, and the use of the dictionary.

All instruction was organized around special units of work according to the interest of each homeroom group, which chose such topics as airplanes, trees, hobbies, our flag, or world geography. Most boys agreed that they had to study and work at camp, but "learning was fun!"

In addition to classroom work, at the end of each day Vesper services were held around the campfire. Also, on each Sabbath, Sunday School and church services were conducted by outstanding religious leaders in the state.

Supplementing the basic academic subjects stressed, the boys enjoyed classes in music, and the camp orchestra played during meals and on all special occasions such as birthday parties and the commencement banquet. Also, an arts and crafts shop was explored by each student and many discovered or developed talents that had been latent.

World current events were discussed as instructors, assisted by students, announced the latest war news. Moreover, each cabin had a daily newspaper, in addition to the *Camp Bugle* which was published weekly by students and faculty.

Additionally, Miss Gray always subscribed to the "All work and no play" theory. Therefore, recreation consisted of hikes to historic Kings Mountain, Saturday night stunt nights, and Wednesday evening hikes and wiener roasts.[3]

176

To determine if the program was worthwhile, one had only to hear the enthusiastic reactions of the campers, who ranged in age from twelve to seventeen years:

> This camp school has helped me in lots of ways. To begin with, the 'excellents' I made on my report card have given me a greater desire to earn them in my high school work this year . . . Mingling with the boys has helped me with my timidness.
>
> The camp taught me better manners, how to spell better and figure better, how to swim, how to make my own bed like the hospital makes theirs, how to be helpful to other people, how to play ball and go by the rules, and the arts and crafts taught me how to build things.
>
> My greatest pleasure did not come from swimming and playing ball, but from being in the presence of a fine group of people.
>
> I learned to identify many trees and shrubs. I was taught how to set and serve a table, and good table manners . . . My memory will stick to the fine talks that were given at camp by different speakers . . . I have also learned by being a friend that I could have friends.
>
> When I got on the bus going home I got up and gave a lady my seat![4]

Not only the boys themselves, but many prominent visitors gave glowing accounts of what went on at Camp Opportunity, Jr. For instance, Mr. W. B. Wilkerson, York County Superintendent of Education, wrote:

> I met these boys at the station when they came in; I saw them many times on the job at school, and I saw them as they caught the bus for home. Never before have I seen a group of boys improve so much in such a short time. If anyone questions the wisdom or value of this camp, my suggestion is that they visit the school this summer. I would like to urge clubs, churches, and individuals to provide the funds and select one or more worthy boys to send to camp. I know of no way to spend money that will bring greater returns.[5]

The Reverend Julian Lake, Rock Hill, wrote after his visit to the camp:

> I am a Kiwanian. It was my good pleasure to visit Camp Opportunity School, Jr. last summer. I am planning to encourage some of our men to send at least one boy there

177

this coming summer. There is no doubt in my mind but what a boy would come away from this camp with an entirely new view of life, of God, and of himself. The word 'Opportunity' is the right word.[6]

As the good news about the camp spread across the state by such visitors, many organizations and individuals made contributions of $25 which sent a boy to Camp Opportunity School, Jr. for a month of fun and learning. Although this camp school was to continue for several years under the capable supervision of Miss Tolbert, Miss Gray maintained a careful watch over this "war orphan" she had come to love.

Campers meeting in Columbia where a special bus would take them to Kings Mountain State Park for four weeks of fun at Camp Opportunity School, Jr.

NOTES

[1]*Seventy-sixth Annual Report of Superintendent of Education* (Columbia: State Department of Education, 1944), p. 46;*Seventy-eighth Annual Report of Superintendent of Education* (Columbia: State Department of Education, 1946), p. 77.

[2]*Seventy-sixth Annual Report*, pp. 46-47.

[3]Ibid., p. 48.

[4]Ibid., pp. 48-49.

[5]*Seventy-seventh Annual Report of Superintendent of Education* (Columbia: State Department of Education, 1945), pp. 65-66.

[6]Ibid., p. 66.

REFERENCES

Seventy-sixth Annual Report of Superintendent of Education. Columbia: State Department of Education, 1944.

Seventy-seventh Annual Report of Superintendent of Education. Columbia: State Department of Education, 1945.

Seventy-eighth Annual Report of Superintendent of Education. Columbia: State Department of Education, 1946.

Return to Columbia College

In 1945, once again Lander College was undergoing extensive renovation and could not accommodate a summer program for Miss Gray's adult students. Miss Gray was determined not to rest until she found a permanent home for the Opportunity School. She knew that she would never be able to build the type of adult educational program that South Carolina needed as long as the Opportunity School had to rely on temporary quarters.

When Miss Gray graduated from Columbia College in 1903, she little dreamed that she was to return to her alma mater forty-two years later to supervise the instruction of hundreds of adult South Carolinians who had not completed their basic education. She was delighted to accept Columbia College's invitation to host the 1945 school on its spacious campus. Since Columbia is the state capital, she felt that there were many opportunities for experience and learning that had never before been available to her students, except on weekend pilgrimages. Moreover, she felt that state officials and legislators were more likely to visit the school due to its proximity. She hoped that when they saw the program first-hand and realized how much progress was resulting in such a small amount of time, a better understanding of the need for a year-round program in a permanent location was possible.

The only Opportunity School to be held at Columbia College, the twenty-fifth consecutive annual session, registered 226 students, of whom 9 were ex-servicemen. A more diverse student body could not be imagined, according to Miss Gray. There were mothers with babies in arms, grandmothers in their seventies, veterans, and a mother in her twenties who enrolled herself and three daughters, aged 11, 13, and 15. One young woman was attending her tenth Opportunity School session. A college student attending for enrichment was from a family of 16 and the only family member to become a high school graduate.[1]

There were children ranging from 12 to 31 months enrolled in the special nursery class. This was a continuation of the program Miss Gray had begun at Lander College two years previously, and was once again sponsored by the Maternal and Child Health Division of the State Board of Health.

There were two dozen faculty and staff members offering the same

180

type of instruction that had been successful the two previous years at Lander College. The theme this year was "South Carolina and Her Part in Building a Better World."

Miss Gray had arranged for a special "relay" class which attracted much attention. This course in South Carolina literature was taught by Dr. Archibald Rutledge, poet laureate of South Carolina; Dr. H. N. Snyder of Wofford College; and Dr. Milton Ariail of Columbia College. These professors lived with the students and talked with them both in classes and during their leisure time. Their well-attended formal lectures were delivered during chapel programs and vesper services. Such close personal contact with these scholars must have opened vistas in the lives of many Opportunity School students, for one student wrote, "Some of the things they said will bless me all my life because they have become a part of me."[2]

During the years, the Opportunity School had continued to observe many traditional occasions which had originally been ideas of Miss Gray for encouraging the social growth of adult students. These customs were continued at Columbia College and reminded Miss Gray so much of the halcyon days she had spent there many years ago. As girls who were enrolled in home economics classes held a reception early in the session, she remembered well attending many such affairs in the beautiful college parlor.

It had become a custom to enjoy a "birthday banquet" to commemorate the anniversary of the Opportunity School as well as any students who had celebrated birthdays during the term. It was at this celebration in 1945 that the students presented their director with four silver candlesticks and an array of lovely flowers.

Perhaps Miss Gray's favorite celebration was the annual Alumni Banquet, when former students from all over the state, and usually representing each year since 1921, gathered for a time of fellowship with their beloved Supervisor and former teachers. At this affair during the Columbia College session, one alumna who had attended in 1924 was present, along with her daughter, who was enrolled in the current session.

The climax of the month's work was always the commencement exercises. Knowing full well the value of positive reinforcement, Miss Gray had always made much of these graduations and found some way to commend each individual for any progress accomplished. At this particular commencement, Superintendent Hope presented high school certificates to three men, two of them ex-servicemen.[3]

And so ended another chapter in the history of the Opportunity School in South Carolina, which could just as well be called the history of Wil Lou Gray. She was about to embark now on a mission, which, if successful, was to be the culmination of all her hopes and dreams.

Along with many others, Miss Gray had been saddened by the death of President Roosevelt in 1945, but on the other hand, she had faith in the fiery Truman's determination and statesmanship. As World War II ended, she was vitally interested in her country's efforts to form world peace organizations such as the United Nations. Too many of her former students had died in action and were being remembered in memorial services at the Opportunity School. Miss Gray now looked forward to an era of peace and the challenge of establishing a year-round permanent school for adults. History was to prove that she was equal to the challenge.

NOTES

[1]*Twenty-seventh Annual Report of the State Supervisor of Adult Schools* (Columbia: State Department of Education, 1944-45), p. 22.

[2]Ibid., p. 25.

[3]Ibid., pp. 29-30.

REFERENCES

Gray, Wil Lou. Columbia, South Carolina. Interview, 7 July 1977.

Twenty-seventh Annual Report of the State Supervisor of Adult Schools. Columbia: State Department of Education, 1944-45.

CHAPTER XIII

A Dream Come True
The South Carolina Opportunity School

Wail not for precious chances passed away!
Walter Malone

For the first time in twenty-five years, there was no Opportunity School session in 1946, for Miss Gray sensed that the time was ripe for establishing a year-round program for adult learning in a permanent location and wished to devote the entire year to the achievement of such a goal. She had been advocating such a program for more than a quarter of a century, and by then had amassed a great deal of evidence that an educational program for adults, even though it might begin on an elementary level, was more than worthwhile. Illiteracy was still a threat to South Carolina's economic welfare since in 1940 census figures reported that 62.3 percent of the Negroes over twenty-five years of age, and 17.9 percent of the white adults had finished no more than four years of school. Furthermore, the number of adult South Carolinians who deserved a chance to complete their education was swelled by the ranks of returning World War II veterans.[1]

Actually, the preliminary salvos in the campaign to obtain a permanent school were fired in late December 1945,when Miss Gray wrote to key alumni in each county, urging them to attend a meeting at the Washington Street Methodist Church in Columbia, on December 16. Although that day dawned bitterly cold, groups arrived from across the length and breadth of South Carolina, in a heart-warming testimonial of appreciation, loyalty, and devotion to their beloved Miss Wil Lou. Typical was a group from Greenville which departed from home at five o'clock in the morning and made the trip in an unheated bus.[2]

At this first organizational meeting, members of the group heard an inspirational message delivered by Dr. Kilpatrick from Teachers College, Columbia University, who had accepted Miss Gray's invitation to speak. After his address, the group pledged to contact General Assembly members to urge their support of a permanent school and to give personal witness to the benefits that could result for those who sought a second chance to complete their education. Miss Gray was prepared with the following facts which she presented to the alumni to use as ammunition in the campaign:

1. More than one-third of the adults twenty-five years of age and over in South Carolina had not completed the fourth grade.
2. The median school year attained in South Carolina was six years, seven months.
3. More than twelve percent of those from South Carolina examined by Selective Service were turned down for educational reasons.
4. Unemployment loomed as one of the major problems of the post-war world, but it could be greatly alleviated if citizens over twenty years of age continued their education according to their needs and aptitudes.
5. An appreciation of world understanding and brotherhood was necessary as a sound basis for permanent peace. This could come only through continued education, since the safest form of government is an *educated* democracy.

Next the group drafted the following resolution:

Since these facts show the imperative need for the universal spread of education among all the people;

and *since* hundreds of folk were forced out of school because of economic reasons through no fault of their own and are now eager for an opportunity;

and *since* people learn most rapidly and economically in the stimulating atmosphere of a college campus;

and *since* there are six colleges in South Carolina to take care of the eighteen percent of the population who are high school graduates, but no state institution to take care of the eighty-two percent who have not reached college level;

185

and *since* the Opportunity School has demonstrated for the past twenty-five years that adults can learn, that discouraged lives can be transformed, that South Carolina's greatest undeveloped assets are her adult citizens eager for further education;

Therefore, be it resolved that the Opportunity School Alumni Association urge the establishment of two permanent state-wide Opportunity Schools (one for white, one for Negroes) as living testimonials to South Carolina servicemen. The doors should always be open to adults who cannot attend day school or college but who feel the need for further training and inspiration to prepare them to meet the changing needs of the present world. The organization should be such that students might attend with their families one month or as long as they desire. The course of study should be comprehensive, ranging from primary through secondary level and should include both general and vocational subjects.[3]

Then these members of the Alumni Association, representing every county and each year of the Opportunity School since 1921, turned their concern into action. They visited their district representatives, telephoned them, and wrote letters to them. Meanwhile, Miss Gray had convinced other friends of the Opportunity School, faculty and staff, and volunteer helpers to interpret the possibilities of such an institution to their representatives in the General Assembly. The state was bombarded with alumni letters, newspaper releases, and personal letters from Miss Gray. She and her office staff prepared a sixteen-page information bulletin, "Twenty-five Years of Opportunity," which told the history of the Opportunity School and the benefits reaped by its alumni, largely through photographs Miss Gray had carefully preserved through the years. This graphic plea for a permanent school was delivered to each delegate of the General Assembly, to the press, the American Legion and its Auxiliary, and missionary societies across the state. Throughout this entire campaign Miss Gray was bolstered by the unremitting support of the Superintendent of Education, James H. Hope.

Finally, Miss Gray and representatives of the Alumni Association were called before the Senate Education Committee, and because Miss Gray's students could speak from the heart of what the Opportunity School had meant to them "in changed lives, new hopes, better preparation for living, and heightened ideals," they presented a most

186

convincing argument. Before the General Assembly adjourned, the Opportunity School was given a $52,000 appropriation, with the added assurance that the teachers' salaries would be paid through general education funds. However, this appropriation was to be contingent upon the securing of a suitable physical plant by the State Department of Education.[4]

What a stipulation this proved to be! Nevertheless, after such a heartening conclusion to the initial campaign, Miss Gray and her triumphant supporters were not about to be discouraged when only one more obstacle stood between them and their long-cherished dream.

After a survey of the entire state, Miss Gray discovered a suitable location and facility right in her own back yard in West Columbia, a portion of the Columbia Army Air Base. During the war the base was used extensively for the training of Air Corps personnel. Since the base had been declared surplus by the War Department even before the cessation of World War II, it had been turned over to the War Assets Administration for disposition. The Air Base proper was returned to Lexington County which had leased it to the government during the war, and the South Carolina Aeronautic Association leased the base from Lexington County to operate one of the largest airports in the Southeast. However, it was the hospital area located on 998 acres that Miss Gray was seeking as a home for the Opportunity School. When she realized that securing the entire plant would be a long, complex procedure, even with the intercession of Senator Burnet R. Maybank of Charleston and other influential Congressmen who were acting in her behalf, she wisely requested an interim permit for use of the hospital area only.[5]

Again, Miss Gray's persistence and determination enabled her to gain an objective which at one moment appeared to be within her grasp, and then in the next instant, tantalizingly vanished into thin air. However, it was characteristic of her that she did not allow miles of red tape nor an intricate labyrinth of military protocol in the Pentagon to impede the realization of her seemingly "impossible dream." She flew to Washington, D.C., and Atlanta several times when there was no more to be done at home by means of letters or the telephone. In Washington she enlisted the aid of alumni, delegates from South Carolina, and anyone else who might possibly be of assistance. At one point she thought the battle was won. Joyfully, Miss Gray left Senator Maybank's office after

187

being assured that the last hurdle for gaining a permit for the Air Base hospital site had been cleared and it was to be only a matter of time before she received official confirmation. Imagine her disappointment and chagrin when within the hour she received word that the War Assets Administration had received a wire from the South Carolina State Health Department requesting that same property for use as a venereal disease clinic, especially when officials seemed inclined to give this request priority.

Miss Gray was not about to surrender without a fight, but she knew she must act swiftly. Within minutes she was airborne en route to Columbia, prepared to engage in a skirmish which threatened to transform a triumph into bitter defeat. Fortunately, she and Superintendent Hope were able to convince the director of the State Health Department that the State Department of Education had made the first application for an interim permit and suggested that he look elsewhere for his needed facility. Like so many others, he found it impossible to say "no" to the dogged determination of the Supervisor.[6]

Not only were other state agencies coveting the property, but so were a group of businessmen who wanted to subdivide the land and sell it as commercial building sites. This group, which included a high-ranking State Highway Department official, had even gone so far as to inform Washington that the State Department of Education had relinquished its prior claim and had no further interest in the site. Miss Gray was shocked at this underhanded intrigue which required another trip to Washington to counteract. One of the group was later asked how he let that little woman get the best of him, and he bitterly retorted, "Have you ever had this little woman stand between you and the door?"

Finally, on July 1, 1946, the State Department of Education was granted an interim permit for use of the hospital area of the former Air Base. The next year, the United States Government presented a quitclaim deed for 998.03 acres of land and 218 buildings, after a similar request for the ordinance area had been approved. That same year Miss Gray had to undergo the same torturous procedure when she wished to add the former military chapel to the campus. Fortunately, the Pentagon complied with all of her requests, with the only stipulation being that there must a residency of ten years by the Opportunity School, after which time a clear title was to be given to the state of South Carolina.[7]

188

Meanwhile, on the same day that Miss Gray received official confirmation that the interim permit was granted, after serving as Supervisor of Adult Education for twenty-seven years, she relinquished her position to her extremely capable Assistant Supervisor, Marguerite Tolbert. Now that the property had been acquired, a thousand-and-one details had to be attended to concerning equipping the plant, soliciting students, and organizing and developing a school program, and Superintendent Hope realized it required Miss Gray's full-time attention.

One of Miss Gray's first official acts as Superintendent of the Opportunity School was to relinquish 175 acres with whatever buildings occupied that land for the development of a State Trade School, which later evolved into one campus of the present-day Midlands Technical College complex. Nevertheless, there still remained for the Opportunity School's use 823 acres of land worth $95,759.[8]

Perhaps an ordinary mortal might have felt disheartened by the unattractive appearance of the buildings and grounds, but not Miss Gray, who already envisioned the beautifully landscaped, spacious campus with its lovely buildings which occupy the site today. This metamorphosis has been wrought from a dismal origin, for in July 1946, the base had been abandoned for two years. The bare shells which had once been furnished buildings efficiently equipped to provide training and care for thousands of servicemen, now had even the radiators disconnected.

A great deal of excellent equipment was secured from the War Assets Administration, the Federal Works Agency, and the Surplus Property Division, but this procedure required months of searching and requisitioning. Then the first two orders finally arrived, but what a disappointment! The one thousand beds that had been ordered arrived without the bolts necessary for their assembly, and the twenty dining room tables proved to be laundry tables, three inches too high, and suitable only for giraffes, according to Miss Gray. However, conditions improved and by the end of the year the Director was able to estimate that furnishings and equipment valued at $60,000 had been purchased for the new school at a cost of only $10,000.

Miss Gray soon realized the total impossibility of having the buildings cleaned, remodeled, and furnished in time to hold a summer session at the new Opportunity School. However, by December, buildings had been cleaned, partitions removed to form classrooms, girls' and boys' dormitories furnished with beds, and makeshift tables placed in the dining hall. She planned for most of the renovation to wait until the first students arrived in January 1947, in order that they participate in a work-study program and assist in making the needed improvements in the facilities. She predicted an increase in students' self-esteem and pride in their school if they helped refurbish it. Moreover, she wanted the students to experience personally making a tremendous improvement in their environment by a few yards of inexpensive material and a little paint. The students themselves were allowed to decorate their dormitory rooms or family apartments as they wished. Under the guidance of skilled craftsmen, the students assisted in transforming barracks into sun parlors, library, chapel, dining hall, canteen, infirmary, recreation hall, workshop, offices, and a kitchen equipped for serving three hundred people. Homemaking and carpentry students assisted in tastefully furnishing and decorating the school. A comfortable, homelike main lounge became a favorite spot for informal student activities. At Miss Gray's suggestion, this lounge was dedicated to the memory of alumni who had died while serving their country in World War II. To the left of this lounge area was an apartment furnished for Miss Gray to live in on campus as the superintendency entailed twenty-four-hour supervision, seven days a week. This was to be her home for the next decade until her retirement in 1957; meanwhile, she leased her apartment in Columbia to a close friend for the duration of her stay on the Opportunity School campus.

Before the school was prepared to receive its first student body, Miss Gray was already fulfilling a promise she had made when making application for the interim permit—the availability of the Opportunity School at all times as an adult education center. The first meeting there was held on October 9, 1946, when a group of welfare workers gathered for a dinner conference on the theme, "How the Opportunity School May Be Used To Raise the Level of Living in South Carolina." On the following evening, a group of Columbia civic leaders met for an informal tour. On December 15, five people from each county were invited to meet at the school for a dinner and discussion on how the Opportunity School might best assist veterans and others who were in need of continuing their education.[9]

Since Miss Gray always found some way of arranging an annual alumni meeting, former students were invited in 1946 to come for the Thanksgiving weekend, even though the furniture at that time consisted only of beds and improvised tables. At a Thanksgiving banquet, Superintendent Hope and James Miles were the principal speakers. Later, former Governor Ransome J. Williams and Governor Strom Thurmond were honor guests and spoke at a luncheon meeting. More than 125 people attended these affairs for four days of group study and recreation. Upon their departure, they donated more than $200 to be used as scholarships for deserving students.[10]

When the first students arrived on campus for the initial session, they were met by an eye-catching slogan emblazoned above the front door, "Why Stop Learning?" Fortunately, Miss Gray had been able to find an excellent faculty to help students answer this challenging question once they entered the portals of the South Carolina Opportunity School. A faculty and staff of eighteen assisted Miss Gray and included Mr. G. W. Hopkins as Assistant Director, a Dean of Women, housemother, business manager, librarian, nurse, dietitian, bookkeeper, secretary, maintenance supervisor, and eight teachers.

The curriculum in the first session included building construction, elementary education, commerce, home economics, English, agriculture, social science, and mathematics. Miss Gray organized the school more like a home and the majority of the faculty and staff lived in the dormitories and shared with the students in making the school-home a cooperative venture. Although classes were scheduled from nine o'clock in the morning until three in the afternoon, and night classes from seven until eleven at night, learning went on throughout the day. Not only was instruction offered in the classroom, but also in the dormitories, corridors, chapel, dining room, recreation hall, and playground. Miss Gray was usually the last person to turn out her lights in the evening, and students who needed to talk always found a warm welcome in her cozy apartment.

Miss Gray continued to plan her curriculum largely as it had always been, built around the needs of individual students as shown by their interests and standardized tests. Since the average educational level of this first class was junior high school, concentration on the basic school subjects was mandatory, with emphasis on remedial reading. However, pupils were also able to take courses leading to a high school certificate, which was earned by successfully passing a state-administered test. It was not until August 1, 1948, that the Opportunity School began to issue its own high school diplomas. These were not earned because a certain number of hours had been spent in the classroom, but by the demonstration of achievement and a personal interview.[11]

Because there were so many veterans with families enrolled at the Opportunity School, there was an emphasis on family living education during the early years of the permanent school. These families either had apartments in Happy Valley, a section of the school property set aside for veterans' housing, or in housekeeping apartments in the main building. The families who did not care to provide their own meals were free to dine with the other boarding students.

An innovation Miss Gray began in order to assist these young families who were on extremely limited budgets was the organization of a Cooperative Club. The homemaking department cooperated by teaching nutrition and distributing scientifically planned, low-cost menus for each club member to follow. Because grocery items were purchased in wholesale lots by the Cooperative, each family was able to save twelve to fifteen dollars per month. In addition to practicing good nutrition, club members also participated in "Home and Family Life Clinics" which stressed the importance of healthful living, intellectual stimulation, and spiritual growth. Members also learned about home beautification through contests in which family units earned awards for home improvement. Last, although not considered the least important, recreation was stressed as a vital part of club activities. Accordingly, once each month parents enjoyed a night out while their children were cared for in the school nursery. These occasions sometimes were festive formal affairs, or informal picnics or cookouts, but members unanimously blessed Miss Gray for her unique idea.

Throughout the years as the needs of adult students changed, the curriculum was altered to meet their requirements. Courses in lip reading for the deaf, Red Cross lifesaving and home nursing, parliamentary law, leadership training, consumer education, orchestra, chorus, interior decorating, sewing, meal preparation, canning, gardening, woodworking, masonry, typing, bookkeeping, office practice, plumbing, ceramics, painting, and wallpapering were added to the course of study as the need arose. Furthermore, Miss Gray was able to entice artists and craftsmen in many areas to come to the Opportunity School as instructors. Perhaps the most outstanding member of her faculty, Mr. Rune Alexandersson, came from the "folk schools" of Sweden to teach woodworking and folk dancing. Moreover, Superintendent James H. Hope, who was always such a staunch supporter of the adult education program, volunteered to teach night classes in woodworking since that was his favorite avocation. With such a broad range of courses to pique the interest of students, and such talented and dedicated instructors, it is no wonder that Opportunity School students were motivated to make giant strides in their educational progress in short periods of time.[12]

At the end of the first three quarters and the summer session in the new school, Miss Gray and other staff members were delighted with the progress of their students. These students made an average gain of one year's progress for each quarter of study, while the average gain for the one-month summer term was six months. Among the most proficient students were four veterans who averaged two years' progress in one quarter of study. At the same time, there was cause for celebration in the new school when seventeen adult pupils, ten of them veterans, were able to secure high school certificates. For these first graduates, for almost three hundred other graduates in its first decade, and for thousands yet to come, the Opportunity School has truly been appropriately called "The School of the Second Chance."[13]

At first the Opportunity School offered three sessions each year lasting three months, plus the traditional one-month summer session, but later terms consisted of two eighteen-week sessions and a four-week summer term.

In its first half year of existence, there were 275 students enrolled, of whom 82 were veterans, with the average age of students being 23. At the end of the first decade in the new facility, Miss Gray reported a total enrollment of 9,458. Before her retirement in 1957, she was expecting the ten thousandth student to register, an expectation that was exceeded. Throughout this first decade, the average age of students was 26. There were more than twice as many students over 21 as there were in the under-21 age bracket. There were also twice as many males as females, largely because of the G.I. Bill benefits which educated 1,934 veterans.

Students came from homes with an average of 6 children, which helps explain why "dropouts" occurred. The average educational level of students was seventh grade.[14]

The cost of attending the Opportunity School has always been quite low because each student is expected to work for the school for a certain number of hours each week. At the first session of the new school, each 3-month term students paid miscellaneous fees of $18; $75 for food; a barracks room was $15, a private room $21, and family suite $54. In contrast, out of necessity student expenses increased over a decade when the miscellaneous fee was $52; $146.25 for board; rooms were from $22.50 to $40.50 for an individual; a family suite was $81; apartments with a bath were $135. These costs were for a term of 18 weeks.[15]

Miss Gray was able to keep food costs low by economizing in the kitchen with food and poultry produced by the agriculture classes. As the campus and curriculum expanded, students learned by managing a dairy and large farm, including a tree farm and seed laboratory. All of these agricultural projects served a twofold purpose: while they were educational, at the same time they reduced the financial support which had to be supplied by the individual student or the state of South Carolina.[16]

Although returning veterans received government allotments, many Opportunity School students arrived without any funds whatsoever to finance their education. Since Miss Gray was never able to turn anyone away who sincerely sought another chance for learning, she continued to solicit scholarships for worthy students. During the decade of her directorship, she ascertained that a total of $68,000 was contributed for full or partial scholarships. On the occasions when organizations or individuals were not to be found to sponsor deserving students, more than once Miss Gray dipped into her own pocketbook to make student loans, which sometimes were repaid, but sometimes not.[17]

During the first ten years of the South Carolina Opportunity School's operation, the total state appropriation was $1,087,838.66, after out-of-state tuition and G. I. benefits were returned to the State Treasury. Nevertheless, Miss Gray has estimated that the benefits which have accrued from the contributions alumni have made to South Carolina's economic welfare have more than repaid the state for its original investment.[18]

Throughout her entire career, Miss Gray has always encouraged many outside agencies to participate in programs for the welfare of Opportunity School students and their families. Perhaps married students have benefited most from the nursery school concept which was introduced on the Lander College campus in 1943, and was further expanded at Columbia College in 1945. At the new school, this program was financed by the Columbia Pilot Club and operated through the cooperation of the Maternal and Child Health Division of the State Board of Health until 1952, when there was no further demand for its services except during the summer terms. In this program, while mothers attended classes at the Opportunity School, a completely equipped nursery school cared for their children. In addition, classes dealing with child welfare and psychology were offered to the parents.[19]

Moreover, once each month the Maternal and Child Health Division sponsored a "Well Baby Clinic," when apparently healthy children were examined and given immunizations and parents were counseled. In 1951 when state funds for this project were curtailed, this service became sponsored by the Columbia City Union of Kings' Daughters.[20]

In the Opportunity School's large recreation hall, the Columbia Recreation Department and the Junior League taught both square dancing and ballroom dancing. Other recreation was planned around outdoor games and the school's scenic lake.

Another agency whose cooperation permitted an expansion of the curriculum was the Red Cross. Instructors from this service organization taught classes in lifesaving, swimming, and home nursing.

Moreover, several agencies cooperated by providing either full or partial scholarships to needy students. These included the Department of Public Welfare, Division of Vocational Rehabilitation, Hearing and Speech Correction Services of the State Department of Education, Family Welfare, and the Children's Bureau.

During the years, Miss Gray continued to operate the school as an adult education center. Furthermore, during her tenure at the Opportunity School, more than 15,000 participants took part in various conferences. Moreover, distinguished visitors from all over the world came to study the methods employed at the school because its reputation had become known internationally. Columbia University frequently sent foreign educators to visit the school, for they considered

195

it to be a model worthy of emulation.[21]

To demonstrate that the Opportunity School has been a bridge to high school and college for hundreds who dropped out of public school, Miss Gray has reported that from 1941 through 1956, 280 students were awarded state high school certificates, 45 of whom had already gone on to graduate from college. Moreover, 68 others either returned to public school and graduated from high school or college or received some credit for college or trade school study before the Opportunity School's certification program went into effect. Not only have Opportunity School alumni received bachelor's degrees, but also many advanced degrees have been earned as well. Physicians, teachers, artists, professors, journalists, pharmacists, nurses, researchers, ministers—these are only a few professions in which Opportunity School graduates have achieved outstanding success.[22] Surely the investment in the Opportunity School by the state of South Carolina had reaped an abundant harvest!

Nevertheless, Miss Gray much prefers to relate warm, true stories of her students' accomplishments rather than to cite cold statistical data. She has told of a young man, age thirty-seven, who came to the school in September 1947. At the age of thirteen he had dropped out of school after completing the seventh grade. He received his high school certificate in February 1948, but remained in school until June when he entered the University of South Carolina. In June 1951, he was awarded his Bachelor of Arts degree and his Master of Arts in June 1953. He had accomplished all of this despite the fact that he worked full-time on a night shift for one year and taught school for another year.

Mrs. L. had been yearning to complete her education for a long time and finally persuaded her husband, an assistant foreman in a large textile plant, to resign and move to the Opportunity School in January 1952, so they both could resume their education. Although she had not gone beyond the fifth grade in public school, her placement tests showed she was capable of functioning at the eighth-grade level. Thus she was able to make rapid progress. Her husband had been an eighth-grade dropout, but in only three months of study he was able to successfully pass the high school examination and was immediately offered a much more lucrative position by his former employer.

When a nurses aide was asked by a hospital patient why she was not a registered nurse, she recited the typical reason of having to drop out of school to go to work. The patient saw her potential and arranged for a scholarship at the Opportunity School. She quickly became a class leader and was soon able to graduate and begin her training as a nurse.

Mrs. D. entered the Opportunity School in September 1947, with only a ninth-grade education. In only three months she earned a diploma and entered Columbia College where she was granted a work scholarship for four years. In college, she was editor of the school journal and state publicity chairman of the Baptist Student Union. After earning her degree in 1952, she became an outstanding member of the teaching profession.

During the years preceding her retirement, Miss Gray carefully preserved the voluminous correspondence she received from former pupils. Perhaps she believed that some day she would have the leisure time to reminisce and relive those busy days which had flown by so quickly.

One student wrote:

> In the summer of 1939 at Clemson College I acquired the grit and determination to go on to school, though little did I realize when I made this statement to you that it would be a reality: 'I'd be willing to go hungry could I only go to school.' I did go hungry for twenty-seven months in a German prison camp. But after my liberation I needed rehabilitation, and I found that readjustment when I returned to the Opportunity School in 1946 upon your request. I began to acquire determination again, and now, Miss Gray, I can see the pay-off—I'm on the Dean's Honor Roll, have had some of my work publicized, and will have finished my four years of work in two more semesters. Had not the 'spunk, get-up-and-go' been aroused in me, I'm sure I'd just be drifting along from one small job to another, with no knowledge of the better things in life . . . The Opportunity School, in my estimation, is the most wonderful of its type in the South.

This student who began studying on a National Youth Administration scholarship in 1939 and earned a diploma from the Opportunity School, went on to become a college graduate and successful artist. He was later offered an opportunity to study art in Paris, France.[23]

Because of the tremendous success of the Opportunity School, in his opening speech to the General Assembly on January 9, 1957, Governor Timmerman stated:

197

... I have examined carefully the accomplishments of the South Carolina Opportunity School and have weighed these accomplishments against the continuing need for the school. As a result of this study I am convinced that the South Carolina Opportunity School should now take its place among the other proud and effective educational institutions of South Carolina as an independent, self-perpetuating facility governed by a board of trustees.

I urge the General Assembly to enact legislation which will make the Opportunity School of South Carolina a self-governing, permanent part of our educational system, thus insuring that the equality of educational opportunity the school has provided for thirty-five years will continue to enhance the welfare of our citizens.[24]

The Governor's recommendation was received favorably by the General Assembly and therefore it was given an independent status and placed under the jurisdiction of an eleven-member board of trustees. Immediately after Miss Gray's retirement she was appointed as Director Emeritus, and has continued to take an active interest in Opportunity School affairs, especially the promotion of a scholarship trust fund for worthy students.[25]

The admitted highlight of Miss Gray's career occurred as she was about to bow out as the Director of the South Carolina Opportunity School. In a joint session, the General Assembly for the first time in its distinguished history, honored a female educator and applauded Miss Gray's service in a final curtain call which was well earned after the starring role she had played for more than half a century in the annals of South Carolina's educational history. After a glowing introduction by Dr. Carlisle Holler, a former supervisor of Miss Gray for many years, not as a prima donna, but with her characteristic humility, she protested that the honor was not hers alone, but also belonged to others who had helped her along the way. Then she dramatically presented to Mr. Solomon Blatt, the Speaker of the House, a deed for the Opportunity School property, now worth more than two million dollars. She had fulfilled the pledge she made to the federal government a decade before, that she promised to occupy the property for a period of ten years while building a training center for adults—those who were seeking further education, with an emphasis on "personal development, vocational efficiency, and effective citizenship."[26] It was almost inevitable that the institution

198

became the Wil Lou Gray Opportunity School.

Miss Gray's only regret during the last decade of her service to the state of South Carolina as Director of the Opportunity School, was that she was never able to gain support for her proposed Opportunity School for Negroes. Even after the Supreme Court decision of 1954 which shattered the bulwark of segregation, an equal opportunity for Negroes at the Opportunity School was late in coming. It seemed that no matter how the Director struggled, the time was not yet ripe, and it was not in her destiny to achieve this final triumph—equality of educational opportunity for all South Carolinians. Nevertheless, it was not she who failed, but an unenlightened leadership not yet ready to concede to the premise upon which she had based her entire life and labors—that each citizen deserved an equal chance to complete an education.

View of the S.C. Opportunity School of West Columbia in 1947

199

Views of the modern multi-million-dollar campus at the Wil Lou Gray
Opportunity School

NOTES

[1]*Seventy-ninth Annual Report of Superintendent of Education* (Columbia: State Department of Education, 1947), p. 30.

[2]*Seventy-eighth Annual Report of Superintendent of Education* (Columbia: State Department of Education, 1946), pp. 63-64.

[3]Ibid., pp. 64-65.

[4]*Seventy-ninth Annual Report, p. 45.*

[5]*Ibid., p. 46.*

[6]*Ibid., p. 67.*

[7]*A government utilization survey of the property was made and ended with the following commendation: "It is believed that the operation of this school . . . reflects one of the best cases of utilization of Government property." Report to the Opportunity School, 2 December 1954.*

[8]*Seventy-ninth Annual Report,* p. 46.

[9]Ibid., p. 49.

[10]Ibid.

[11]Wil Lou Gray, *Opportunity School Handbook*, 1949, p. 3.

[12]*Seventy-ninth Annual Report*, p. 51.

[13]Ibid., p. 56.

[14]*Eighty-eighth Annual Report of Superintendent of Education* (Columbia: State Department of Education, 1956), p. 277.

[15]*Seventy-ninth Annual Report*, p. 57.

[16]Ibid.

[17]*Eighty-eighth Annual Report,* p. 278.

[18]Ibid., pp. 277-78.

[19]Ibid., p. 280.

[20]Ibid.

[21]Ibid., p. 277.

[22]*Eighty-seventh Annual Report of Superintendent of Education* (Columbia: State Department of Education, 1955), p. 272.

[23]Wil Lou Gray, "Opportunity School Bulletin," 1955.

200

[24]Wil Lou Gray, "Steps in Obtaining the Opportunity School Property," 1957, p. 8, unpublished.

[25]Ibid.

[26]*Seventy-ninth Annual Report*, p. 46.

REFERENCES

Gray, Wil Lou, and Tolbert, Marguerite. *A Brief Manual for Adult Teachers of South Carolina.* Columbia: State Department of Education, 1948.

Gray, Wil Lou, and Tolbert, Marguerite. *A Brief Manual for Adult Teachers of South Carolina.* Columbia: State Department of Education, 1952.

Gray, Wil Lou, and Tolbert, Marguerite. *A Brief Manual for Adult Teachers of South Carolina.* Columbia: State Department of Education, 1954.

Gray, Wil Lou. *Opportunity School Handbook,* 1949.

Gray, Wil Lou. "Steps in Obtaining the Opportunity School Property," 1957.

Gray, Wil Lou. "Year-Round Opportunity." *Mountain Life and Work,* Fall 1946.

Eightieth Annual Report of Superintendent of Education. Columbia: State Department of Education, 1948.

Eighty-first Annual Report of Superintendent of Education. Columbia: State Department of Education, 1949.

Eighty-second Annual Report of Superintendent of Education. Columbia: State Department of Education, 1950.

Eighty-third Annual Report of Superintendent of Education. Columbia: State Department of Education, 1951.

Eighty-fourth Annual Report of Superintendent of Education. Columbia: State Department of Education, 1952.

Eighty-fifth Annual Report of Superintendent of Education. Columbia: State Department of Education, 1953.

Eighty-sixth Annual Report of Superintendent of Education. Columbia: State Department of Education, 1954.

Eighty-seventh Annual Report of Superintendent of Education. Columbia: State Department of Education, 1955.

Eighty-eighth Annual Report of Superintendent of Education. Columbia: State Department of Education, 1956.

Eighty-ninth Annual Report of Superintendent of Education. Columbia: State Department of Education, 1957.

Seventy-eighth Annual Report of Superintendent of Education. Columbia: State Department of Education, 1946.

Seventy-ninth Annual Report of Superintendent of Education. Columbia: State Department of Education, 1947.

CHAPTER XIV

Retirement - Never!

> The only true retirement is that of the heart . . .
>
> William Hazlitt

Miss Gray officially retired on August 29, 1957, the occasion of her seventy-fourth birthday. Early in December she wrote a letter to all of her alumni friends which read in part:

> You'll be interested to know I have had no retirement heartaches. Nothing has been taken away from me. I still have the school, my church, and my community to serve when they need me. I have the pleasant task of getting the scholarships this year. What could be nicer than asking those who are able to invest in fine students? I am assisting with a project for Senior Citizens at my church, and I am now able to accept my share of responsibility with community activities and various clubs which helped us at school. I still have my family and my friends to love and enjoy, and my house to develop into a home. Tomorrow, with the help of a specialist, we'll begin to turn my yard into a garden, and thus create beauty by painting a picture through landscaping. Tomorrow, also, I meet with an Opportunity School Alumni Committee to complete a task I had hoped to do before August 29, but the sun just wouldn't stand still.

Then almost a year later, when many retirees begin to wail the "retirement blues," Miss Gray wrote:

> You will be interested to know that I am enjoying retirement, with days too short, and never a dull moment.

203

I can't see why time flies so rapidly now, when it used to be so long between Christmases. Neither do I understand why I see so many things to be done. The first four months after retiring I struggled with the painters, the plumbers, and the decorator in getting re-established in my home. Incidentally, I made the most and easiest money per hour I ever made, by chiseling two rows of brick off of a mantel I wished to lower, before calling in the brick mason! Three months of 1958 were spent in Miami with my sister who was ill. Two out-of-state educational conferences have been enjoyed, one in Louisville on Education beyond the High School, the other the Adult Education Conference in Cincinnati. The rest of the year I have been catching up on loose ends in life—working with the AAUW, BPW, SFWC, College Alumni Club, Garden Club, Church, and other organizations, as well as soliciting money for scholarships and running a home. It has been a joy to have time to read books and papers without hurry. Just today I enjoyed vicariously a Winthrop Alumnae Seminar on moral and spiritual values . . .

In this same letter Miss Gray explained what prompted her to begin her volunteer service to the Senior Citizens of America. She wrote:

Because I have seen the pathos of older people giving up and living only in the lives of their children, I have agreed to act as State Director of Senior Citizens of America. It is a volunteer job, but then I believe that after retirement if it is possible we should give the rest of our lives in service to our community which has done so much for us. The challenge in the field of aging is unlimited. I'm convinced that only by being interested in people beyond our family groups can we stay mentally and socially alive, so I'm trying to be alive as long as I live.

Because Miss Gray's retirement had not changed her, she determined to expend most of her time and still quite considerable energy in assistance for the aged and aging citizens of South Carolina because she recognized that this was another neglected portion of the state's population. Her pugnacious spirit as she organized a publicity campaign and contacted powerful state leaders, including the governor, was quite the same spirit in evidence as she battled for her permanent Opportunity School.

The first state-wide effort to pinpoint problems of the aging and aged was a conference workshop, "Live Long and Like It," which Miss Gray organized in January, 1957, at the South Carolina Opportunity School, under the auspices of the American Association of University Women and the Opportunity School. She became chairman of a temporary steering committee which formulated two goals: (1) appointment of a legislative committee to study the problems of senior citizens; (2) organization of a branch of Senior Citizens of America, to encourage personal growth and community service. However, it was not until May 1959, that the State Branch of Senior Citizens was organized in another meeting at the Opportunity School and Miss Gray was elected State Director. In September 1959, the State Commission on Aging was organized and received a federal grant of $15,000 for a state-wide study. By 1960 Miss Gray had organized all counties in the state, and had enlisted the help of 500 volunteers, many of whom were members of Senior Citizens of America. That same year 200 citizens, laymen, and professionals met in Columbia for a local White House Conference on Aging. This group compiled a survey, "The Aging Population in South Carolina" and forwarded it to the Secretary of the Department of Health, Education and Welfare. Then in January 1961, when President Kennedy called the White House Conference on Aging, Miss Gray was among 24 delegates from South Carolina attending this meeting.[1]

It was not until 1966 that all of Miss Gray's efforts bore fruit, for it was then that the South Carolina General Assembly created the South Carolina Interagency Council on Aging. This council was designated to administer federal funds available under Title III of the Older Americans Act of 1965. In 1971 the Council was transformed into a Commission, and its organizational structure altered to allow for a more efficient, responsive administration. That same year this group presented to Miss Gray its "Distinguished Older South Carolinian Award ...in recognition of achievement and influence beneficial to community and state."[2]

In the meantime, Miss Gray singlehandedly organized and sponsored another agency, the South Carolina Federation on Aging, which acted as a more direct voice of the state's senior citizens, working in conjunction with the South Carolina Commission on Aging. It was in recognition of this service that the Federation in 1973 elected Miss Gray to honorary life membership in the organization, and in 1974 named her as a co-recipient of its "Outstanding South Carolinian Award."[3]

Miss Gray had become a close personal friend of the founder of Senior Citizens of America, Dr. Joy Elmer Morgan, and she had embraced wholeheartedly his philosophy: "The unused talent now going to waste among persons who think they are on the shelf could win world peace, mitigate racial tensions, help economically less advanced peoples to gain the advantages of progress, and give a new sense of adventure and hope to life throughout the earth."[4] Therefore, Miss Gray developed a program to assist the state's senior citizens, and encouraged their participation in many activities that might broaden their horizons.

When the General Assembly in May 1961, enacted a resolution providing for celebration of May as Senior Citizens Month, this was the first recognition of its kind to older citizens in America. The next year Miss Gray inaugurated "Senior Citizens' Day" at the State Fair, where prizes were awarded for the oldest man and woman present, the couple married the longest, and the county with the most representatives. The day was so successful it became an annual tradition. A nutrition program provided people aged sixty or more and their spouses with low-cost, nutritionally sound, hot meals five days a week. The University of South Carolina made an in-depth study of the institutionalized elderly in this state. A Social Indicator Survey made a study of the needs of older persons by personal interviews in the home. Radio station WNOK broadcast a program for and about older South Carolinians. Educational television developed slide-tape programs to disseminate information about aging. An awards program was initiated to recognize outstanding older persons and those working in behalf of the elderly. Also the Commission on Aging cooperated with Clemson University's Department of Park and Recreation Administration to sponsor a camping program at Oconee State Park for those who would have no other opportunity for a vacation. An "Open House for Senior Citizens" observed "Older American Month," coordinated by the Commission on Aging and the University of South Carolina. The finale of this celebration occurred as 1500 senior citizens gathered at Carolina Coliseum,and observed as Miss Gray became the co-recipient of the "Outstanding Older Citizen Award" for 1974.[5]

Since Miss Gray is a firm believer in learning "from the cradle to the grave," she planned a "College Week for Senior Citizens." These one-week sessions at Clemson University were mini-semesters, modeled after a college schedule, and sixty recreational and educational courses were designed for senior citizens. Participants elected such courses as nutrition, fabric care, art history, personal finances, scrap sculpture, physical fitness, self-concept, painting, drawing, poetry workshop, housing for the elderly, financial planning, the ethics of death and dying, writing a living will, early history of South Carolina, and "retired and ready to help."[6]

Miss Gray is still vitally concerned with these social service organizations. It will continue to be her goal to assist other senior citizens in maintaining their economic self-sufficiency and in their continuation as contributing citizens of their communities. In recognition of her continuing efforts on behalf of senior citizens, she has been awarded citations in 1976 and 1978, as "an advocate of programs to uplift the aging and the elderly, and the moving force behind the creation of the South Carolina Commission on Aging and the South Carolina Federation of Older Americans."[7]

At the same time Miss Gray was actively engaged in promoting the cause of South Carolina's senior citizens, she continued to demonstrate her concern for the welfare of the students at the Opportunity School. When she had retired as the Director of the South Carolina Opportunity School in 1957, she did not intend for her service to the school to terminate. During the past two decades, she has promoted and secured scholarship funds for worthy students.

Miss Gray had first planned to retire at the conventional age of sixty-five, but the acquisition of the property in West Columbia and the fruition of all her hopes and dreams for a permanent school presented a challenge to which she had to respond. She felt compelled to witness the Opportunity School become a functional, independent entity under her leadership. At the same time she decided to delay her retirement, she pledged that any salary she might earn was to be returned to the school in the form of scholarships.

At first, this pledge was to be a provision in her will, but Miss Gray soon decided that she preferred to see the money being used by deserving students. This was to be her "thank you" to the South Carolina General Assembly, to churches, civic and fraternal organizations, business and industry, and thousands of individuals "who have made it possible for the school to be giving such wonderful service to the people of the state."[8]

In December 1961, Miss Gray issued a challenge to the Alumni

207

Association to match her offer of $12,500 as the beginning of a campaign for one hundred named scholarships given "in appreciation of," "in honor of" or "in memory of," individuals who have been builders of a greater South Carolina. On July 16, 1966, her challenge was met; the scholarship fund reached approximately $100,000.

Not content with this achievement, Miss Gray in 1968 "electrified those present at the South Carolina Opportunity School's Alumni banquet, Friday, December 6, by the announcement of a trust fund of $50,000 for scholarships to the school." However, again there was the stipulation that the funds were not available for use until the Alumni Association could raise an equal amount.[9]

Since then, Miss Gray has envisioned an even more ambitious philanthropy:

'The Builders' Trust' is the culmination of a dream I've had for many years: the dream of helping a great many South Carolinians along the road to better citizenship by giving them a chance they never had before.

I'm thinking about the thousands of people, whatever their ages might be now, who were forced to drop out of school in their early teens and go to work out of necessity.

Many of these people have been helped by the Opportunity School over the years, of course, but there are still so many more to be helped.

This is why we have established 'The Builders' Trust'— to help build a few more monuments to human kindness and good citizenship.

What we have is a trust fund, with two million dollars as our goal, to provide scholarships in perpetuity to the Opportunity School for one hundred of these deserving folks. (It takes about fifteen thousand dollars to produce one scholarship of six hundred dollars a year.)

Our special thanks to the many special people who have been so generous . . . $5,000 from Dr. Jane Bruce Guignard . . . $12,500 from Mrs. Russell Grumman . . . over $15,000 in Winn-Dixie stock from Mrs. Hubbard Harris and a like amount in Sonoco stock from Mrs. David Coker.

But equally important are the gifts and pledges that have come from the alumni of the school and others connected with the school. One of our graduates did well enough with his 'second chance' that he pledged $12,500 to the trust . . . another graduate who was one of nineteen children sent in a $50 gift not long ago, her entire take-home pay for a week . . . and another young lady pledged

208

$45 to the Trust and faithfully sent in a dollar a week for almost a year until she had paid her pledge in full.

We'll name the scholarships for each of these people, and for everyone who contributes, and we'd like to name one for you, too. Anyone who can give or pledge to 'The Builders' Trust' will be warmly received and it will help to build the most valuable gift we could ever give to our State.

Not only has Miss Gray made large contributions to the Opportunity School, but in 1978 she gave property worth more than $50,000 to her alma mater, Columbia College. Any funds which accrue from this investment will be earmarked for the "Wil Lou Gray Endowment Scholarship Fund."[10]

In 1975 Miss Gray wrote in one of her many letters to the alumni of the Opportunity School, "There's never a dull moment. I could live two lives and both would be interesting." One project she undertook at this time which certainly lent interest to her "retirement" days, was the development of an educational game called "Palmetto Patriots."

Miss Gray has always been concerned about a large segment of society that apparently feels no loyalty or appreciation for America. When the Retired Teachers Association asked her to serve on the Bicentennial Committee, "Pride in America," she felt it was appropriate to develop a game that encouraged better citizenship and loyalty. Another purpose was to add to the Opportunity School trust fund for scholarships from the proceeds of sales.

Miss Gray, despite her ninety-two years at the time, was the moving force behind the game's development. Patterned after the game of "Authors," "Palmetto Patriots" features men and women who have made "valuable contributions to the quality of life" in the Palmetto State throughout the years. Four prominent South Carolina historians were asked to select the thirty patriots whose faces appear on the double-deck of cards and to write an accompanying booklet giving their biographical profiles. Miss Gray hoped that the game was to become an enjoyable way for South Carolina school children to learn about their heritage. Her admirers feel certain that one day Miss Gray, herself, will be among the Palmetto Patriots.

Wil Lou Gray at the age of 90

Wil Lou Gray, State Director, Senior Citizens
of America, on April 29, 1962, as Governor
Ernest F. Hollings signs a proclamation for
celebrating the first Senior Citizens Month

Wil Lou Gray II, a student at Columbia College, unveils the portrait of her distinguished aunt at an alumni banquet in 1958. This gift from friends, faculty, and alumni, was painted by Mrs. Katherine Clark, head of the art department at the Opportunity School.

NOTES

[1]"South Carolina . . . The Aging and Aged," *Progress Report of State Branch of Senior Citizens of America,* February 1962.

[2]On display at Archives of Wil Lou Gray Opportunity School, West Columbia, South Carolina.

[3]Charles M. Aull, Director, South Carolina Federation on Aging, to Wil Lou Gray, 20 November 1973.

[4]"South Carolina . . . The Aging and Aged."

[5]*Eighth Annual Report,* South Carolina Commission on Aging, 1974, p. 16.

[6]*Clemson College Continuing Education Center Bulletin,* 1959.

[7]On display at Archives of Wil Lou Gray Opportunity School, West Columbia, South Carolina.

[8]Wil Lou Gray to Opportunity School Alumni, January 1958.

[9]*The Journal*, West Columbia, South Carolina, 11 December 1968.

[10]*Columbia College Magazine*, Spring/Summer 1984, p. 5.

REFERENCES

Clemson College Continuing Education Center Bulletin, 1959.

Columbia College Magazine. Spring/Summer 1984.

Gray, Wil Lou. Columbia, South Carolina. Interview, 10 March 1979.

Journal. West Columbia, South Carolina, 11 December 1968.

Progress Report of State Branch of Senior Citizens of America. "South Carolina . . . The Aging and Aged," February 1962.

South Carolina Commission on Aging. *Eighth Annual Report*, 1974.

CHAPTER XV

The Gray Mystique

> I shall pass through this world but once.
> If, therefore, there be any kindness
> I can show,
> Or any good thing I can do,
> Let me do it now.
> Let me not defer it or neglect it,
> For I shall not pass this way again.
> Attributed to Etienne de Grellet

Three major forces have directed Wil Lou Gray's destiny and molded her personality: (1) her deep religious convictions, (2) close family ties, and (3) the philosophies of other educators whom she has sought to emulate.

Wil Lou was born into a family of devout Methodists. Her parents loved their church and brought up their children to be regular in their attendance at worship services and to contribute their tithes and service cheerfully. The Gray children were taught to obey the Ten Commandments and to follow the Golden Rule. From the time Wil Lou was a tiny child, she knew how to pray, and all her life she has been comforted in times of bereavement or travail with what she called "conversations with my Creator." No matter how long her day has been, or how late the hour, Wil Lou has never gone to sleep without saying her prayers.

In a letter written to her family on Easter Sunday, 1975, Wil Lou recalls the vivid religious emotion she experienced when she was a young student at Columbia College:

... It was a beautiful Easter day in 1902. I did not go home for the holidays, an extra expense for Papa. Alone in my room I was reading the story of Jesus' death and resurrection. I found myself crying for I had not realized the sacrifice he made for me. Since then He has been my guiding star, freeing me from many of life's frustrations. Here I am, 1975, seventy-three years afterwards, alone in my sitting room, reading the same story . . .

Very early in her career, Miss Gray had stated that "ours is a Christian challenge," and "our work is applied Christianity." Hence, she never planned a curriculum without scheduling specified times for devotions. Also, she planned chapel and vesper services in all of the Opportunity Schools, and students were expected to attend, for she considered their exposure to the spiritual realm to be fully as important as the enrichment of their intellectual lives through education.

Not only does Wil Lou have complete trust in God, who is always solicitous of her welfare, but she also has a sublime faith in other human beings. For example, she often used to travel across the state at night, both to avoid the harsh rays of the sun—the bane of her existence—and to save time. Her family and friends fussed and fretted over this habit, and suggested she find a traveling companion when she knew she was to be on the road at night, for they feared for her safety. They knew also that when she saw a hitchhiker on the road, she was unable to pass him by.

Late one night she realized she was to travel over the desolate old Highway 76, which then twisted and turned over the many bridges of the great Wateree River Swamp. For once she heeded the advice of those concerned about her safety as she wondered what was to happen if she had a flat tire or other car trouble on such a deserted stretch of road. Therefore, she stopped at a hotel in Sumter to inquire if there was anyone waiting to ride a night train or bus to Columbia who might be willing to ride along with her instead. As she made this inquiry to the desk clerk, a perfect stranger sitting in the lobby spoke up and volunteered to accompany her. When her family the next morning protested at what she had done, Wil Lou replied that she was simply doing as they had suggested, to put their minds at ease!

Perhaps Wil Lou does have a guardian angel protecting her throughout the years, but more than likely people perceive the deep trust she communicates, and they feel they cannot betray that trust. There are thousands of former adult students who have completed an education,

212

led more successful lives, and repaid student loans, because Wil Lou had trusted them and had faith that her trust was not to be betrayed.

At times this deep trust has been construed by those closest to her as naiveté. One former Opportunity School student, the son of a poor sharecropper, became a multi-millionaire a few short years after entering the business world, and in 1969 pledged a perpetual endowment of one million dollars to the Opportunity School. In 1972 he was the principal speaker at commencement and presented a check for fifty thousand dollars to Superintendent Willis, the interest from the endowment fund. In 1973 his "empire collapsed under an avalanche of legal challenges" and his trial dragged on for several years.[1] Throughout the entire ordeal Wil Lou's faith in him never wavered, and she was one of the few to believe his statement that he had "unknowingly violated security laws." Moreover, her total faith led her to stipulate that his first contribution, the fifty thousand dollars, was to be held in reserve to aid in conducting his defense, if necessary!

Not only was Wil Lou fortunate in having a family with profound religious convictions, they also inculcated in their offspring a strong sense of family solidarity. She was further blessed with parents and grandparents who encouraged ambition, sobriety, industry, and integrity in their children. They also were firm believers in the best education possible for all members of the family.

Wil Lou vividly remembers attending her first family reunion in 1893 at Gray Court, at the home of Uncle Bob Gray. At that time every member of the family lived within a twenty-five-mile radius, but today they are scattered from the Atlantic to the Pacific. Then there were fifty family members, while today there are more than two hundred.

The Gray family has always been very close and enjoyed many family get-togethers through the years, but they will never forget one special reunion which Wil Lou planned. This occasion was on March 31, 1968, when a luncheon was held at the Opportunity School to honor Wil Lou's grandparents, and every descendant then living was invited to attend. They were to come for a time of family fellowship and visitation and to develop the Gray family archives. Wil Lou further wanted to give recognition to her family for the supportive roles they had played as she had starred in the dramatic struggle to free South Carolina from its shackles of illiteracy.

213

Ever since Dial's donation to the school at Tamassee, her family has been her staunchest supporters. Her father often visited the Opportunity Schools in their various locations and became a campus favorite with students and faculty alike. Moreover, five of her first cousins had served as teachers in various schools she supervised. Additionally, seven distant cousins have served as volunteer teachers or librarians, without pay.

At all family reunions Marguerite Tolbert is the family historian. As such, she keeps careful records of these events, traces genealogies, and writes editions of the Gray Journal so each relative can be aware of his heritage.

Through the years, Wil Lou has survived as most members of her immediate family have passed on—her father in 1932, her stepmother some twenty years later, and her half-brother in 1976. She was devastated in November 1946, when both Coke and Dial, the brothers to whom she was so deeply devoted, died within twelve hours of each other. It was fortunate that this occurred during the same time she was frantically attempting the acquisition of the site for the Opportunity School because she was forced to stifle her bereavement and use her work as a catharsis for her grief.

Her half-sister Hattie, a writer and poet whose work has received critical acclaim in literary circles, is the only surviving member of her immediate family. Although Hattie lives in Florida, she visits Wil Lou in Columbia for several weeks at least once each year, and stays in close contact at other times with frequent telephone calls and letters.

Perhaps Wil Lou's closest relative at the present is Marguerite Tolbert, both in proximity and relationship. As she lives in the apartment across the hall from Wil Lou, the two cousins are available at any hour of the day or night to visit or to lend assistance to each other. They still feel especially close since they worked together and shared the same experiences for so many years. Wil Lou is the first to admit that through the years, she always turned first to Marguerite to "help her pull her chestnuts out of the fire," as she sometimes assumed too much responsibility for one human being to undertake. More than once Wil Lou remembers driving over muddy country roads with Marguerite on the way to end a frantic daily schedule as honorary guests at a commencement or banquet. As one of the cousins drove at a breakneck pace to reach their destination on time, the other was changing into her long gown brought along for the special occasion. Then the drivers alternated positions in order for both to be appropriately attired. One time Wil Lou felt "undressed" for the occasion, for her long petticoat had flown out of the window into a mud puddle as Marguerite raced down the bumpy road.

Marguerite's great love, admiration, and unselfish support of her cousin is attested to in the following letter which she wrote to the committee chairman who was planning to bestow yet another honor upon Wil Lou on the eve of her retirement. She wrote:

> There is only one Wil Lou Gray and there will never be another like her. Hence, I long to be a Boswell who could give a real appreciation of this wonderful person—not just a panegyric.
>
> First, let me comment on her imagination and vision. Her dreams are as big as the earth, but somehow she can always make her dreams come true. She had to buck traditions and the leading educators of this State to get them to agree to awarding an equivalency high school certificate to citizens who successfully passed a State high school examination. This was quite an innovation back in the thirties; now it is an accepted pattern of procedure. One of her students, Mr. Charles L. Magalis, Jr., President of Vogue Press, has the distinction of having attained the first high school equivalency certificate . . .
>
> A clique of businessmen in Lexington fought Wil Lou's efforts to secure from the Federal Government the hospital area of the Columbia Army Air Base, the site of the present Opportunity School. They wanted to use this valuable area for their personal financial aggrandizement. But, with her stubborn determination, she was successful in obtaining this two million dollar property, almost single-handed, for the State of South Carolina. Not one cent was ever charged to the State to defray the costs of her many trips to Washington to promote this project. What a legacy to leave the State! However, the thousands of lives she had touched will prove a greater monument to her love and unselfish devotion—the greatest legacy of all.
>
> Wil Lou is the soul of generosity. Her heart is as big as the world itself. When one considers that she could have remained in a lovely home, surrounded by comforts and luxuries, one is amazed that she has dedicated her life without stint and without limit to others. She has worked

indefatigably, denied herself, worn old hats and coats, taken boarders, that she might have more money to invest in others who did not have the educational opportunities they merited.

Wil Lou could have been a top-flight financier and rivaled her brother who was a business genius. She is a regular King Midas; anything she touches turns to gold. Thus, the unselfish dedication of her life to education and people—she began with $35 per month and worked for years for not more than $150—is all the more amazing when one considers that she might have accumulated a fortune for a life of ease and pleasure.

Wil Lou's spirit of hospitality is one of her many gracious attributes. Her home and her heart are always open to her friends, the millionaire or the illiterate. She has the rare charm of being able to make everyone feel at home; she just sets another place at the table.

The greatest miracle of all is how one woman could accomplish so much. A pioneer in adult education, she has made a name for herself around the world. What began as a volunteer service in her country school developed into her life work. Learned and popular magazines have told the thrilling story of her life and achievements. She has won every coveted honor. Her spirit is still young. She has grown old gently and gracefully. She still dreams dreams. Her dynamic drive still inspires her to greater achievements, and we are all holding our breath, now that she talks of retiring, with: 'What next, Wil Lou?' On her lips is the answer: 'Come and grow old with me. The best is yet to be.'

Finally, Wil Lou's appreciations have colored her entire life: fine family traditions, her love of people, beauty, spiritual values, the commonplace, and understanding and consideration of the lowly and the poor in heart. I believe that she has been more thrilled over a family from the mountain fastnesses of Pickens County than with her wonderful friends from Vassar, Yale, and Randolph-Macon. Her life has been an inspiration to us all. . .[2]

In addition to the members of her family, Wil Lou acknowledges that she has been greatly influenced by other educators with whom she has come in close contact. As she worked with W.K. Tate, her Rural Supervisor in Laurens County from 1910 to 1914, she began to see the need of a militant stand against illiteracy as he broadened her understanding of the educational needs of South Carolina's citizens, whether young or old. In 1912, Mr. Tate had written to his young

216

protégée his definition of "true culture," which was adopted by Wil Lou as a vital part of her philosophy. He wrote:

A wholesome optimism and a broad, deep human sympathy are necessary elements in any true culture. As the truly cultured man mingles with his fellow men of every rank and station, he will have joy in their worthy successes, respect for their honest failures and forgiveness for their human frailties; he will meet his own life problems with a triumphant faith in God who rules for ultimate good the destinies of the universe.[3]

Another learned educator to whom Wil Lou is greatly indebted is Dr. Patterson Wardlaw, the Chairman of the first active Illiteracy Commission in South Carolina, and for many years the Dean of the School of Education at the University of South Carolina. Dr. Wardlaw made her aware that the search for truth is a never-ending quest which we must make available to all citizens. The following poem, "A Christmas Sentiment," written in 1918, embodies his philosophy:

I plead the right of the unlettered man
In a larger world to live
Than is measured by his senses' span
And the word his neighbors give.

I plead 'gainst slavery of the mind.
That none dependent be
On his group, but each for self shall find
The tools that shall make him free.

Then from her year of graduate study at Vanderbilt University, Wil Lou was more than a little influenced by attending the classes of Dr. Jones and from living in the home of Dr. Vaughan. From these two scholars she learned to follow the precepts of being a good citizen, being actively concerned about the condition of others less fortunate, serving her state and community as repayment for her education, and sharing whatever she has with others.

There are other facets to her personality which cannot be attributed to any particular influence, but nonetheless have come to be known as Wil Lou's trademarks. Wil Lou is still actively concerned in the politics of her nation, state, and community, and as an avid Democrat, she supports her party wholeheartedly. She chose this party because "I am old enough to remember early days of my life when under Republican regimes we lived in nearly a moneyless world and only a limited number had the advantages of education." For her many years of political involvement, the Democratic Women's Club of Richland County granted a life membership to a "dyed-in-the-wool Democrat."

Wil Lou has a shrewd mind for business, just as her father before her. As an example, in 1931 she built the three-story brick house which is still her home. This was in the midst of the Depression when she had absolutely no funds in the bank and remembers not being able to pay all of her bills. When she had first come to Columbia in 1918, she had saved enough money to build a home, but she lost her entire life savings when her bank in Columbia failed. However, she did have three residential lots which her father had advised her to buy while he was a member of the General Assembly. By 1931 these lots had greatly appreciated and she was able to exchange two lots as a downpayment to the contractor who was to build her house. She also still had some stocks her father had advised her to buy years before, and these were given to the bank as collateral for the mortgage on her new home. There were five apartment units in her new home, and while she lived very comfortably in one, the other four were always easily rented so the house in reality paid for itself, just as she had planned.

Another of Wil Lou's projects allowed her to indulge in a favorite pastime while she was also making use of her business acumen. She has always had an absolute passion for travel, and since it usually requires a substantial amount of money to indulge a wanderlust, she shrewdly organized the "Gray Tours," a way for her to travel at a profit. By taking groups to various places such as Canada, the New York's World Fair, the Chicago's World Fair, and Washington, D.C., she had all of the fun of making the trips herself, plus the challenge of making all of the arrangements and seeing that all members of the tour had a good time. Sometimes assisted by her brother Dial, beginning in 1921 Wil Lou conducted these tours during her vacations in the summer. However, they had to be discontinued in 1946 when she became totally dedicated to the establishment of the Opportunity School. Even earlier, in 1915 Wil Lou had planned a tour for herself, Marguerite, and several other friends. They traveled by train to New York, stopping off at various points of interest along the way. For the sum of $65, each person enjoyed three weeks of travel; this included all transportation, food, lodging, and entertainment.

Wil Lou's passion for people and worthy causes has prompted her to become a "joiner." She is a devout member of the Washington Street Church, an honorary member of the Wednesday Club of Laurens, Daughters of the American Revolution, American Association for Adult Education, Woman's Club of Columbia, Columbia College Alumnae Association, Columbia College Club, and the South Carolina Rehabilitation Association. In addition, she has been an officer in many other organizations, such as the American Association of University Women, Southeastern Adult Education Association, South Carolina Teachers' Association, South Carolina Federation on Aging, and the South Carolina Commission on Aging. She has been on the Board of Trustees of Columbia College and currently is Director Emeritus of the Wil Lou Gray Opportunity School.

Evidently, Wil Lou is a most gregarious person who not only loves to travel and meet new faces, and enjoys club activities, but she also loves to entertain. She is a gracious hostess whose hospitality and delicious food are well known by any who have visited in her home or at the Opportunity School. Today, she still delights in her maid's day off when she can go to the kitchen and putter to her heart's content. Moreover, she still has her friends over to play Canasta and other card games.

As we review the accomplishments of Wil Lou Gray, we realize that it all would not have been possible without an extraordinary physique. Wil Lou can recall missing very few days of work due to illness other than her bout with influenza in 1918. She was advised to lighten her work load twice, once in 1923 and again in 1937, but after a few weeks of rest she was back on the job, as busy as ever. Her family recalls the time she fell and broke an arm on the way to deliver an important speech, but her tremendous will power enabled her to continue to the meeting, deliver the speech, and only then did she consent to go to her doctor to have the arm attended to.

She did not have a serious ailment until the age of eighty-five, when she suffered a coronary occlusion. Doctors saved her life then by installing a pacemaker. As far as her health was concerned, 1972 was a bad year for her because she had to be hospitalized twice. First, she fell at her home breaking her hip, and this injury took several months to mend. Also that same year she became blind in one eye, but fortunately doctors were able to save her vision after cataract surgery. Except for the usual aches and pains of arthritis, Wil Lou today is extraordinarily healthy. Just recently, after doctors had installed her fourth pacemaker, as she jokingly refers to it—"recharging my battery,"—they assured her she would be good for another twenty years.

It is such fortitude and perseverance that prompted Superintendent James H. Hope to say of Wil Lou:

> Got any rivers they say aren't crossable?
> Got any mountains that can't be cut through?
> We specialize in the wholly impossible
> Doing things no one else can do.
> That's Miss Wil Lou Gray.

Although Wil Lou would not have been able to have achieved all that she did without a tremendous amount of perseverance, there have been those who did not think this an admirable trait, but felt she was downright obstinate. As one state senator put it bluntly: "She is worse than chewing gum in your hair." Although she had to fight for the present Opportunity School site, the conflict was comparatively short-lived. However, there was an interminable battle with some members of the General Assembly to finance adult education through the years. A particularly formidable foe was Senator Edgar Brown from Barnwell, who was never in favor of supporting her program, according to Miss Gray. She has never been able to forget one budget hearing when he unkindly remarked, "Well then, let's give her a little bit to play with."

Today, Wil Lou is no less persevering in her pursuit of the "Builders' Trust." Although there are those who will hide in office closets at her approach, this goal, too, must eventually be attained, if history is an indication of future success.

NOTES

[1]"Glenn Turner, the 44-year-old salesman whose $300 million pyramid sales empire was toppled by fraud litigation, is back in the motivation business with a new line called 'Challenge to America.' *New York Times*, Sunday 27 May 1979; "Glenn Turner, founder of the 'Dare To Be Great' motivational program, is led from court in Phoenix, Arizona, after being sentenced to up to seven years for conspiracy and fraud. . ." *Columbia Record*, Friday 21 August 1987.

[2]Marguerite Tolbert to Russell Grumman, University of North Carolina, 12 March 1956.

[3]W.K. Tate to Wil Lou Gray, March 1912.

REFERENCES

Columbia Record, 21 August 1987.

Gray, Wil Lou. Columbia, South Carolina. Interview, 4 April 1979.

New York Times, 27 May 1979.

CHAPTER XVI

Epilogue - The End of an Era

All lovely things will have an ending,
All lovely things will fade and die...
                                    Conrad Aiken

Miss Wil Lou Gray's final public appearance occurred as a host of friends, relatives, and former students and co-workers assembled at the Opportunity School to celebrate her ninety-eighth birthday on August 29, 1981. As the climax of this gala occasion, "This Is Your Life, Miss Wil Lou Gray," was presented. As the Master of Ceremony, Mr. Joe Pinner of WIS-TV narrated the highlights of Miss Gray's life and career, memorable scenes from her past were projected onto a huge screen while "voices from the past" were introduced.

The first voice Miss Wil Lou recognized was that of her half-sister, Harriet Gray Blackwell:

> Wil Lou Gray is one of the first people I met when I entered this vale of tears. She is my sister. Knowing my disposition it is strange that during all of these years I have never been angry with her, for I have a short fuse which is proper for one with red hair and anger close to my mouth.
>
> The fact that Wil Lou has not faltered in her fight against illiteracy, and that her innate love for humanity has been steadfast, regardless of frailties of the flesh that might have slowed a less arduous member of the human race, have been like a flower growing in the wilderness. It has also made me think that she is truly a disciple of Christ, even in the confusion of today.

222

Aside from her angelic disposition, her human side is delightful. Many of the older generation remember the time when Wil Lou and Miss Agnes McMaster were returning to Columbia from a meeting. There had been an ice storm and the car slipped off the road into a gulch. When the two were rescued, the only available hospital room was in a place for unwed mothers. The headlines screamed that two of the city's most respectable educators were in such a place, but this did not upset Wil Lou.

Wil Lou's success as an educator is well-known, but not everybody is aware that she cooks the best fried oysters ever tasted and that her waffles are beyond belief, but most of her cooking was before the reign of Evelyn.

When I was a child, I cringed every time a visiting missionary spoke at our church. If Wil Lou happened to be present, I could see her going off to 'darkest Africa or some other beknighted place to carry the gospel. I also visualized boa constrictors dropping on her from the jungle and I had to pray extra hard to keep her in this country. Of course, I don't take any credit for her staying here, but I am so glad she did!

Then the words of Miss Wil Lou's first roommate from Columbia College, Mattie May Morgan Allen, were heard:

I first met Wil Lou at Columbia College in September 1901. She was a lovely girl of seventeen years, with red, curly hair, and a beautiful peachy complexion. I was a homesick freshman, crying my eyes out after my father left me saying he would 'see me Christmas.' Wil Lou dashed in, grabbed me, and said, 'Get up and come with me. I have something for you to do.' Since that day, she has always had something for me to do, and I've loved her dearly. (Since her health prevented her attendance, Mattie's words were read by Eugenia Bechtler.)

Mary Nelson Crowe, the first student to enroll at Tamassee, related:

I have always said that Wil Lou should have been named 'Will You,' for she was always asking, 'Will you do this?' or 'Will you do that?' But I always say that she will be remembered among the great people of the world like . . . Dwight L. Moody, who in his zeal for Christ, turned two continents upside down. He begged so much money for his work, he asked them to put on his tombstone, 'The beggar died!' From the meager beginning I remember at Tamassee, Miss Wil Lou's 'Will you's?' have accomplished the wonderful institution we have here

223

today. Her zeal and inspiration, like dropping a pebble into a pool, have been far-reaching to so many people for the enrichment of their own lives and those around them. She taught not only what was in the books but that YOU are someone special, and the world and life have so much to offer if you are willing to reach for the stars.

Miss Wil Lou's cousin, Marguerite, next spoke of their long association working side-by-side for the cause of adult education. Although Marguerite played an important role in the dramatic struggle against illiteracy, she never attempted to share any of the glory accorded to Wil Lou. This evening was no exception as she paid homage to her mentor.

As the pages of Miss Wil Lou's life continued to turn, a succession of former students spoke to her, evoking many memories from the past. Wreford Nabors of Joanna spoke of attending the Opportunity School beginning in 1927. One of his most cherished memories of Miss Wil Lou came from the pilgrimage of 1930 when she carried night school students to Washington and presented a basket of fruit to Herbert Hoover.

Two of four sisters who attended the Opportunity School during the 1930's were in attendance. Laura Stringfield Barkley addressed Miss Wil Lou with these words:

> I shall always remember how you met our group with outstretched hands as we arrived very late at Clemson. The bus coming up from Charleston had mechanical trouble and we had waited in Aiken for hours. Needless to say, we were hot, tired, and hungry, and you hurried us along to the dining room for supper. You have been my friend and guiding light since that first meeting.

Then Laura's sister, Hazel, spoke:

> Knowing you, Miss Wil Lou, since we first met in 1939, has been truly one of life's extras. One of our fondest recollections is that of your bringing a picnic supper a few nights after the burial of our dear mother, and your words of comfort gave us the courage to carry on. You have been our dear friend for forty-two years.

William C. Poole of West Columbia is a second-generation adult student who came to honor Miss Wil Lou with these words:

> I little dreamed as I tagged along with my father as he attended classes at Youngs School near Gray Court, that I would ever be a student of Miss Wil Lou Gray. After my discharge from the military, I was among the first veterans

224

to attend the Opportunity School in its permanent home. I moved from Woodruff with my wife and young son in 1947 because I wanted an education in order to go into business for myself.

I remember the wonderful teachers, good classrooms, and a fine library. We all worked to improve the school, participated in community affairs, raised the money to buy our first bus, and really felt that this was our school. Miss Gray personally taught me in a class she held for those with reading difficulties, but more importantly, she taught us that we could make something of ourselves. So thanks to you, Miss Gray, I have been conducting a successful restaurant business for thirty years.

The final tribute from a former student was paid by Glenn Turner who came from Florida to speak of being Miss Gray's chauffeur as she traversed the state recruiting students and soliciting scholarships for worthy students who had no means of continuing their education.

The last "voice from the past" was that of Mary Major, who spoke of first meeting Miss Wil Lou in 1914 when she was five years old and her father was the pastor of the First Methodist Church in Laurens.

I was a close friend of the Gray family through the years, and became your secretary and sole office assistant in the State Department of Education from 1937 to 1944. I recall that I was your traveling companion and chauffeur at all hours of the day and night, all over South Carolina, up and down the Eastern Seaboard from Miami to New York, helping with tours and pilgrimages, visiting former and prospective students, attending teachers' conferences, contacting Congressmen and legislators, searching for antiques, and just plain visiting for the fun of it. My primary duty, however, was keeping up with your purse!

I have to confess that since the age of five I have felt somewhat guilty because I failed to accomplish something that you asked me to do. When you discovered that Henrietta, the twelve-year-old daughter of our cook, could not read or write, you offered a quarter to me if I could teach her to read from my first reader. When Henrietta proved too stubborn and refused to even try, I had to admit defeat. I have always remembered your genuine disappointment and you worried about Henrietta for years.

The next distinguished guest was Governor Richard Riley who was unable to attend personally, but who extended greetings and

225

congratulations via videotape as he expressed the gratitude of the state government for all Miss Wil Lou had accomplished for the citizens of South Carolina.

As Glenn Turner escorted Miss Gray to the podium, she received a lengthy and most enthusiastic standing ovation. Then Miss Wil Lou again expressed her gratitude for all of the assistance given her throughout all the years, and repeated that she could not have accomplished anything without the help of all those who had assembled on this occasion to honor her. This was to be the final curtain call for Miss Wil Lou as she entrusted the care of her beloved Opportunity School to those whom she was to leave shortly, in body but not in spirit.

During the years of 1980 and 1981 Miss Wil Lou remained in relatively good health. She had learned to live with her fourth pacemaker and the intense pain of arthritis. She was able to remain quite mobile with the help of her "space shoes," which she was quick to point out to one and all, had cost $136 a pair.

Miss Wil Lou had a frightening experience in 1981 when she became confused and activated the elevator in her home to lower it, while she was standing under it, not knowing it was at this time on a higher floor. The elevator knocked her to the floor and she was pinned under it for some time until a hydraulic jack could be found to raise the elevator. However, she remained very calm throughout this ordeal, much calmer than the fire department, police, relatives, and other residents of 1851 Devine Street, who were attempting to free her. She received a slight abrasion on her head, but otherwise was unharmed. All concerned agreed that perhaps the elevator should remain off-limits unless someone was able to accompany her.

Some months later it became necessary for Miss Wil Lou to undergo major surgery to remove her gall bladder. Again she amazed her family and doctors by breezing through this experience and recuperating as quickly as an adolescent.

Inexorably, however, the time arrived when family members admitted that Miss Wil Lou could not be adequately cared for at home and medical expertise was necessary at this point to maintain her comfort and well-being. Until this time she had received the very best possible care from her housekeeper, chauffeur, and friend of twenty-four years, Evelyn Branch. When around-the-clock care had become necessary, Mi, a lovely Vietnamese Lady, remained with Miss Wil Lou each night until Evelyn arrived in the morning.

Miss Wil Lou was admitted to Providence Hospital in April of 1982 after she became bedfast. She remained there for three weeks and then was transferred to Manor Care Nursing Home. On the day Miss Wil Lou went to Providence, Evelyn resolved to accompany her and remain with her until the end. Each day Evelyn was with the patient from 9 a.m. until 1:30 p.m., then from 8 p.m. to 3 a.m. As many geriatric patients do, Wil Lou refused to use utensils or indicate any interest whatsoever in eating, unless the food happened to be her favorite vanilla ice cream; therefore, Evelyn fed her with a food syringe twice daily in order to prevent intravenous feedings which she knew were quite painful. Evelyn also dressed Miss Gray each day and positioned her in a wheelchair, taking her for frequent rides to give her a change of scenery. At least once each week they went to the beauty shop in the nursing home where Miss Wil Lou's beautiful white hair was shampooed and set.

Evelyn recalls that during this time Wil Lou would not attempt to communicate with family members who were frequent visitors. When the news of Marguerite Tolbert's death reached them on July 6, 1982, Wil Lou refused to acknowledge that she had heard. However, she did talk to Evelyn, who believed that Miss Wil Lou realized she was not her former self and did not want to become embarrassed by her failing memory. Evelyn also recalls that when Miss Wil Lou received a telephone call from Governor Riley on her one-hundredth birthday, she appeared to recognize his voice, smiling and nodding her head, as he undoubtedly was mentioning the Opportunity School.

Fortunately, Miss Wil Lou was not in pain during this time. Occasionally, she required oxygen, but no other medication was necessary. About ten days before she died, she became comatose, but in one last lucid moment, she opened her eyes, looked at Evelyn, and with great clarity declared, "Evelyn, I love you." Soon after, when the faithful servant and true friend knew the final hour was imminent, she was compelled to leave her charge in the care of the nursing staff because she could not bear to see her die. It was on March 10, 1984, at the age of one hundred years and seven months, that Miss Wil Lou Gray experienced physical death; yet she achieved an immortality as her spirit lives on in the lives of the many thousands whose lives she has touched.

When Miss Gray's family, friends, and former students gathered the next day at Dunbar Funeral Home, it was with joy rather than mournful sadness as they remembered the legacy they had inherited. They now had a lifetime of beautiful memories of an unbelievably altruistic teacher who had influenced their lives so tremendously.

Then on Monday, March 12, 1984, services were held at Washington Street Methodist Church which had been her church home for sixty-six years. There were no tears in evidence as those who had gathered to pay their final respects quietly smiled as they imagined that Miss Wil Lou was already in heaven wearing her well-deserved star-studded crown as she busily organized reading and writing classes for all of God's angels.

Governor Richard Riley eulogized Miss Gray as one "whose unique talents proved her to be a true visionary . . . who could change and expand as the times dictated . . . She perceived very early the value of an education . . . She knew how to get things done without waiting on the 'system' . . . In the 26,000 graduates of the Opportunity School, the spirit of Wil Lou Gray lives on . . . Her name will forever be synonymous with education."

Then a lengthy procession accompanied Miss Wil Lou Gray to her final resting place on this earth in Laurens, South Carolina. Miss Wil Lou had returned home; she had fought a good fight. Miss Wil Lou, may you rest in peace.

Wil Lou Gray was a trail blazer who turned obstacles into stepping stones, whose passion was humanity and whose creed was democracy. Like St. Matthew, she "laboured not for myself only but for all them that seek learning."

As Wil Lou Gray laid down the gauntlet and issued a challenge to others that her work for the good of mankind might continue, may the torch of learning which she enkindled in the souls of so many thousands be passed to future generations. Then her cry shall not have been in vain, "Let my people learn!"

Dr. Wil Lou Gray in 1980 as the recipient of the Rotary Club's "Paul Harris Fellow Award," the only woman to receive this honor

APPENDIX
Accolades

1934-35	Who's Who in South Carolina	
1937	University of South Carolina	"Algernon Sydney Sullivan Medallion"
1941	*Anderson Daily Mail*	Scroll of Honor for "outstanding public service"
1944	Opportunity School Alumni	"Friendship Portrait" presented to Columbia College
1946	Pilot Club	"Woman of the Year"
1947	Wofford College	Honorary Doctor of Law Degree
1947	Clemson College	"Woman of the Year"
1948	*Progressive Farmer*	"Woman of the Year"
1948	Governor Strom Thurmond	Honorary Colonel
1949	South Carolina State College	"Certificate of Merit"
1950	Kappa Alpha Gamma	Honorary Membership
1950	South Carolina American Legion	"Distinguished Service Award"
1952	Columbia College	"Distinguished Service to Church and State
1953	Bob Hope	"Woman of the Week"
1954-55	National Association of Public School Educators	"Special Merit Award"
1956	South Carolina Moose Association	"Citizen of the Year"
1956	Southeastern Adult Education Association	"Outstanding Service to Region"
1957	Joint Session of South Carolina General Assembly	"Recognition for 54 years of public service"
1957	Board of Trustees and General Assembly	Appointment as Director Emeritus of South Carolina Opportunity School
1959	Sertoma Club	"Service to Humanity"
1959	South Carolina Council for Common Good	"Distinguished Service Award"
1961	Sertoma Club	"International Service to Mankind"
1963	National Retired Teachers' Association	"Honorary Life Membership"
1963	Senator Olin Johnston	Tribute printed in *Congressional Record*
1967	South Carolina Association for Public School Education	"Contributions to Education for Adults"

1967	South Carolina Rehabilitation Asociation	"Award of the Year"
1969	South Carolina Opportunity School	"for 66 years of dedicated service to her fellow man"
1970	Winthrop College	Doctor of Humane Letters Degree
1971	South Carolina Commission on Aging	"Distinguished Older South Carolinian"
1972	Union Oil Company and WIS Radio	"Spirit of '76 Award"
1972	Woman's Club of Columbia	"Certificate of Appreciation"
1974	South Carolina Commission on Aging	Co-recipient, "Outstanding South Carolinian Award
1974	South Carolina Hall of Fame	Induction and Portrait
1975	National Retired Teachers' Association and American Association of Retired Persons	"Continuing and outstanding service to others"
1976	South Carolina General Assembly - South Carolina Opportunity School	Named the Wil Lou Gray Opportunity School
1976	South Carolina Federation of Older Americans	"Certificate of Appreciation"
1978	Columbia College	"Distinguished Service Award"
1978	Columbia College	Doctor of Humane Letters Degree
1978	South Carolina Federation of Older Americans	"Citation of Appreciation"
1980	Rotary Club of Columbia	"Paul Harris Fellow Award"
1981	98th Birthday Celebration	"This Is Your Life, Wil Lou Gray"
1981	Clemson University	Doctor of Humanities Degree
1986	Joint Assembly of South Carolina General Assembly	Unveiling of Portrait by Michael Del Priore

The subject of articles in the following magazines and books:

The Youth's Companion

Survey Graphic

South Carolina Magazine

Holland's, the Magazine of the South

The State Magazine Section

New York Mirror

Colliers

Senior Scholastic

Friends

Coronet

Newsweek

Independent Woman

Senior Citizen Magazine

Columbia College Magazine

South Carolina's Wil Lou Gray,
by Mabel Montgomery

South Carolina's Distinguished Women
of Laurens County

Senior Circle